Make it a Double

Make it a Double

FROM WRETCHED TO WONDROUS: TALES OF ONE WOMAN'S LIFELONG DISCOVERY OF WHISKY

SHELLEY SACKIER

PEGASUS BOOKS

NEW YORK LONDON

This book is dedicated to all the words that did not make the final cut. There were scores of you, superfluous redundancies like nobody's business. Please don't take it personally. It is not dedicated to all misplaced modifiers, however, because they make my writing hilarious without my being aware of it.

———

This book is memoir and the author's truth. The conversations in the book all come from the author's recollections, but as memory is slippery, they are not written to represent verbatim transcripts. In all instances, the essence of the dialogue is accurate. It reflects the author's present recollections of experiences over time and her emotions, reactions, and interpretations. Some names and/or identifying characteristics have been changed to protect privacy and some events have been compressed.

———

MAKE IT A DOUBLE

Pegasus Books, Ltd.
148 West 37th Street, 13th Floor
New York, NY 10018

First Pegasus Books cloth edition June 2022

Interior design by Maria Fernandez

Library of Congress Cataloging-in-Publication Data is available.

ISBN: 978-1-63936-179-3

10 9 8 7 6 5 4 3 2 1

Printed in the United States of America
Distributed by Simon & Schuster
www.pegasusbooks.com

May we all one day realize the ripple effect of a warm and welcoming hand.
And may one of those hands be ours.

———

No one can build you the bridge on which you, and only you,
must cross the river of life.
There may be countless trails and bridges and demigods
who would gladly carry you across;
but only at the price of pawning and forgoing yourself.
There is one path in the world that none can walk but you.
Where does it lead?
Don't ask, walk!

—Friedrich Nietzsche

Contents

PART ONE: LOVE AFFAIR WITH SCOTLAND

Whisky? Or Jet Fuel?   3
Days of Yore   5
A Beginner's Tour Guide   9
The Royal Mile   16
Barrel Hugging Tours   20
Win by a Nose   24
Peatrified   28
Balmenach: Professionally Licensed Peat Shed   34
Bagpipes   36
Spirits—Both Ghostly & Drinkable   41
Gleneagles   43
Bowmore's 100 Degrees Proof: Certifiably Explosive!   48
The Unending Sky on the Isle of Skye   51
Smuggling & Struggling: A Bad Guy Gone Good   55
No Toys for Mommy   57
Whisky, Women, and *Wham!*, You're Wedded   61
Spelling Lessons   65

PART TWO: YOU CAN TAKE THE LASS OUT OF SCOTLAND . . .

Pipers on Sale, Aisle Three   71
Ernest Shackleton: The Women, the World, the Whisky   74
Go Fetch Me a Pint   78
Old Pulteney: The Demon's Drink   82
What to Wear for Burns Night: Getting Your Plaid to Work for You   84
Men in Plaid, aka Highland Games   89
Burns Night Takes Virginia   92
Bottoms up for Burns   96
The Calamity, Chaos, and Conclusion of Burns Night   98

PART THREE: AN APPRENTICE OF THE MOTHERLAND

Ardbeg's Whirlpool Whisky   105
Apprenticeship 101   107
Barley   110
Fear Realized   117
There's Trouble at t'Mill   119
A Messy Return   122
The Bugs in Your Bourbon, the Growth in Your Grog, the Spores in Your Spirits   127
Attagirl   130
Yeast   134

Chicken and Clapshot 140

Burn, Baby, Burn 145

Solving the Mystery of Oysters 149

Breathing Room: Whisky's Wooden Lung 157

Squeaky Clean 161

The Water of the Water of Life 164

Sage Words from the First Lady 168

Well, Well, Well. Aberlour's History Runs Deep 171

The Best and Worst of *The Wizard of Oz* 173

Tipping the Hip for a Sip of the Tipple 177

The Distillery's Source of Confusion 180

Whisky Coproducts: The Extra Bits and Bobs Part 1 (Draff) 184

Field Trips 187

Whisky Coproducts: The Extra Bits and Bobs Part 2 (Pot Ale and Spent Lees) 192

Whisky Thieves Are My Best Friends 195

Whisky Coproducts: The Extra Bits and Bobs Part 3 (The Heat Is On) 199

How to Impress Your Boss with Bovine Ailments 202

Whisky Coproducts: The Extra Bits & Bobs Part 4 (Biofuel) 207

Graham's Great Exam 209

PART FOUR: FROM ENTHUSIAST TO WHISKY WOMAN

When Opportunity Knocks 215

Belly Up to the Bar (Part 1) 217

Trusty Rusty Research 220

Belly Up to the Bar (Part 2) 226

Challenge Accepted 231

Belly Up to the Bar (Part 3) 238

Proper Whisky 243

Belly Up to the Bar (Part 4) 247

Please . . . Let Me Explain 249

Boozy Broads & Whisky Women 253

The Malting, the Making, the Whisky, the Waiting 257

Cardhu and Helen Cumming: Cunning Doesn't Even Come Close 260

The Lass Gets a Title 263

When the Spirit Moves You 268

PART FIVE: EXTRAS TO SIP ON

A Nip, a Novel, and Knowledge 273

The Distiller's Handbook: The Mirth of Mixology 277

Singing the Praises of Whisky: Drinking Songs 284

Here's to All That Gives You Pleasure: Toasts and Tributes 287

Where to Find Your First (Or Next) Whisky 290

Acknowledgments 294

PART ONE

A Love Affair with Scotland

Q: HOW DO YOU GET TWO BAGPIPES
   TO PLAY IN PERFECT UNISON?

A: SHOOT ONE OF THEM.

Whisky? Or Jet Fuel?

I winced with my first sip of scotch and pulled back from the glass to eye it with suspicion. "This tastes like someone found a burnt log at the bottom of the sea, dragged it up, and squeezed it out over a glass," I said.

"Fabulous, isn't it?" Jonathan, my then husband, responded with a nod. He took the tumbler from my hand, and I gave him what would shortly become a well-practiced look of incredulity mixed with pity. I had married a man with no taste buds and a penchant for things curiously fetid. I would be expected to share meals with him for the rest of our lives. How had this happened? He was a smooth-tongued, dark-haired, and handsome Brit, who made his living as either a man of medicine or a walking encyclopedia, depending upon the company he kept. How could someone so educated make the grave mistake of thinking the liquid in his glass was "fabulous" let alone safe for human consumption?

I glanced at the label to check for the skull and crossbones sticker, or at least the green Mr. Yuk face that was pasted on all our cleaning fluids under the kitchen sink. The label said "Oban." It should have said, "Oh bad."

"You're tasting the smoke with a slight hint of iodine," Jonathan said, nosing the glass before taking another sip.

"No, I'm pretty sure I taste an accident someone happened to scoop up into a jug." I wondered how much my husband had been suckered into paying for taking this toxin off the hands of a snickering retailer.

"So . . . this comes from the *higher* lands?" my dad asked, changing the subject. He'd been standing with us in the kitchen he shared with my mom, tasting the gift from his new son-in-law.

"The *Highlands*," Jonathan corrected. "A rugged, mountainous land where hairy-assed Scotsmen steal each other's cows and pillage neighboring clans."

"And that's the booty?" I pointed with a wrinkled nose toward his glass.

"It's an acquired taste," he said with a supercilious smile.

"Or a lack of one," I mumbled, not wanting to spoil my dad's present. I couldn't imagine anyone getting used to the noxious fumes in that cup, let alone desiring it. And after shaking my head to rid my tongue of the attack it withstood only moments ago, I vowed never to afflict my senses with that kind of gruesome behavior again. Except I'd married a person who wrongly believed I could be molded into someone else's concept of the perfect wife, and as a result, a profound, unquenchable longing slowly surfaced when I sought my authentic self: a woman who chose her own path of motion, not because someone else pointed her sharply in that direction, but because she was indisputably and fervently drawn toward it.

Later, I would come to recognize this moment as a threshold. The decisive instant where I grabbed the latch, opened the door, and stepped into my whisky life, a distinctly new epoch where more than twenty-five years of struggle, grit, and glorious reverie would help spin a long yarn of sagas, both horrid and happy.

As I stood in that kitchen *oh so long ago*, the whitecaps of churning, troubled waters were just downstream of our lifeboat. Not only did I end up breaking the vow with the whole "*till death do us part*" bit, but I also reneged on my oath to give a wide berth to that foul brown spirit.

Both choices brought me bliss.

Days of Yore

Distilled spirits have been around almost a thousand years—about when Birkenstocks became fashionable. Likewise, there is a long list of people to whom all whisky drinkers owe a giant "thank you" fruit basket. We'd be remiss if we did not direct a hardy "Well done!" shout to the Chinese, who had a lot of extra rice and time on their hands; but it seems most history books suggest the first horn of plenty would simply be addressed to *the Moors*, who were gracious enough to be the first to bring the art of distillation to European monks.

While we're looking for a hand to pump and a back to thump, those Benedictine monks were adamant about not letting their Muslim teachers down. As if there wasn't enough on their plates already, these indefatigable fellows made sure to slip brew mastery and elixir manufacturing into their already overstuffed monastic know-how. It's a wonder the monks ever got around to practicing the whole *Let's-ferment-our-morning-mush* idea when their daily to-do list also included the husbandry of animals, insects, and fruit, making cheese, building dams, ironmongery, mining, quarrying, forging, and don't forget, perfecting their penmanship. Not only did they have to create and maintain their very own little village universities and vocational tech schools, playing both teacher and student, but they got to throw themselves out of their own college bars for acting like frat boys gone bad. These men learned to do it all. I assume some of their ingenuity stemmed from deft calculations that answered the question *how can we make this better?* And some simply addressed the ever-so-crucial aspect of *how can we put off death*? Making liquids safe to drink turned out to be a helluva lot more fun than manning the smelting furnace.

Although there is muddled evidence and great debate as to who brought distillation methods from Ireland to Scotland, there are some who insist we need to show some gratitude to St. Paddy. Despite Ireland's patron saint having Roman Britain listed on his birth certificate as "origin of birth," he spent ten years in Ireland, having been snatched up and enslaved in his mid-teens. Upon returning to his homeland, he shared the magic recipe with a few guys off the west coast of Scotland who, I like to imagine, must have looked like they needed a stiff drink. I could be wrong, but as a writer of mostly fiction, I am trained and encouraged to invent the missing threads between historical events.

It's also been mentioned that it's not St. Patrick, but St. Columbanus (or Columbán) who established a monastery on the island of Iona to spread the feel-good message of God and grog. Regardless of which holy man brought the holy spirit to the wholly appreciative, it goes without saying, a fan base was born.

At the time of introduction, aqua vitae—the water of life—was used medicinally. King James IV was particularly fond of his medicine and made repeated requests for refills on his prescription. Soon everyone needed this marvelous new tonic. Determined to show those pesky, overbearing Romans that they'd had enough Latin lessons shoved down their gullets, the Scots changed the name to the much more lyrical *uisge beatha*, which can only be pronounced properly—along with most Gaelic—by someone thumping your back while you're in the middle of a sneeze.

God forbid something as wondrous and beneficial to the masses should be left in the hands of the ignorant and exploitable. Cue the British government. Commercial development could not go forward without the fine leadership of Parliament. And who doesn't love Customs and Excise men? These skilled Gaugers (or more accurately *gougers*) led Scottish distillers to the marketplace, where they were more than happy to help carry away their bags of heavy coins. Like, way away. Usually over castle drawbridges and up the stairs past guards with pointy spears and the equivalent of itchy trigger fingers.

Thankfully, the Scots were a canny bunch and knew how to hide. Whether camouflaging themselves and their stills as heather, rocks, or waterfalls, or leading taxmen away from their illicit activities with wild-goose chases after fair-faced maidens, whisky-making blossomed (as did a good number of those fair-faced maidens). No matter how determined those pesky taxmen grew in the hunt for unlawful stills, it must have felt like they were battling a Hydra—for every one they confiscated, two took its place.

Finally, in the defeated effort of an "*If you can't beat 'em, join 'em*" type ruling, Great Britain's government began passing licensing acts, allowing distillers to pay a fee in exchange for legitimacy. It still took thirty-odd years to gain a foothold on the illegal distilling and smuggling activity in the country, but once the Excise Act of 1823 passed, the days of digging seventy-yard-long peat-smoke tunnels from illicit stills to farmhouse cottage chimneys were diminishing rapidly. And in what I'm sure is more than one incident of serendipity, the discovery of a few forgotten barrels, opened and sampled after a year or three, revealed a melodious spirit—a far cry from the fiery liquid produced and distributed at that particular time.

There were plenty of seminal individuals who, from that era onward, shaped the future successes of whisky distillation. Among them was Aeneas Coffey, who improved the design of the column still and furthered production capabilities. Other men, whose last names are now synonymous with the spirit—Ballantine, Walker, Chivas, Dewar, and Teacher—helped advance the trade by either selling the product in their grocery stores or, like Robert Haig and William Grant, practicing the art of distillation themselves. Where are the women, you ask? Most often behind the scenes and unacknowledged, although I'll do my best to shine a spotlight on that dark corner.

Of course, one must not churlishly offer thanks, but rather acknowledge that the deadly phylloxera aphids—creators of the Great French Wine Blight, which in the mid–19th century nearly wiped out France's wine industry—also chipped in to boost demand and increase the drive for whisky production. Surely the upper crust of Great Britain and Europe could not be left without something to fill their claret goblets and cognac snifters.

Within a short period, trade regulation was the talk on everyone's lips, and after a few years of attempting to gain brand loyalty, many of the independents gave in to the economic pressures of corporate strategy, falling in line with what would soon become part of your average *How to Grow Your Business* manual under the chapter "Mergers and Acquisitions".

As the decade, and then centuries, went on, this made way for companies like Diageo, the world's largest producer of spirits (until recently), to buy up everybody else. That might be an artful statement, but when making a visit to an ancient distillery, way off the beaten path and in search of rousing authenticity, one may feel disheartened by the long reach of social media giants—written in shorthand as GAFA or FAANG, or in this case the PLC (public limited company)—for being present on the tour. Somehow, one player controlling all the goods is a little like one guy owning almost every spot on the Monopoly board and putting up all the expensive hotels. It makes you want to gather up your marbles and go home early, because all the fun has been sucked out of the game.

Still, when holding a dram up to the light before taking that anticipated first sip, most whisky lovers care not whether it was made by the shine of the moon or the shackles of management. They feel only gratitude at the wonder of it being made at all.

A Beginner's Tour Guide

I sank into one of two chairs facing a love seat in the small library in Balbirnie House outside of Edinburgh. It looked as though Laura Ashley and Rob Roy had collaborated in decorating this lush country house hotel. Floral upholstery, a Chinese-style rug, and tartan curtains covered the furniture, floor, and walls. Rob had also wrestled a few heads with sharp hat racks into place above the mantel and bookshelves. I half expected one or two of them to introduce themselves à la an animatronic show at Disney World.

It likely wouldn't have surprised me at this point in the day. I had encountered more jaw-dropping moments in the last twenty-four hours, experiencing Scotland with Jonathan, than I could remember collecting in my lifetime. Of course, that lifetime was merely twenty-two years, so it didn't hold a helluva lot of weight just yet; but all the same, apparently my first trip to this magical land required a great deal of scouring castles, traversing mountains, and slithering along gleaming lochs. The leaves were flashing flags of autumn's choicest colors, and the nip in the November air dictated the need for heat.

"What's that smell?" I finally asked, questioning the pungent and curiously enticing aroma heavily lacing the atmosphere.

"Decomposed vegetable matter," Jonathan said. "It's burned and used for fuel."

"People are burning their compost piles?" Typically, back in Wisconsin where I grew up, we just spread it onto our spring garden beds.

"It's called peat."

"Well, peat is my new favorite smell. And I'm pretty sure we're going to name one of our kids after it."

It was as heady as a drug. And decades later, I am still seeking someone to agree to either burn my corpse on a pyre of peat or lower my casket into a grave where I am nestled between small burlap sacks filled with it. It doesn't matter. I just wish to have it accompany me into the afterlife.

Peat is often described to the newcomer's nose as the only other thing that keeps the Scottish warm apart from wool and whisky. Before I got a small lecture on this vegetative source of warmth, I was introduced to what I would refer to as another enkindling experience.

Little was I prepared for the heat-inducing incident of seeing Scottish men in Highland dress. Yes, Jonathan had made prior references to this suborder, tagging them as "hairy-assed Neanderthals who dragged their women around by their hair." This had left a worrisome (not to mention erroneous) impression in my head. But apparently, my body was reacting in ancient biological ways. I won't admit to swooning, but something happened to my knees, and what normally locked them securely in place acted unhelpfully like Jell-O.

Seeing a true Highlander is like spotting a prehistoric relic: endangered and fascinating, a Komodo dragon, a golden tabby tiger, a lone red wolf. Now perhaps my mind played tricks on me, convincing my eyes that what I saw was a towering, bewhiskered Titan, a strapping, rugged man robed in complicated plaid packaging, further enhanced with weapons of destruction tucked into various belts, socks, and shoulder straps. And in my foggy state of befuddled euphoria, I was confident he was holding onto either a brace of freshly killed rabbits or the head of his clan's enemy.

What I doubtless saw was nothing remotely close. It might have been some tourist geezer outfitted in a spanking new skirt, freshly made for Edinburgh Woolen Mill—a mass-produced, high-street chain that will have you dressing like a local from the 18th century, just like clansmen from your family tree. He was probably carrying his sporran like a man purse—a teeny tiny, hairy briefcase (hence the hanging head illusion)—rather than strapped to his waist and dangling in a region where most women try to keep their eyes from lingering.

The other possibility is that I witnessed a bookshop owner setting up a large signboard featuring the front cover of the newest bodice-ripping, neck-sucking romance novel, nothing left to cover our muscular hero apart from his broadsword and the fiery, well-placed hair of the damsel in distress. It's easy to get confused when you've had a pint of Guinness with lunch. And then one for the road.

Regardless of whether it's real or imagined, the combination of a dank, smoke-sodden atmosphere, a heavily sedating lunch of venison pie and sticky toffee pudding, and an afternoon filled with visits to the seats of dead kings and fabled warriors, the stage was set for my last rite of passage. Immersing oneself in Scotland is a little like getting sucked into a time warp—a *Doctor Who* episode with bagpipe music. The only thing missing was encapsulating the entire experience into liquid form. And evidently, this is possible.

Jonathan and I sat across from one another in the softly lit library, balancing colossal dinner menus in our laps and listening to the faint clink of glasses and dinnerware from the dining room next door. A pallid slip of a girl stood before us; a leather-bound volume that could have passed for a large-print edition of the Bible stretched from her hands toward my husband.

"Would you care to peruse the wine list tonight, sir?" she said with a thick Polish accent.

He looked at the tome and then at her. "Will there be a test?"

The girl fell coy and giggled, dropping the list into his hands. "*Nie martw się!*" She waved at him. I knew what she'd said. I'd learned some Polish as a kid growing up in a house full of unpronounceable last names and heavily doughed desserts. It was something like, *English idiot!* (Or maybe it was *Good morning, how are you?*) Whatever it was, it sounded familiar. Perhaps she was just counting to three.

My husband looked at me and cocked his head. "Answer her," he whispered.

My eyes went wide, and I felt the slow creep of panic slide up my neck. "*Dziękuję,*" I mumbled, which means *thank you*, although I've been told that my pronunciation of it sounds more like a hiccup.

"Oh!" she gasped and rattled off a few foreign words. She paused. "You speak Polish?" Her eyes were hopeful with longing for a piece of her homeland.

"Umm . . . not really," I admitted. "Unless you happen to be looking for the train. And I know a lot of swear words." (Thank you, Grandma.)

Her face scrunched and after a moment of attempting to further translate my answer, she shrugged and left the library. It was a split second later that the hotel's barman, who had been silently polishing tulip-shaped glasses in the corner, came to stand beside us.

"Care for a wee drink? Ye might need one if you're planning to crack the spine of that tale." He nudged an elbow toward the wine canon.

"Definitely." Jonathan nodded and looked to me. "Gin and tonic? Martini Rosso?"

The barman put a hand on the back of my chair. "Perhaps the lass would like a dram of something warmer?"

I glanced up at him.

"Scotch?" Jonathan said and rolled his eyes. "No. She hates whisky."

The barman took a small step back and clutched at his chest. "Hates whisky? What have ye tried?"

Jonathan shook his head and opened the wine book, looking for inspiration within the pages. "Took one sip of Oban and thought I'd handed her poison."

The barman clucked his tongue. "Ye did, sir."

Jonathan snorted, looking up. "Don't tell me I've come across a Scotsman who can't stomach his own country's most winning feature."

"I willna do that, but ye've done your wife no favors by ruining her tongue straight away."

I watched my husband's nose flare with the challenge. "How so?"

"Well, if ye'll allow me a moment." The Scotsman raised a finger and dashed back to the long, polished slab of wood that stood beneath multiple shelves stacked with whiskies. He returned with a tray holding four tall and two stubby bottles. CLASSIC MALTS OF SCOTLAND was etched in gold on the front of the platter. He placed the tray on the coffee table in front of us and crouched to be at eye level with the display. Clearing his throat, the barman ran a practiced hand across the label of each bottle. "Here, we have a mindfully chosen representation, every bottle distinct to each region and style of whisky."

I sat forward to get a better look at the foreign words on the bottles. "Do you mean each region has its own special flavor of yuck?"

The barman chuckled. "I'll wager a bet that I can give ye something ye'll want to have again tomorrow."

"Are we still talking about whisky?" I asked, and then I bit my tongue, remembering we were in polite company.

The barman made a small choking sound and looked to the ground.

Jonathan gave me a look that said, *Behave yourself,* but hardly a serious one because had I not asked the question, he surely would have.

"Sorry," I mumbled. "Okay, I'll take your wager, but this better be on the house or at least one my husband likes, otherwise it's going to be a waste of money."

The barman picked up one of the stout, thickset bottles and pulled the cork stopper from the neck. "This here is a fine single malt from the 'Garden of Scotland.' It's a delicate whisky, sweet and custardy."

"Sounds more like ice cream," I said.

The barman pulled a dainty tulip-shaped glass with no stem from his front pocket and tilted the bottle. A pale gold liquid burbled into the glass. Corking the jug, he ran the glass beneath his nose. "Vanilla . . . cut flowers . . . lemon cheesecake."

"Seriously?" I said. I laid out my palm. "Hand it over. You make it sound like a marmalade cosmopolitan. And one that requires an umbrella."

The barman shook his head and placed the glass in my hand. "Not at all, but this particular malt is referred to as a *Lady's Whisky.*"

I took a long whiff and closed my eyes. *What am I smelling? Where are all these scents?* I exhaled and looked to my husband. "Well, the good news is, it doesn't smell like turpentine." I glanced to the barman. "May I taste it?"

He nodded. "Not too much or too fast, aye? Let it sit in yer mouth for a second."

I took a slow sip and swallowed. A trail of embers followed the liquid down my throat and settled into a small campfire in my belly. I looked at the tartan curtains and thought about the Highlander. Earlier I'd asked my husband the age-old question of what a Scotsman wore beneath his kilt. He responded with the new-to-my-ears but oldest comeback to that query: "Lipstick, if he's lucky."

It made me focus on the heat thrumming from inside me. This had to be one of the smartest reasons to drink whisky. It was like having a mini Jacuzzi just below your sternum. I took another sip and closed my eyes. Everything about today filtered through my mind. The scent of smoldering peat fires. The gray smudge of sky that released only a constant mist instead of a day-ruining downpour. The pub with its heavy local fare and even heavier local dialects. The highly alcoholic beer—leaving me anesthetized and inarticulate. The soft hush of the ancient hotel with faint whispers of its past inhabitants. The awe-inspiring mountains, castles, and lochs. And of course, the Herculean Highlander sans Underoos.

I must have sighed with pleasure because both my husband and the barman started laughing. Flushing with embarrassment—and probably the effects of the alcohol by now—I couldn't reveal the real reason for my lustful pining. I smiled, tight-lipped, and announced à la Dudley Moore when describing what it's like to be on a yacht, "It doesn't suck."

So, this was how it all began. I fell in love. Of course, there was no way in hell I was about to reveal to Jonathan and some stranger that I was having a Harlequin hallucination, but it's not the real reason I developed a mad crush for whisky. The truth was, I was falling in love with Scotland. Bringing whisky home was like purposefully drenching yourself and your clothing in your lover's cologne and waving it in front of your spouse. America was going to hate me.

It became apparent to me, in no short amount of time, that I wanted to be reminded of my unmitigated list of the perfect experience. Not only did I see this country, I smelled, chewed, and drank it. I felt its ghosts slither through me. I stepped off an airplane in Glasgow, and within an unimaginably short period of days found myself pulled into someone else's past—a history enrobed in devotion, pain, and deep desire. It felt like it was mine. It felt more important than it should have. I was embarrassed when trying to articulate it, and to this day cannot conjure the words to convey that strange and mystifying feeling—like I belonged somewhere else.

How do you reveal such lunacy without people passing surreptitious glances between one another, concluding that you've held your head in the oven for too long while last cleaning it?

In the end, it stopped mattering—or maybe I stopped disclosing this bit, but the truth was that I had been, and remain, tethered to another place and all its other times. History had never been a fascination of mine, nor studying the cultures of other countries, yet it seemed with each further taste of whisky, I had developed an unquenchable thirst.

The Royal Mile

V isiting Edinburgh for the first time was a little surreal. Back in the nineties, walking the Royal Mile was like visiting the Scottish equivalent of Disney's Magic Kingdom. There were attractions, theaters, restaurants, and gift shops, each leading you closer to the crowning siren, Edinburgh Castle. But instead of touring Snow White's Scary Adventure, you'll find Margaret King's Close—a section of old tenement housing where folks who caught a touch of the plague were "quarantined," but just until they "got better," circa 1644.

Yes, in Disney you might have a chance to cruise the popular ride It's a Small World, where you can ogle three hundred toucan-colored animatronic children from around the world, joining hands and singing Disney's own mind-numbing version of "Kumbaya"; but on the Royal Mile, you can climb to the top of the sixth floor in the Outlook Tower to spy on living people through the Camera Obscura. Only here you can watch as they argue with one another in the street over how much they got suckered into paying for tartan garden clogs and a sporran barbecue apron.

Hungry? Well, instead of eating lunch at the Pinocchio Village Haus, chugging from beer steins and measuring the accuracy of Geppetto's cuckoo clocks, try dining in The Witchery at the gates of the castle. Count the lingering distant screams of the myriad women (and men) burned at the stake after *thankfully* someone discovered they were witches. See if you can finish your plate while the images of flames licking the feet of these charm-casting she-devils play with your sense of security—but careful how you lay your fork down. It's one of the indicators of whether you're a card-carrying member of the local coven.

And lest you think you can't get a decent ride like Splash Mountain or the Magic Flying Carpets, you'll be delighted to discover you can pop yourself into the middle of a barrel and float through the entire distillation experience—from barley sprout to bottling—complete with the apparition of a dead Scottish distiller and his wee cat, Peat, as your guides. How much more Walt can you get?

Even though the Scotch Whisky Experience, located at the top of Castle Hill across from the Camera Obscura, may have morphed into something close to an Epcot attraction, I'd still recommend you purchase a ticket. Your average tour price will provide you with not only the barrel ride—sorry, no waterfalls—but also entrance into the Sense of Scotland, where staffers fill in any gaps you have on the history of whisky and introduce you to a more thorough understanding of Scotland's assigned olfactory districts. (And yes, I agree, it seems like they should have named it the Scents of Scotland.)

Strange as it may be to some, the museum has assigned four scents to major regions of whisky making. Belly up to the bar and take a whiff from an aroma pot that will identify the Lowlands as "biscuity," the Highlands as "floral," Speyside as "fruity," and the Islands as "smoky."

I sigh a little when writing this, as I find it nearly impossible to label an area as a smell; that is, with the exception of the seaside, where the mixture of brine, wet sand, and breeze should be bottled and sold; whatever real estate my hound occupies that will forever emit the odor of cowpie patty; and the financial district of New York, where it just stinks of corruption. Of course, I now know that not all the whiskies of Islay smell of peat, and there are ample beautiful Speysides for the smoke addicted.

The distilleries of today have ventured well beyond the typical regional choices of your kindergarten Crayola starter kit and have since moved on to the master series edition. Producing a whisky indicative of each distillery's region no longer seems as important as making a spirit that is a credit to the art itself. Yet, as hard as distilleries try, they may find they're still labeled by their postal codes. It's as if they were each a slightly different variant of Miley Cyrus: no matter how much leather and fishnet stockings she wears, how many racy videos she produces, or how many YouTube leaks we find of her smoking from a bong, she will always be squeaky clean and thirteen to the rest of us.

Nevertheless, at a time when I was only just discovering what version of "me" I wanted to explore, maintain, or protect, experiencing this Edinburgh attraction lured me further down a spiraling rabbit hole, across some magical footbridge that connected the spirits to their homes and histories. Still so fresh to the world of whisky, The Scotch Whisky Experience invited me to peek curiously, cautiously within. It made me hunger for more—or whatever the "nose" equivalent is of *thirsty*.

At the end of the tour, we were encouraged to pick our favorite square off a "scratch and sniff" card—a reflection of the scent-assigned regions. After you choose an aromatherapy flavor, someone hands you a dram to take into the next room where, if you're like me, you'll have some minor heart palpitations witnessing the Diageo Claive Vidiz Scotch Whisky Collection. A remarkable gathering of 3,384 bottles, the collection showcases everything from routine favorites to the rare and unseen.

Claive Vidiz, the Brazilian responsible for spending thirty-five years amassing this compilation of both single malts and blends, is humbly described as a "whisky enthusiast"; I'm sorry, but that's like saying the Pope is "a touch Catholic." I'm fairly sure that, like anybody else who took up a new hobby, someone in the family recognized the red flags of obsession.

Here's how I see it: What started as something a little out of the ordinary for old Claive, at home, soon became out of the question for Mrs. Vidiz as she wondered whether her husband was out of his mind pulling so much money out of their pockets. And shortly after a new wing of their abode was built to house this *hobby extraordinaire*, I can only imagine Mrs. Vidiz was simply out of humor and wanted nothing more than to have the collection out of sight. Possibly, she offered Diageo her husband as part of the bargain. I'm sure Diageo gave it some consideration but soon realized the weather-beaten face of a silver-haired eighty-something wouldn't sell too many T-shirts.

I moved from one display case to the next, my head coming to rest against the glass whenever I'd come across a bottle whose spirit was truly ancient.

"I wonder who touched you last?" I asked a 1950-something Lagavulin.

"That would be me," a voice said from behind me.

Startled and a little embarrassed, I turned to see one of the fresh-faced tour guides, beaming with the claim.

"I was dusting just this morning," he said, chuckling, before pointing out a second historic bottle with a name that rolled off his tongue but skidded past my ears.

It didn't matter. None of the names were familiar to me, but the scent drifting upward from the glass I cradled was cementing itself within all the nooks and crannies between the tip of my nose and depth of my brain.

I slid along the fluid shelves and was soon deftly guided into the McIntyre Gallery, where I discovered there was more to learn and sample (especially if one forked out the big bucks for the Supreme Tour Experience).

Of course, what kind of a tour would this be if the folks at "The Experience" hadn't also been trained in the three basic principles of Disney's gold standard for entertainment:

1. Smile with your upper teeth.
2. Think "Zip-A-Dee-Doo-Dah" thoughts throughout your entire shift.
3. End the tour by chucking folks right into the mind-boggling maze of shiny key rings and sparkly glassware, plus bottles of whisky exciting enough to make your head spin and your pocketbook empty.

No doubt these people have earned their ears.

The sun may not shine 365 days of the year on the Royal Mile (more like fifty-six), but it's fair to say that there's a new kingdom in town and it's well worth the visit. It's A Whole New World in Edinburgh. Or maybe it's a really, *really* old one, but they've finally learned how to cash in on it and entice people, even without music and fireworks.

Barrel-Hugging Tours

With more than a hundred working distilleries to visit in Scotland, and an absolute slew of closed or "silenced" ones you can drive past or trek to, chances are you're going to have to make a list of those you absolutely *must visit* if lucky enough to travel to this gorgeous country. Your other alternative is to rent yourself a big ol' Airstream and plan a three-month sabbatical. I have done the first route a bazillion times; the second is still on the bucket list.

My first distillery tour was in Oban—to get that "here's how the sausage is made" feeling from the very first sip of spirit I'd ever had. Maybe I'd discover a section of the walk-through where, in Willy Wonka fashion, they added the flavors I wasn't fond of, so I would now give a wide berth to whatever the equivalent of "hair toffee" and "candy floss sheep wool" was, but if there was a recipe to this wienerwurst, my widened eyes read it to be unwieldy and garbled at first glance. There were vast wooden buckets of foamy slosh, pipes twisting around corners and snaking up walls, copper pots that belched steam, and a guide who spoke a version of English the BBC's linguistic landscape library would be eager to record and pass on to NASA as a follow-up version of the Golden Record.

A variety of people milled about as we made our way from one damp, chilly room to the next. When I think back on my visit to Oban, what I see most clearly are their faces—faces I now recognize as representative of the same group I would tour distilleries with throughout the first decade of my whisky journey. Faces in a flock mostly comprised of men.

Things have since changed, but back then the patchwork of participants was this: There was the keen-eyed husband, thrilled to see the birthplace of his favorite malt, and his sighing wife, rubbing her arms in the cold, repeatedly turning to her husband to whisper, "What did he just say?" (Surely this wasn't just me?) Next to them were three Swedes, one of them translating each sentence of brogue coming from the guide with absolute precision. In the front were the barrel-huggers, on holiday from America—usually three or four men making comments comparing the five or six malts they'd had last night at their hotel and asking questions they already knew the answers to in order for the rest of us to practice raising our brows (and eventually rolling our eyes).

In the back were three Japanese men. Taking pictures. Making notes. There might have been a smattering of women, but if they were there of their own volition, they likely felt somewhat soreheaded on the way home as most of their time was captured by the act of shifting a whining child from one hip to the other whilst their spouse got chatty with the guide.

Regardless of the typical makeup of a touring group, a survey commissioned by the Scotch Whisky Association proves the economic contribution of distilleries and Scotch whisky tourism is nothing to sneeze at. In 2010, 1.3 million tourists graced the visitor centers and facilities of some fifty-two working distilleries, spending somewhere close to twenty-seven million pounds (or well over thirty-six million US dollars). In 2019, those numbers reached more than two million tourists dropping nearly eighty-five million pounds (more than 114 million US dollars). This is a massive change from my "novice days," when back in the early '90s, visitor centers were few and far between, and the more usual reception upon knocking on a distillery's door was, *Yes, you could have a wee peek, but don't stick your head in any vats as the CO_2 will knock the wind from yer breath and the strength from yer knees.*

Now, if one were to compare the recent stats above to the report prepared for Scottish Enterprise, which reveals golf's contribution as a whopping 286 million pounds for 2017, and a late 2018 estimate of 325 million pounds, one might scoff at the "Drop by for an hour and have a wee dram" advertisement distilleries were offering. Clearly, with such cash up for grabs, the Scotch Whisky Association is starting to pay attention.

As the years go by, wherever working distilleries with visitor centers or tours exist, then hotels, pubs, and shops soon spring up. If one were to see it from the optics of a cynic, commerce recognizes the smell of money—even if it's hidden beneath the scent of malted barley. But perhaps it's simply further proof of the business community putting on their thinking caps. ScotlandWhisky, or the Scotch Whisky Tourism Initiative, was equivalent to the result of two noble families making an arranged marriage and anticipating a better bloodline. Thankfully, their brainchild shows no signs of crossed eyes and a receding chin.

Instead, the initiative encourages Scotland's public and private sectors to search for mutually beneficial ways to use one another to pay their bills—a very handy "You scratch my back, I'll scratch yours" kind of a deal.

I've had the great fortune to visit distilleries in Scotland over the span of thirty years, and during that great sweep of time, I've watched the industry change its approach toward visitors. The affable, if some-what perplexed greeting I received when showing up at a distillery long ago—half due to befuddlement that *anyone* would care at all for a glimpse inside and half because it was a *girl* who wanted that glimpse—has morphed into a much slicker and more streamlined operation. In my early days, I often felt compelled to point at an object and ask for some bare-bones particulars:

"What is that fellow pouring into that massive wooden tub?"

To which this might be the reply:

"Fergus over there is s'posed to be dumpin' yeast into the washbacks, but there's every chance the numpty has grabbed a bag o' rock salt instead. We'll ken soon enough."

Today, the tours are optimized to present you with an abundance of tantalizing information, an experience that touches upon the sensory per-ceptions of sight, sound, scent, and taste. You view the operations—from grinding grain to glossy pot stills. You hear the mechanics of it—the hissing steam and gurgling spirit safes. You smell the aromas—all yeasty, fruity, briny, peaty. And you taste the results, results that typically leave you in a state of reverent incredulity.

As I began those early days of touring, I quickly learned that, for some, traveling to a specific distillery was the equivalent of finally seeing a mecca—perhaps only visited once in a lifetime, but thought about with alarming frequency. How many people can say that about the products they consume on a regular basis? Ever visit your French fries' potato field? How about any of McDonalds's great slaughterhouses? Either of them make you feel warm and tingly inside? "Hey, Chuck, would you mind taking a picture of Beverly and me? And make sure you get as much of the feed lot in the photo as you can." Yeah, didn't think so.

There is something so special about making a distillery trip. Many people cannot envision what goes into the process of creating their special drink. Is it the source? The local water or spring that gives the whisky its distinct taste? Or perhaps the barrels in which it's stored? The more of Scotland I saw—and drank—the more I wanted to know (and drink).

My earliest theory was this: The enchantment is one part distillery and all its myriad functions (many of which I will eventually dive into); one part distiller, whose experience, intellect, and schnoz are vital; and two parts magic. All this gets swirled about and bottled. There might be the odd eel that gets thrown in for good measure and a few bawdy pub songs belted out while tending to the mystical elixir, adding to the spirit's depth of character (or lack of it).

To the layman's eye, it's dead easy. To an artist, beneath the simplicity are layers and layers of cunning, masterful craftsmanship. To me, having raised two children on a fifteen-year steady diet of *Harry Potter*, it's pure wizardry.

Win by a Nose

There's an old adolescent joke: "You can pick your friends, and you can pick your nose, but you can't pick your friend's nose."

Long ago, when my son was elementary school–aged, I recall a slew of his buddies gathering around the dinner table, working on a few riffs off that wise crack. My favorite: "You can pick your friends, and you can pick your nose, but you can't wipe your friends underneath the car seat."

What I'm trying to say here is that right around this booger-oriented time I found myself up to my ears in the desire to learn as much as possible about whisky and, in some absurdly peculiar way, it may have taken a handful of those goofballs for me to realize that our rhinencephalon is super important to that process.

I like to call this bit of your brain "Scent Control." (Or maybe the "Command Scentral?" Don't groan. It's cute.) Some folks call it the "Smell Brain." Less creative, but it gets to the point. And as all these endearing nicknames suggest, it handles your sense of smell and includes the olfactory bulb and limbic system.

Whatever you call it, it's my favorite part of my body, and even though it shows no reflection in my mirror, it must have an ego the size of a planet as a result of my constant adulation.

Let us take note that "Whisky noses are made, not born." This belief is clearly restated in much of the whisky literature and becomes more obvious the longer you participate in the delightful training exercises that eventually allow you to discern the difference between a typical Islay and a traditional Lowland at fifty paces.

How is this done, you ask?

Well, you could compile a list of the most frequently noted flavors and scents profiled by some of the great nosing experts—think toffee, honey, biscuits, and heather—and then proceed to line them up on your kitchen counter. Now simply pass by and sniff each a dozen times a day. Maybe two dozen. Make it an even three if you're the true Hermione Granger sort. It's not the most practical way to approach the vital step of memorizing each scent, but it could happen. And probably has.

Except, what can you do about the lesser noted, but still commonly found, scents in some of your drams? Where do you find a bucket of wet cement, slightly green-edged peat, or ripe forest fruits? I don't think I could locate any burnt cough-linctus if my life depended upon it. In fact, I'm wondering if it's just the symptomatic smell of a certain disease.

Instead of giving up before you begin, here are three approaches:

Fake it—I would of course advise against this, as I've seen it done enough times to know *it's not worth it*, and you're denying yourself both new knowledge and pleasure.

Pay attention to your nose like it's your new BFF—send it surprising gifts, help it study for exams, and maybe compliment it in front of other people (yes, a little lame, but I was working a theme here).

Or—purchase yourself a Nosing Kit.

I chose what was behind doors number two and three long ago and have since benefited immeasurably.

Options two and three are how many experts began their climb to such prestigious fame. Of course, if it's celebrity status you're after, I'm not sure there's enough room for both you and master blender Richard "The Nose" Paterson to share a stage. I would imagine his rhinencephalon is large enough to occupy most concert halls on its own. In fact, it's valuable enough to have been insured by Lloyd's of London for over €2 million ($2.4 million). Well, his nose, anyway.

So, realizing the bar had been set high, I recall just how keen an interest I had in developing my own Jimmy Durante–quality schnozzola.

At first, I simply spent more time focusing on my nose than putting it to the test. Instead of subjecting it to training sessions per se, I tried a solid week of catching myself at frequent intervals and taking stock of what scents were present around me. Here's what I mean:

Does the inside of my car have a specific scent? What about my skin? My hands? The closet, a jacket, my son's hair?

I'd pause before picking up my fork. I'd close my eyes and try to identify what my spouse, the chef, or PepsiCo put into my food before I ate it. If it smelled faintly of almonds and I didn't order almonds, I wouldn't eat it. It meant my mother-in-law was cooking and she'd likely located a vial of cyanide.

I especially paid attention to my whisky—those early training bottles of Glenlivet, GlenDronach, and Glengoyne with their grassy, appley, sherried notes. Going beyond the usual routine I may have previously gone through—"Ahh, look at that color and *sniff, sniff* what a heady aroma!"—I stopped looking at the back of the bottle for tasting notes.

Eventually, I was shown the wrist test where you dip your finger in your whisky and dab it on the back of your hand.

You blow on it to allow the alcohol to evaporate.

Then inhale.

I would ponder, reach back and up to that great rhinencephalon of mine, and take a stab at what might be integrated and wedded within my glass. *Then* I checked the tasting notes.

I practiced the small exercise of nose drills until I no longer needed to put sticky notes with reminders up around the house to "stop and sniff."

With that preparatory work in full swing, I purchased a simple "beginner" whisky nosing kit, which can easily be found online. Twenty-four *mostly* lovely scents had been captured in little bottles and were accompanied by a handy-dandy booklet. I soon learned a few interesting bits of data:

1. Your nose needs a nap. Too many scents assaulting your sniffer equals "nose fatigue." Try one or two, then take a rest. Sniff neutral air. Sniff coffee beans. Eat chocolate-covered coffee beans, do some dishes, and then come back for another two or three scents.

2. Scents stir up memories. As I found it hard to recognize what I could not see, I began to rely upon the flashback

through time that took me to a place or event where that aroma was present. Neuroscience is amazing.

3. I will never grow fond of the scent of decay.

With each day and week and month of practice, I remember growing more excited with the results, writing about it online, and especially sharing my newfound appreciation for my nose with absolutely anyone close enough to get trapped into a conversation. Discovering a cool reception from most strangers, I began to limit my enthusiasm to family and friends.

Especially the ones I couldn't wipe underneath the car seat.

Peatrified

P eat (or amateur coal as I like to think of it) is one of the greatest dis-
coveries of humankind. It embodies the true smell of Scotland—apart
from wet wool, which I'd have to say is your everyday eau de parfum on
your average Scot.

One of those average Scots—a distiller doppelgänger of Sean
Connery—once told me that a whisky without some degree of measurable peat was comparable to a tree without leaves. Still beautiful if you
can appreciate the skeletal aesthetics, but not quite fully fleshed out. Some
would even go so far as to say whisky without peat isn't worth watering
plants with, let alone quenching one's thirst. I'm not saying *I've* ever said
that, but let's just say I have heard it uttered. Okay, yes, this quote was
also from the same Connery-esque curmudgeon. Most of his avowals
were prickly as hell.

To truly understand peat, one must visit a peat bog. And not simply
to view from the inside of your car. Instead, arrive fully outfitted in
rain slicker rubber, sealed at every potential opening with surgical
hosing, and thrust yourself into the middle of it during a typical
Scottish island summer day. The wind is whipping with the frenzy
of a *Price Is Right* contestant flying down the aisle when their name
is called. The rain is falling horizontally and occasionally pitching
itself upward from whence it came. You can hear nothing apart from
the roar of both said wind and rain. You will be handed a slippery
mud-caked instrument that looks like a wooly mammoth's dental

pick. The goal is to harvest the ground. Except the ground is actually soup, so good luck.

Peat, for those of you who have never had the memorable opportunity to attempt farming consommé, is just dead plants. And occasionally the remains of a deceased relative everyone agreed would not be missed. Millions of years have gone into the making of this material, billions of plants and, don't forget, trillions of raindrops. After all this time, nature has produced a rather unremarkable boot-filling bog. Except that somebody somewhere said to someone else, "Hey, why don't we try to burn this stuff?"

To me, it's like wondering who came up with the idea of deep-frying butter. There are plenty of wannabe Ferran Adriàs out there who will pursue this dream until it is a reality.

There are two different layers of peat—one that looks like chocolate ice cream when it comes out and the hairy layer. Yep—hairy. Folks cut peat and burn it for warmth in their homes, while distilleries use it for flavoring their barley. The hairy kind gives off more smoke than a Pink Floyd concert, so the homeowner's choice is the hairless variety. Distilleries, on the other hand, have found that peat smoke oils stick best to the barley. I occasionally imagine a distillery manager on the phone calling in an order of peat bricks. The peat harvesting head says, "Are you ordering the catotelm or the acrotelm?" And the distillery manager responds, "Doesn't matter, just send over something that looks like Hugh Jackman and Tom Selleck had a baby."

———

Measurements of peat in whisky are done on a scale of *ppm*, or parts per million. And unless you're a scientist with pertinent equipment, it's a little tricky to calculate the degrees of peatiness in your dram.

At some point I searched for an easier definition and "mental" visual, and I came across an article written by Zane Satterfield of the National Environmental Services Center. He defines *one ppm* as simply "one part in one million" and suggests picturing someone placing four drops of ink in a 55-gallon barrel of water then giving it a good solid stir. This is the formula for creating an ink concentration of one ppm.

He also provided a few other analogies from the University of Minnesota to help you picture the scale. One ppm is like:
- one inch in 16 miles,
- one second in 11.5 days,
- one minute in two years, or
- one car in bumper-to-bumper traffic from Cleveland to San Francisco.

It's the last one that really clears things up for me.

Regardless of which layer or what amount of peatiness someone prefers, peat has a way of participating in more than making hooch and heating hearths.

I remember traveling to the northern regions of Scotland during that first life-altering trip. After a long day of hunting through heather to find obscure stone circles and mystical fairy rings, I relished the thought of a hot soak in our hotel room's huge claw-foot tub. Jonathan ran the tap as I was unpacking, and when I stepped into the bathroom I recoiled with alarm. The water's color was revolting. It looked like the toilet pipes had backed up.

"Umm . . . Sir Sackier? We've got ourselves a problem here, and I'd stop unpacking if I were you. I think we might have to move rooms, if not hotels."

"What is it?" Jonathan called from inside the closet.

"We've got feculent froth for bath water."

"Wha—?" He rushed into the bathroom.

I made a grand Vanna White gesture toward the lurid liquid.

"Oh." He rolled his eyes. "I forgot."

"You forgot what? Is there some sort of backwash valve that needs to be stoppered? Have we just filled the tub with poo?"

He frowned at me. "No. I just forgot to tell you about the water."

"Did we get a cheap rate because of faulty plumbing?"

He sighed with slight impatience. "This is northern Scotland. The water is peat-colored. Enjoy your bath."

"You've got to be joking."

"I am not. It offers up no scent, it's simply the tannins from the plant matter."

I mumbled quietly, "I like my tannins in wine glasses, not bathtubs." But he'd heard and simply shrugged.

"As I'm currently blond, will I come out as a brunette?"

Jonathan pressed his lips together, thinking. "I wonder if that's why so many Scots are red-headed. The peat-tinged water."

"Except that a good chunk of them are fair-skinned. If it would taint their hair, wouldn't it color their flesh as well?"

"Good Lord, just get a move on. I'd like a bath, too, so this is not the day to enjoy an epic steeping."

"No worries," I said, dipping a toe into the large cup of tea I was about to bathe in. "This will be record timing."

And it was. Within five minutes I'd had all I could take. I propelled my body from the pond water and studied myself in the mirror. It was hard to tell if I was clean because I didn't *feel* clean, although I reminded myself that if I was planning to be buried in a casket full of fragrant peat then I'd best get used to bathing in tubs stained with it.

I got dressed anyway and thought about dinner. In hindsight, upon first bringing me to the United Kingdom, my ex-husband had probably done himself a huge disservice. He'd introduced me to what he referred to as "proper places to stay"—that is, country house hotels. I sigh even just saying the phrase.

Staying in such "proper places" is like having extremely wealthy friends invite you for the weekend, except you never have to see them—only their staff. The food, the service, the history is all wrapped up into a blissful experience and usually plopped onto the grounds of someone who stayed up late retracing the faded sketches of Capability Brown. Everything is drenched in antiquity, aristocratic luxury, and floral fabrics. And you never have dinner before drinks. Or salad until after dinner—just before dessert and then cheese. This all took a while to get used to, but I didn't mind suffering through it. Even if I always used the wrong fork. Being married to an Englishman whose accent got crisper with each passing birthday, I became wholly used to his glances filled with disapproval. I grew inured.

After my peat bath, I was thinking about the whisky I'd get to try. Thus far, I was taking the advice of the barman of Balbirnie House: stick with the "ladies' malts," the "gentle drams." The Glenlivet from

Speyside, Bladnoch—a perfect Lowland—or even Auchentoshan, whose distillery sits overlooking the great River Clyde. Each of these drinks I was tutored to view as my gateway whisky. They were the introduction to subsequent malts that wouldn't be described like a dessert menu. Although it was nearly impossible, and often a laugh, to pick up on the tasting notes described on the bottles (a decaying chrysanthemum and socks piled up in the corner?), I became quite focused on at least attempting to make an interpretation of my own, to begin to identify the scents my nose was discovering.

Usually, I was out in left field. What the distiller described as "peaches in syrup," I tasted as something from my grandmother's medicine cabinet. Or if the label prepared me for the smell of "honeyed lavender with a dusting of talcum powder," I'd take a whiff and open my eyes expecting to see my mom's cousin Teresa standing in front of me, all big-bosomed and freshly coiffed from Marge's Hair Emporium and Oil Change.

Reading the labels or listening to the barman tell me what I'd be tasting ended up being depressing, plus I was disappointed when my mom's favorite cousin did not magically appear. I decided to attach my scents to experiences instead. One whisky reminds me of standing in the wind at the top of a twisting and wall-less staircase at Urquhart Castle—earthy, fresh, and ethereal. Another tastes like the battlefield of Culloden—dark, serious, and tinged with cannon smoke. There are stories that go with many of them, colors with others, but most of the time, each whisky smells and tastes of the distillery that created it.

Sitting in the drawing room before dinner that evening, I was eager to try something new, but whisky is something you don't quench your thirst with, so I found it a good practice to have a glass of water beforehand. Except I'd forgotten that tonight I'd be served a glass full of sludge-colored liquid.

I looked up at the barman. "It's safe to drink this?"

"Oh aye," he said with a wink. "Some women say it's a fine weight-loss aid."

I shuddered. "Is it because they lose all their water weight by not drinking any of it?"

"No worries. I'll bring ye some bottled. We have two. One is High-land Spring, and the other is a bit pricier. It's Aquagen."

"Why does it cost more?"

The barman wiggled his eyebrows. "It's oxygenated."

I glanced over to Jonathan, who was knee-deep in another wine bible. "What does that do for you?" I asked him.

He raised his eyes to meet mine. "Gives you expensive burps."

"Never mind," I sighed. "I'll just have a whisky. Neat."

Balmenach:

Professionally Licensed Peat Shed

Mark Twain said that the only difference between a tax man and a taxidermist is that the taxidermist leaves the skin.

Perhaps James McGregor, a farmer and illicit distiller who lived in the early 19th century, held the same sentiment and therefore did his utmost to wine and dine the local excise officer in search of a few unlawful stills.

It could have been the first overly generous dram McGregor served the visiting officer that raised a small red flag in the tax man's mind before receiving a tour of the farm, or that McGregor was too eager to divert his attention with the answer "That'll just be the peat shed" when asked about the purpose of the little shack beside the stream. Maybe it was the second charitable offering of whisky after the walkabout.

Whatever tipped off the exciseman, it was surely unexpected to hear him offer up, "If I were you, Mr. McGregor, I'd just take out a license for yon 'peat-shed.'"

Thankfully for whisky lovers everywhere, Mr. McGregor did just that. And thus, one saw the birth of Balmenach Distillery.

Personally, I think what saved old McGregor was not his generosity, but his skill. Was it any wonder some were pleased to turn a blind eye now and again if it meant they'd be assured of the continued existence of a good thing?

No doubt this historic distillery, huddled close to the deeply heathered hills of Cromdale, is deserved of honor and credit. They've had ample time to perfect the production of a fine spirit.

Before its founding in 1824, McGregor may have reviewed the two criminal activities his family was prosperous with and successful at—distilling and smuggling—and considered going legal with one of them, revealing a safer method of creating income. I have no real facts to draw from, as sadly, Balmenach does not have a visitor's center where I can hold a dram up to the light and say, "So this is what smuggling tastes like."

But having discovered the recipe for success for the McGregor line, the family remained true to the formula: a cast-iron mash tun, Douglas Fir washbacks, and worm tubs (the bygone practice of submerging a coiled copper pipe—containing the distilled vapors—into a tank or tub of cold water to condense the vapors and return them to liquid form).

The "conversation" between copper and vapor is an interesting one, where (in a nutshell) if the vapors pass slowly over the copper, its flossy, scouring-pad threads hold on to the heavier elements, resulting in a lighter spirit. Less of a "chat" creates heavier, richer flavors. Since Balmenach's worm tubs are less loquacious and work "true to spirit," the end product is generally dense and deep, meaty, and a measurable mouthful.

Alas, this distillery is one of only thirteen or fourteen that continue the tradition of the worm tub technique, and much of Balmenach's boodle is branded for blends such as Peter Dawson and, at one time, Johnnie Walker. In fact, as described by Inver House Distillers, which currently operates Balmenach Distillery, the spirit is "ideal for adding weight and grunt to blends." I have never heard such terminology, but it seems fitting if one is a smuggler attempting to pilfer goods in less-than-ideal situations. If a taste of history is what you seek, Balmenach's hidden gems are worth the search. Just ask the tax man.

Bagpipes

I have heard more jokes about bagpipes and pipers than I've had hot dinners, yet each time I've attended an event where a musician plays a set, the crowd is hushed, becomes reverent, and usually someone strains a neck muscle from craning to see over the heads of others. The bagpipes are mystical, cabalistic, and yes, meant to be played far away. They were intended to rally the troops, and anyone who has spent time in or around the military knows that exploding gunpowder is a noisy event. Obviously, something akin to a musical drill sergeant was needed to pierce through that thunder, and the Celtic harp just wouldn't cut it anymore.

It's true the pipes were also used as an accompaniment for dancing. That's no surprise as kids love loud music, and back then, in ancient times, parents had no way to make them turn it down.

Bagpipes have been around for at least three thousand years—their origin story beginning likely somewhere in the Middle East. History clearly displays that, cool or not, bagpipes are impossible to get rid of. Sort of like gravity, bedbugs, or the Kardashians.

Each experience I've had hearing them has led me closer to wanting to join an online fan club. I'm not saying I would go all out and print flyers and T-shirts, running for cochairman of the club, but I am a silent admirer of anyone who cracks open an old case and starts to inflate a wheezing bag. And I assure you, it is *not* simply because most bagpipers I've seen are men in full Highland getups. That's merely a perk.

The first time I heard one played in a typical Scottish tradition was when Jonathan and I visited Inverness. We stayed a few miles outside the town in a beautiful hotel called Culloden House. It was breathtaking . . . and nerve-wracking. The house was close to the Culloden battlefield and, apparently, formerly used as headquarters for Bonnie Prince Charlie. If you've read up on all your Scottish battles—or even breezed through the Cliffs Notes version of them (and there were a good handful of those clashes for each person who received a chance to hold the Scottish ruling wand), then you'll know that Chuck had a few problems when it came to fighting. Namely, he sucked at it.

Chances are it was either because his dad never allowed him to play rough with the other boys at sleepovers, or because he liked to dress in constricting women's clothing. Personally, I think it might have been the latter as nothing ticks off the English more than a copycat.

As a result, the souls rest uneasily around Culloden, and disgruntled ghosts abound. It was difficult to sleep. Let me rephrase that. *I* had difficulty sleeping. My *husband* did not. Nor did he ever. It has become clear to me that if you are British, you are very accustomed to having your dead ancestors roam about your bedroom at night. I find this particularly bizarre seeing that Jonathan would spring from sleep with heart-palpitating surprise the second our living cat walked across the foot of the bed. Puzzlingly, Great Aunt Edwina stroking his cheek with her cold dead fingers was nothing to raise the hair on the back of his neck over, but one must put their foot down when it comes to Fluffy looking for a warm place to curl up into a space the size of a gumball.

When we arrived at Culloden House, we dropped our luggage and jumped straight back into the car, making our way to the battlefield and its visitor's center. The day, naturally, was ashen and bleak. A calibrated mist, the envy of any greenhouse owner, subtly irrigated the ground and my clothes.

The visitor's center had plenty of informational walls, displays of armaments and costumes and, of course, the requisite twenty-minute film covering battle strategy and death tolls, all neatly narrated by a monotone former hypnotist. Despite the 1970s-style Driver's Ed film voice-overs, I managed to be captured by the documentary's content. Nearly two thousand men died within the short span of an hour, the climax of the Jacobite rising of 1745–46. As the film ended, I was left with the echoing and unforgiving sound of clanging armor and the battle cry of crazed Highlanders. What I craved was a breath of fresh air. What I was offered was a tour of the actual battlefield. I'm not sure the two can occupy the same space.

The sliding glass doors parted, revealing a path of stone, not unlike the one Dorothy Gale got to skip along, except ours was not of yellow bricks and definitely did not lead us to a dazzling verdant city complete with hair salon and townsfolk hyped up on hashish.

The wind blew with swirling gusts, flapping at the sides of my woolen wrap. We walked past memorial stones revealing the clan names of those who lay beneath them. Hundreds of men clumped together, where nothing apart from plant sprigs in their bonnets identified their allegiance.

My ears prickled with the whispers of these voices. The coiling breeze fooled me into turning right and left, searching for the source of these sounds. The echo of men expressing frustration, developing stratagem, challenging their enemies, crying for reinforcements, falling in combat, and suffering with demise.

In the end, I discovered this battlefield was less about the loss of life and more about the loss of a *way* of life, as following this bloody assault, the Scots, who were desperate to reclaim the throne for Prince Charles Edward Stuart, were at last defeated, and their fate was to see their culture literally erased before their eyes. For those who were not captured and imprisoned, nor sent to the United States as indentured servants, life was a whirl of escaping the British commander's long reach of consequence. Men commanded by the Duke of Cumberland ("The Butcher Cumberland") burned their homes and stole their livestock. The government banned their Highland dress and weaponry, and soon thereafter, stringent laws sprang forth to banish their clan system. No bagpipes, no speaking Gaelic in public, no celebrating anything Stuart-related. Persecution defined.

After returning to the hotel, we found out we were the only guests staying that night. A quiet bath led me into a further reflective mood. When I finally stepped from the now-tepid liquid, I wrapped myself in a hotel robe and sat down in front of the dressing table mirror. I must have been staring off through the window, gazing at the gardens around the hotel, because I jumped as Jonathan slid a tumbler of whisky in front of me along the tabletop.

"A wee dram to warm the cockles of yer heart—or better yet, the heart of yer cockles." He laughed at his own joke. "This one's Glen Ord. Not far from here. It might be a little strong for your liking, but I thought something local might be appropriate."

He left to fill his own bath, and I returned my gaze to the greenery outside. Fumes from the glass, situated directly beneath my nose, drifted upward. There was the hint of smoke, or peat—I couldn't tell which at this early stage in my learning—and something warm and fragrant. I felt the idea of an embrace.

In the distance I heard a buzz, a slow hum, keening a soulful tune. I picked up my glass and moved closer to the window. The sound grew louder until I recognized the bray of a bagpipe. I closed my eyes and took a tentative sip of the whisky, unsure if I'd like it or even want it.

The piper's tune echoed through the estate's parkland like a siren's song, and as he passed beneath my window—had I not been wearing only a robe—I would have followed him like a rat to a watery grave. The whisky slid down my throat, melding itself to the lyrical chant that penetrated my bones. I saw those men, I smelled that battle, I tasted their defeat. The whisky's flavor spoke of history. It held secrets and pain and loyalty. I felt its warmth, its steadfast determination, its ideology. I was left yearning for something that did not belong to me.

I stood for the next twenty-five minutes listening to the piper's wail advancing and receding as he paced the perimeter of Culloden House, a mother encircling her babes, now long gone, but pushed by memory and instinct.

When Jonathan appeared après bath, I'd finished my drink—every last drop of it—but was still left with the echoes of the piper.

"Did you hear the bagpipes?" he asked, putting on his socks for dinner.

I nodded. "What was he doing?"

"He was piping down the sun."

I tilted my head, confused.

"It's a tradition for some pipers to play as the sun sets."

"Oh," I murmured. "I thought he was playing funeral rites or something." The men of Culloden were still singing in my blood.

"Yes, well I'm sure bagpipers are the cause of many a funeral."

I gave him an unappreciative smirk, slightly miffed that he could not intuitively discern my wistful mood. "Why is it that he walks while he plays? Why doesn't he stay in one spot?"

Jonathan raised an eyebrow. "Just like everyone else around him, he's trying to get away from the awful sound."

Spirits-Both Ghostly and Drinkable

I am always drawn to lovely drams that provide stories of a *shady* background. Some are a bit shiver-inducing, but after a sip or two of those heavenly malts, the heebie-jeebies fade away and I'm left wanting more details. Sadly, with no one from those distilleries at my elbow to fill them in, I sometimes make them up to suit my mood. Rest assured, this story is researched and, despite my attempts to find even more to add to the tale, it does not fit into my overflowing file of story snippets titled, "This would make a great novel if I just spice her up a bit."

There are beautifully spun rumors about Glenrothes's distillery that I can't help but think about every time I reach for the barrel-shaped bottle up in my pantry. This particular story provides a few enticing details involving the patch of earth it resides upon, revealing that it has had more than its fair share of deadly encounters. The first happened back in the 18th century in the town of Rothes, where the villagers had a taste for body snatching—as one was wont to have in that era. Thankfully, the snatching took place *after* the body had expired, but still, relatives were growing miffed.

The solution was to build a grave watcher's house: a place where family members of the recently deceased could station themselves until they were sure their mum or dad, granny or gramps were thoroughly and completely ravaged by the thoroughness of decomposition, and no one could benefit from their corpses any longer.

Of course, one couldn't be expected to do their shift without something to shore up jangling nerves. Watching the dead, and hoping they'd stay that way, was a business that required a hefty dose of courage—real or liquid.

Therefore, it comes as no surprise that a distillery (Glenrothes) was shortly founded nearby. If you tour that graveyard today, you'll find them furred with *baudoinia compniacensis*—black sac fungus that is typically found happily residing around distilleries, bonded warehouses (where those sleeping spirits mature), and bakeries, because who doesn't love a little cake with your after-dinner dram? It's clear to see, with a quick examination of the blackened headstones, exactly where the bulk of the "angel's share" is going, and I'm willing to believe that being dead is thirsty work.

One of those gravestones belongs to a man named Biawa Makalaga, who was brought to Rothes in 1898 by Major James Grant of the neighboring distillery, Glen Grant. Apparently, Grant found him "orphaned" on the side of a road during one of the major's hunting expeditions in Africa. The young lad became the newest manservant to Grant, lived in Rothes until his death in 1972, and was buried in the cemetery overlooking Glenrothes Distillery.

In 1980, Glenrothes opened a fresh stillhouse, but it found that the new still, number three, was acting a tad cantankerous. It appeared that Biawa wasn't particularly thrilled with some of Glenrothes's distillery updates and was making his displeasure known to a few workers within the shop by . . . showing up. Strange that he would care so much about Glenrothes and not Glen Grant, but who am I to question the motives of ghosts?

Regardless, the following year, the boys in the distillery got together and decided enough was enough. Despite upper management's deep skepticism, they were given permission to make a call to the local ghostbusters. They set up a visit from amateur paranormal investigator and University College Dublin's professor of pharmacology, Cedric Wilson.

Professor Wilson was reportedly successful in his search to discover the problem: the positioning of the new still had rattled a ley line. Time to adjust some furniture—or it might be adjusted for you.

After hammering two iron stakes on either side of the disruption and a quick but conciliatory conversation with Biawa's headstone, the professor deemed all was well again in the land of spirits. Both paranormal and potable.

Gleneagles

There is a place I have traveled to that has left a deep impression upon my soul; a land where one man cooks so well, it makes you weep; falcons beckon when called, landing heavily on your leather-clad arm; and children drive miniature Range Rovers on woodland trail courses designed specifically for their pleasure. It's also the place where I learned how to make a Scotsman blush.

This enchanted kingdom rests in the heart of Scotland near Perth, perched atop a mass of soil they've named Gleneagles. Royalty has dined there, presidents have golfed there, and anyone footing the bill has experienced cardiac arrest there.

Somewhere a few years deeper into my headlong dive toward the meaty marrow of all things "spiritual," Sir Sackier thought it a splendid idea for us to stay in one of the world's grandest estates. I was right behind him on this one and pretended not to notice anything like prices on menus, the jewel-bedecked women followed by insurance company–hired security guards, or the fact that every day the hotel ripped up yesterday's plush carpeting and replaced it with a new one, varying only slightly in pile and color.

If I walked down any of the hotel's long wood-paneled corridors without my sticky-fingered children trailing behind me, sword fighting one another with 18th-century butter knives they pilfered from the dinner table, I could pretend—for about thirty blissful seconds—that I'd married into wealthy aristocracy and was simply retiring from a long

day of entertaining wannabe friends. The bubble repeatedly burst when
Sir Sackier would catch up behind me, usually after debating the dinner
bill and the fair market price for fish, then *tsk*, saying something like:

"Do you know how much that place makes in a night? If you assume
fifty head per sitting, two seatings per night and let's see . . ."

Then his brain would calculate while snippets of phrases would
slip past his lips including, "one bottle between them at an average
bottle cost of . . ." and "if you figure in the overhead . . ." or, "plus
the cost of the eleven-man kitchen crew then you come up with . . ."
Most times I pretended he was the head of my household staff and
waved him off with a dismissive hand. He rarely had time to notice
because usually, by this point, some child had knocked over a large
oil painting by throwing themselves against the hallway wall in an
effort to die theatrically, and the real household staff came running
up, assuring us not to worry because that painting was going to be
replaced tomorrow anyway.

At Gleneagles, the motto is something like, "The avowed intention
of the management is to create happiness," but I think they left off a
tiny portion of the print that includes the words, "at whatever price you
have to pay."

They certainly deliver. No one can quibble with that. Yet they've set
the bar so high I find myself wanting to leave snarky comments in the
guest books of charming but cheap B&Bs with remarks like, "Not bad,
but you're no Gleneagles."

Apparently, while playing make-believe during my short stay at the
Riviera of the Highlands, I donned a hat so heavy in the back that it
ratchets your nose up three income brackets, and I forgot to take it off.
I became a snob without the bank account to back it up. I really should
have felt ashamed, and I did, but once you start running your fingers
down the wainscoting of everybody else's corridors, it's nigh on impossible to stop the tutting from escaping along with your sighs as you flick
away the dust.

At this point, while visiting the valley of preying birds, I had
come to understand my taste buds were changing—or perhaps
developing—specifically, when it came to the single malt whiskies I was
sampling each night. I'd left behind the softly rounded hills of Lowland

and Speyside spirits and year by year was inching westward through the Highlands. In fact, one evening I had finally considered dipping my toe into the seawater off the coast.

With the hopes of fitting in at supper, I applied my best Fanny Cradock lipstick interpretation. If you aren't familiar with Fanny, she was a real ball-breaking BBC celebrity with a cooking show and the mindset that staying within the lines of anything meant compliance. I'd seen this style on scores of women in the bathroom the night before, but I suppose it becomes harder to precisely reapply anything on your face when your features are swimming in the mirror's reflection. I'm not sure, but this might be a result of popping the cork on your third bottle of Château Margaux 52 B.C.E.

After setting up the children with room service, a movie, and a nanny that charged more than the price of my first car, Sir Sackier and I waded through the three-quarters of a mile of freshly laid carpeting, outside our door, that led to the restaurant's bar. The bar staff glanced at us skeptically, likely assessing whether we could foot the final bill, or perhaps wondering why I let my children apply my makeup.

We were seated in a corner, behind a potted palm that was larger than most California redwoods, and handed a dinner menu, an aperitif menu, and another wine bible—Volume A–C. Having sauntered through one of the hotel's endless gift shops earlier, I'd spotted a shelf filled with names of whiskies I'd not come across before. All of them heralded from a little island called Islay.

I'd seen a few maps and knew of the Hebridean islands, but little else. Not included in the "little else" was how to pronounce the name of the place that at least one third of the bar's whisky menu offered up as an aperitif.

I slaughtered the names, which was par for the course while visiting the United Kingdom. If I ever paused to consider how to pronounce a word, after I proceeded it always became clear I had chosen the wrong way. "How about I select an *Iz-lay* whisky this time and you try something else in case I don't like it?" I'd asked Sir Sackier.

He scanned the menu up and down, making a great show of it. "Hmm . . . sorry, don't see any *Iz-lay* whiskies. In fact, I've not heard of them."

I gave him a withering glare. "Fine. *Eyes-lay? Izzle-lay?* What?" I said, growing frustrated. I threw out my last card, which usually consisted of me tossing a combination of letters together that generally carried a fine spray of my frustration with it.

He laughed, as he always did, and paused professorially until I finally gave up and actually looked at him. He then said, *"Eye-lah."*

I snorted. "No way."

"Yes way."

"Who taught these people how to spell?"

"The English. Just as we have tried to teach most of the world how to do everything."

He did not see my second scowl of the evening, but I was just warming up. Surely there'd be others.

I glanced through the offerings and nearly choked at the cost of some whiskies. "Who would pay one hundred dollars for just over an ounce of scotch?"

Sir Sackier smiled. "Surely not us."

"I wasn't asking for permission." I bristled.

"And I wasn't giving it," he assured me.

Out of the corner of my eye, I saw one of the older barmen push a younger one in our direction, perhaps sensing a brewing spat.

The young man kept glancing over his shoulder as he made his way to our little table. He was stick-thin, splotchy-faced, and clearly nervous, but he also appeared determined to prove himself.

He wrung his hands and looked at my husband. "And how might I be of service this evening?"

Sir Sackier didn't lift his eyes from the wine bible but used his eyebrows to gesture at me. "My wife would like to order a whisky."

I nibbled on a fingernail, having no idea what to order, and looked up at him. A small drop of perspiration collected on the tip of the young man's nose. I smiled a little, trying to be encouraging. "Umm . . . I'm still undecided." I thought if I could engage him in helping me choose, he might relax somewhat. I wasn't going to bite.

"I've tried whiskies from just about every region except the islands and thought I'd give one of those a go."

He wiped at his brow and refused to make eye contact. Instead, he stared straight at the menu I held. "Are ye thinkin' Islay, Orkney, Skye, or Jura?"

My eyes went wide. I hadn't recognized anything he'd said. His accent was incredibly thick. Sir Sackier's head was deep in reverent bliss with the wines, so there was no help in translation there.

"How about something from the island of *Eye-lah*?" I said with great distinction. No one would accuse me of ignorance a second time.

"And what would ye like, then?" He swallowed and looked back over at his senior colleague.

"Any Scotsman in a kilt, as I've come to find out," Sir Sackier said dryly from behind his book. Yes, it was true. In the early years of my repeatedly returning to this country, I couldn't help swooning, just a little, whenever seeing a man in his dress plaids.

The young barman suppressed a cough. I let my husband's joke pass and smiled up encouragingly.

"What would you choose? What do *you* think is outstanding?" I asked.

Straightening his shoulders and drawing in a breath, he thrust his chin forward and said, "Well, everyone's taste is different." His voice cracked, but he swallowed and tried again. "Men and women don't often go for the same thing. What appeals to one might not t'other, but I always choose Bowmore as my measuring stick."

I beamed. "Well, then it's settled. I would *looove* to taste your measuring stick."

The young Scotsman blushed a shade of red so deep, it was almost purple.

"Good heavens." My husband choked with laughter. "You little minx!"

The young man bolted from the room. I'll wager that was his first and last day working at Gleneagles. That's okay; they were going to replace him with a fresh barman tomorrow anyway.

Bowmore's 100 Degrees Proof: Certifiably Explosive!

It's a bit of a bummer to find out that you've entered a competition and lost. It's a major bummer to enter a competition and find out *you've won* but have been dead for the fourteen years it took for the judges to adjudicate.

This historical irritation happened to poor Bartholomew Sikes, inventor of the hydrometer chosen as the victor by the British government in their 1802 search for a more accurate instrument to measure liquid density, or for distillation purposes, alcohol levels.

His wife, on the other hand, probably wasn't as bummed out as old Bart, who was likely kicking the inside of his coffin. She received the tidy sum of £2,000 for the rights to his invention; in today's purchasing power, that's the equivalent of around $220,000. By 1818, when his hydrometer was finally adopted as the new legal standard of measurement, she was probably off in Monte Carlo living the good life and not bothering to measure *anything* about her alcohol.

The hydrometer (including those that existed before Bart's big winner) was a welcome development. The term "proof" is synonymous with the Royal Navy. Sailors were given a daily tot of rum from 1655 until the ration was abolished, as recently as 1970. Originally, it was given to sailors neat once the beer ran out; for a good period of time, water wasn't safe to drink, becoming rancid very quickly at sea and often sourced from polluted rivers, such as the Thames.

Now, determining the strength of the rum was a wee bit challenging before 1816, when Sikes's hydrometer was finally adopted, but the Royal Navy worked out a simple over/under method: they mixed a small sample of the spirit with gunpowder to form a paste and did what all mothers of teenaged boys fear most—they tried to light it on fire. Although the results may have been dubious, it was said that if the liquid blazed, you could rest easy; you had your *proof.* If it flashed, your fusion was *over proof.* No fire? No good. Apparently, sailors in the Royal Navy had it nailed down to a science when testing the daily rum rations. See? Science *is* fun.

We now know that this strength is 57 percent alcohol by volume (ABV). This was just a way of "proving" that spirits were at or above a certain strength, hence the term "proof." And every sailor wanted their full measure of strong hooch. The perfect whisky to illustrate a nod toward that magical number brings us right back to Bowmore.

After visiting Gleneagles, and trying my first Islay whisky, Bowmore became one of my own measuring sticks. That initial sip not only unearthed the new-to-my-tongue pungent flavors of smoke, peat, and leather, but swirled them about with sea spray, seaweed, and iodine-tinged herbs. From that moment on, I was fascinated with the distillery by the sea. I'd not yet seen it, but I knew what she tasted like, and lucky for me, she had a wide spectrum of flavors.

Bowmore Distillery, located on the beautiful island of Islay, has since moved on to more updated and more accurately calibrated techniques for securing proof results—the likely choices being a hydrometer, thermometers, or a densitometer. Certainly, in many countries, distilled spirits are taxed on alcohol content. In the United States, spirits are taxed at the rate of $2.70 per proof gallon. A proof gallon is one liquid gallon of 100 proof spirits or 50 percent ABV at 60° F. The tax on *80 proof* spirits would be .8 x $2.70 or $2.16 per liquid gallon. See? Math is hard.

Taking pride in the long-established practices that have created some of my favorite bottles, Bowmore produced an expression that gives a robust salute toward that fascinating historical proofing method—their powerful 100 Degrees Proof small batch release single malt. I like to think of it as certifiably explosive.

Bottled at a higher alcohol strength, the distillery's potency choice allows consumers to determine how much water they'd like to add to open up the beauty of this dram. Many expert tasters recommend adding a touch of water to truly experience whisky at its finest, and that is certainly sage advice when facing Bowmore's particular masterpiece.

A whisky so intense and multifaceted, 100 Degrees Proof has proven its worthiness to me with each successive sip—no fire necessary. It now happily lives on a shelf among my kingdom of bottles. To borrow (and take creative liberties with) a phrase from Oliver Cromwell, I'd suggest you *"Trust in Bowmore and keep your powder dry!"*

The Unending Sky
on the Isle of Skye

I grew up in Northern Wisconsin, where the summertime—because of its latitudinal proximity to the North Pole—allowed for extra daylight hours. Flashlight tag was pushed back, the dinner hour was fuzzy, and many a child whined over the fact that they'd been sent to bed at what must be an ungodly hour, as the sun was still up and shining.

I thought we had a fair amount of daylight to brag about, but that was before I went to the Isle of Skye. As a kid back in the Midwest, come 9:30 or 10:00, we delighted in knowing that summer was fully upon us because it was finally getting dark and nearing the time to set up the campfires. When I visited Skye during the month of June one year, I gave up on sleep and finally got out of bed to go jogging at 11:15 P.M.

It was just too bright outside. And with a sky refusing to give an inch toward the defeat of daytime, one feels propelled to do anything other than toss around fighting the losing battle of losing consciousness. Any other activity seeps into your mind as a fine idea: dusting, sock folding, practicing the art of spoon-bending. It doesn't matter. It simply needs to keep your mind occupied until your muscles eventually give up the ghost.

Then, just when I thought it was getting dark enough for some shuteye, the sky brightened again around 3:30 A.M., and up comes the sun less than an hour later. Well, back to spoon-bending.

I will admit to having a few other activities in mind on this trip—almost all of them involving food and whisky, topped off with more whisky—but nothing is open at 3:30 A.M., and thus, I am left staring at the ceiling and mindlessly recalling the dumbfounding and most surreal landscape that brought me to this marvelous chunk of earth.

To get to the Isle of Skye from mainland Scotland, one must take a bridge, although one can still take a ferry there, as well. The bridge to Skye was built and opened for use in 1995. As a lover of bridges in general, I found this one rather breathtaking with its large, swoopy concrete arch against the lush background of the mainland's Highland landscape.

The bridge caused a bit of a stir with the folks on either side of it, as for a time there was a pricey toll to pay the German engineers—and private investors—of this gliding roadway artwork. The intent was to recoup the cost of their talents.

With enough protesting, the government of Scotland rubbed their twisted arm muscles and finally opened the country's wallet to purchase the grand gateway. People breathed a sigh of relief at now being afforded the luxury of getting gas and groceries on either side of Loch Alsh; that is, until in a few months' time, they realized they could now afford neither gas nor groceries, as the government quickly added a tax on air inhalation and the viewing of seawater to recoup their own costs.

Okay, I'm not entirely certain about that last part, but I swear that's what my ears picked up one night while eavesdropping in a local pub on Skye.

Regardless, when I visited I was granted access for free and sent up a round of thanks for all involved—builders, designers, and protesters alike.

Now, to get to Skye Bridge, one must drive through lands that are paralleled only by those in Tolkien's trilogy.

Riding with two thoroughly unhappy children and a husband who believed himself to be in a car more akin to a 1964 Triumph Spitfire than the Peugeot hatchback we were neatly folded into, gives one pause for thought as to why any consideration was given to a trip such as this.

I'll tell you why. Because Talisker was on the other side of it.

Oft-uttered phrases such as—

Stop touching me!

This tin box has absolutely no pickup!

This time, I really, seriously have to pee.—were nearly muted by the other locution drumming steadily in my head: *Whisky will make a balm of it all.*

And lest any reader feel I use alcohol as some sort of precarious psychoactive calmative, then let me assure you, you're spot on—I do.

Under most circumstances, it's merely meant to enhance a meal or make me weep with joy at the talents it took to create something so memorable and special.

But I will not apologize for the gift man and God created that alleviates back pain, head pain, or heart pain. If you have a product that advertises a motto such as *Pain begone!* then yes, I will peruse that label with curious and thorough interest.

On this particular trip—one I had begun to fantasize about months in advance once the first sip of Talisker passed over my tongue—I was willing to put up with the humdrum family dynamics that can dampen the spirits of any vacation, but I was unprepared for the gift that unspooled before me. A gift that would wipe away any memory of small-car discomfort and whining child chatter.

The road we traveled upon was one unlike any I'd experienced before. Thin—as are most Scottish roads I directed us toward—and winding, though this time, not entirely my fault as this is bog-standard with nearly all Scotland's byways. My jaw dropped incrementally with each mile and each bend. I had never encountered beauty so majestic, imposing, and lush with greenery.

We were traveling along the A87, a road that takes travelers past *Sgùrr Fhuaran*. Now, I'm no mathematician, but when I later asked a local about the view we'd driven straight through, the answer he provided was one that left me wondering if Scotland employed some new form of computation that the rest of the world had yet to catch up with. The other explanation for his confusing logic of quantity was evident by the heavy perfume of hard liquor that came with his story. Anyway, try to follow along:

Sgùrr Fhuaran is one of three mountains with four main ridges that make up the Five Sisters of Kintail, there being seven altogether.

I swear, that's exactly what he said.

The story goes that a couple of dodgy sailors—brothers at that—landed their foreign boats in Loch Duich and fell head over heels for the two youngest sisters of a farmer's large litter of seven daughters. When the farmer refused to hand over their hands until the older gals were all hitched, the sailors grew canny, stating they had five other brothers who would be more than pleased to land such a lot. They took off with the two fresh-faced lasses and vowed to send the promised suitors on in no time flat.

Except "no time flat" was a little longer than everyone expected. These five girls waited and hoped, dreamed and desired, until what usually happens to women in such a state as this occurred—they turned to the local sorcerer, who said he'd be happy to help preserve their youthful beauty whilst they waited and promptly turned them into stone. Legend goes that their feet are in the rivers and their heads are in the clouds, where they remain, forever vigilant, forever foiled.

And now, like Lilliputians, we trample all over their lovely heads and shoulders because Scotland has declared those sisters the best hiking and ridge walks known to mankind.

Legend and lore aside, it does not matter if you are at the feet of these sisters or among their crowns in the clouds, via car or backpack, the trek to see and be within them leaves you breathless.

Smuggling and Struggling:
A Bad Guy Gone Good

C an you remember the times when you were in class as a kid, and everyone hated the teacher? Remember how you'd break the rules in devious alliance behind the teacher's back?

Now, do you remember that one kid who was all for participating in the illicit activity, right there with you as everyone took turns writing something forbidden on the chalkboard, snagging something from the teacher's desk, or coming up with the next scheme to wreak havoc in the classroom—just until he figured out he liked the perks of the other side better? A goody-goody, more satisfied with working for the enemy?

Remember the anguish of betrayal and how you all lamented that you'd obviously lost him to adulthood, but you remained stubbornly steadfast in the blissfully ignorant joys of immaturity?

Well, after reading about George Smith, raffish whisky smuggler of the early 1800s and founder of The Glenlivet distillery, I was immediately reminded of those early school day shenanigans.

George started off on the same side as the illegally distilling High-land farmers living beside him—skirting authority. They were brothers from another mother, right? They all hated the English. Chances are they all had FREEDOM & WHISKY GANG THE GITHER tattooed on their upper arms.

Except George got cozy with his landowner, the Duke of Gordon, laird of Aberlour. Maybe it was because the duke filled him with flattery, praising George's fine Latin handwriting, or rugged good looks, or the way he spun a good yarn while sharing an hour at the local watering hole, but whatever the reason, George moved over to the dark side and went straight.

The laird helped sway the government to make whisky distilling a legal venture, convincing them that the fellows in his neck of the woods—tenants especially—were going to make whisky come hell or high water (or maybe hell or high taxes). Distilling was in their blood just as much as the high content of alcohol. And if the government passed the new bill with "reasonable" duties, the duke and his cronies would all help stamp out bad-boy behavior. Once the Excise Act of 1823 was passed, it was time to get a few folks to sign up and show the rest of the valley just how much fun behaving like gentlemen would be.

Shortly after putting up his shiny new shingle as the rule-following teacher's pet, George had to *"shower, shave, and shan't be long"* all with one hand because the other one now always needed to hold a gun. For several years after his decision to follow Darth Gordon, George was in constant threat of being shown the inside of his own kiln. This animosity was a blatant message revealing just what his neighbors thought of the new law.

Nevertheless, George was not one to give up. People could call him a toady all they wanted. He was going to continue making whisky—and making money from making whisky. He simply wasn't going to be invited to any potlucks if his plus-one was the duke. Yet he persevered in the face of danger and continued to make a spirit that grew from good to great, and eventually, to hugely enviable.

It's tough to be the guy who changes the game, but sometimes by taking a chance and sticking it out, you'll also change history and become a notable part of it.

A few years ago, I was lucky enough to come into the possession of a bottle of Glenlivet, bottled in March of 1979 and ready to drink at thirty-three years of age. It's a beautiful dram that reminds me of freshly mown hay, crumbly shortbread, and sticky golden raisins in my lunchbox. I'm guessing these are exactly the scents I was smelling and the food I was eating in my very own schoolyard thirty-three years ago—right before I joined a bunch of other kids to leave a ransom note for the classroom's pencil sharpener on our teacher's desk.

No Toys for Mommy

Driving around Skye is an activity that will surely provide you ample opportunities to catch flies—or midges, I suppose, as this was the height of summer. My mouth hung open a lot. The scenery is stunning, with places to visit that sport titles like Fairy Pools, Garden of the Gods, and Kilt Rock, the latter being one of my all-time favorite natural formations. It looks like a pleated kilt—it's just missing the man beneath it.

The village of Portree is Skye's tiny capital. A fishing hamlet that has been perfectly painted for postcards and snapshots, it's ripe for visitors to happen upon and believe they've landed inside an undiscovered Hebridean fairy tale.

But in my case, the fairy-tale ending was a mental picture: me with a glass of treasured Talisker in my hand—no prince, no castle, just the happily-ever-after drink that would leave me deliriously gratified for years. Or at least until the following week, when I'd trade any nonessential organ for another round.

Sadly, my plans were foiled. By children. And by Talisker, which I'm guessing hates children.

After we'd arrived at our B and B and tossed our luggage into two tiny rooms that would make an airplane toilet feel spacious, we took off to explore the fine island. Without much time left in the day, we visited Portree, and the giant skirt made of rock, then headed back toward our rooms to change for dinner.

Dinner, I was told, was going to be one of the best I'd had in Scotland. As in *ever*, which was an incredibly high bar to reach as I have had some of the best meals of my life in squatty old pubs that specialized in pies, pints, and the occasional punch-up.

Also, in Italian gas stations. And that is no lie. Those people seriously know how to cook anything, anywhere, and make you sigh like you've just had your first kiss, but this I'll save for another story, another time, another book.

Dinner, I was told, would be at the world-renowned, nearly impossible to get to, and more impossible to book, The Three Chimneys.

It also had a Michelin star.

That two-word descriptor is another thing that can make you sigh like a schoolgirl. Having the good fortune to eat at an establishment worthy of that award will likely make you feel like the other checkmarks on your bucket list pale in comparison—though maybe that's just me. My whole life is basically a series of moments between meals.

The Three Chimneys promised oyster foam and pickled sea lettuce, scorched langoustine tails and wood-fired Skye red deer. By this point, after reading the menu, I could have just eaten that and probably been equally thrilled. Everything smelled divine and looked heavenly. Clearly, God was cheffing that night. I was sure to say an extra line of grace before unapologetically licking my plate clean.

The walk home was a needed one. Bright with the northern summer evening light, it helped burn off about twenty of the three thousand calories I'd consumed during the previous two and a half hours.

Then I found myself in bed. And bored. And then jogging. And way too full for jogging. So, it ended up being a bit more of a slogging close to midnight.

The next day, our chipper family would be wedged into the sardine tin with wheels, and we'd be off to finally experience the great spirit wonder of Skye's whisky world.

During breakfast with the delightful older couple who owned the cottage, I began to list all the spectacular, heart-palpitating facts about Talisker to (1) make the older couple envious enough to wish they were coming along, and (2) excite my children to a fevered pitch for yet another distillery outing they would *never forget*.

"Did you know that when Talisker was being built in 1830, the local clergy were prophesying hell and damnation to the MacAskill brothers, the owners?"

"Hell and damnation?" the older gentleman repeated with a crooked gaze directed at me.

"Err . . . something like that. Well, they were against it for sure."

He nodded.

"And did you know that they used to do triple distillation and then switched to double somewhere in the early 20th century? And that they lost five stills in a fire in the sixties? Those are a couple of little golden nuggets of interest most folks don't know about," I said, spearing a sausage with my fork and pointing at him.

"Aye, canna say that they made much of a dent in this old noggin'," he said, pouring more tea for everyone.

I was losing him, I could tell. "And how about the fact that they're shutting down, and this is their last week due to the fact that they've been caught sabotaging the restoration of the old Torabhaig Distillery under construction, one that's going to be a massive competitor?"

"What?" the old guy said, alarmed.

"I'm kidding," I said quickly.

"Cool," one of my children chimed in.

"Well, time to go," I said, popping up from the table.

"You're off to the distillery then?" the elderly missus asked, wiping her hands on the large and delicately embroidered apron around her waist.

"Finally," I said with a giant smile and added, to the children, "And we all know what a brilliant time people have looking at giant copper pots, don't we? All those potions and magic machines?"

They each shot me a dour glance as the missus asked, "And what of the children? Where will they be?"

"With us. Of course." I felt a tiny itch of *uh oh* creep up my neck.

"Oh no," she waved a hand. "Talisker doesna allow the wee bairns on-site. Ye'll need make other arrangements. Ah well, I'm off to bingo!" she shouted over her shoulder.

"Right behind ye, darlin'," her husband called.

And that was that.

No Talisker. No copper pots, nor five new stills. No stories of the takeover by Johnnie Walker and John Dewar and all their many sons. No peaty, peppery, salty, smoky, heady, dream-inducing malt from Skye.

I plopped down again at the table and did a head dive where my forehead met with egg yolk so orange one wonders if the chickens around here aren't scarfing down sackfuls of annatto seeds to give themselves that lovely Wisconsin-cheddar hue.

"Take them to the Glendale Toy Museum!" I heard the old woman shout as she slammed the front door shut.

Toy museum! Toy museum! I heard echoing from the bedroom where the children were getting their gear together.

"We were *going* to a toy museum, dammit," I mumbled. "An explosively dangerous and operational one, but now . . . no toys for mommy."

Whisky, Women, and *Wham!*, You're Wedded

Back in the car, plowing across roads barely stretching from front tire to front tire and stopping every other mile to shoo sheep off the road, I read about the full-family excitement we were in for. The pamphlet in the B and B advertised that Glendale's Toy Museum is sited directly upon Skye's "stark and lunar edge," and the single most heard phrase echoing about it was, "Oh! We used to have one of those!"

Goody.

There were sheep everywhere when we arrived. Not to mention a good number of wandering wild goats. After stopping to chase more frenzied unfarmed animals, I ushered the kids inside with a hiss of, "Seriously, the sign out front says that if either one of you break something in the museum with your adorable jammy fingers, the owners get to decide which of your internal organs they can carve out and place in a jar upon their mantel. So, watch it, wee ones."

At least an hour had passed when I finally looked up from a whole shelf dedicated to Donny and Marie Osmond and remembered that I actually came with two children.

A few *dammit*s later, I found them. Two floors up. Under a pile of wooden trains and sock puppets.

"Where's the 'on' button?" said my son, looking up, confused.

"It's back in the car. Come on, let's go. I heard a massive coach of German tourists has just arrived, and I'm guessing they've just finished admiring their lovely bridge. Time to skedaddle."

On the car ride home—or rather back to the mainland—I took in the island animals. The sheep and goats, the red stag and six-foot wingspanned gannets, the puffins and—if you squinted just so and thought yourself lucky enough—the bobbing gray seals.

I sighed with a long, deep note of sadness at the fact that I'd missed out on Talisker. When would I return? Ever?

Jonathan stopped for gas and came back with a look of self-congratulation on his face. "We're going to a *ceilidh*—one of those Scottish parties you've been on about. They put them on for tourists each Sunday afternoon in the next town over. That should put a stop to your miserable mood."

Miserable? I questioned myself. Oh, good Lord no. I wasn't the slightest bit miserable. I was in Scotland. The land I loved more than any place in the world. How could I be miserable?

I was regretful. There's a big difference. But I was well aware by this point that empathy was beyond my companion's aptitude. Spelling out the dissimilarities between the two emotions would only fall on deaf ears. I was supposed to celebrate. He'd fixed everything. Now be happy, dammit.

But going to a ceilidh would only be considered a great idea if it were a real one. Not the type he had booked for us—the equivalent to our American Medieval Times Dinner and Tournament, which this clearly and unmistakably would be.

A true ceilidh is one where you do not leave through a gift shop, or with snapshots of a cast, or wishing you hadn't decided to "what the hell" it with the buffet. It is not the last day of a Gaelic Experience Tour.

Now, I know. The word looks unpronounceable. And after you've been to a real one, pronouncing anything is nearly impossible, so no one cares how you end up slaughtering the Gaelic. A ceilidh (pronounced *KAY-lee*) is basically a social gathering. A party. With booze. Copious amounts. But more important, it's one with singing, dancing, and a whopping dose of camaraderie.

The term *ceilidh* derives from an old Irish word that translates into "companion," but you cannot have a ceilidh with only one. It's not that people haven't tried, but the Scots have ears like an owl who can hear a mouse pass gas from three hundred yards away. It's impossible to pop the cork from a bottle of whisky or draw the bow across a fiddle string without fifteen Scots showing up within thirty seconds, rubbing their hands together in anticipation.

I think what I like about these gatherings, more than anything else, is the spontaneity. No one sends out invitations. There are no dreadful e-vites piling up in your inbox. It's more the sound of the opening of the pub door that brings folk running.

I've witnessed these get-togethers in both the middle of the night and the middle of the day. If you've got a distilled spirit, a cup, and someone who can whistle in time, you've got yourself the makings of a grand event.

Now, if you're thinking this gathering sounds no more involved than your average backyard barbecue, you might find yourself surprised when attending one. Normally, our garden variety parties are more drink in hand, stereo on, bowls of chips and guac, and friends milling about in the kitchen or living room and checking your bathroom cupboards for info to spill or goods to filch.

A ceilidh is a drink *in each hand* (unless you're one of the musicians, in which case you balance it on your knee), a shouting match over the music, recitations of your favorite poetry and tales (the musicians need a couple of minutes to enjoy their whisky, after all), ballads sung, and marriages made. How many people have come to *your* village shindig with the intent of finding a mate and announcing their nuptials—all in one night?

Maybe it's old fashioned, maybe it's quaint, but I find it to be as close to perfect as possible. The language is bawdy, the women brazen, the clocks are hidden, and no one sits for longer than it takes to tell a story. If you've met a Scotsman, you may come to the same conclusion as I did. I'm sure they've got a third lung.

So, in fact, there might be time to recover from the last reel or strathspey, but don't get comfy. Musicians get itchy, and the publican knows that dancing people are thirsty people.

But, by far, the best way I've heard a ceilidh described was like this: You will dance. You will be made to dance. And you will love it. And you will love the fact that you can't remember any of it the next day. Except for the part of yourself that relentlessly reminds you of what you've done. It shouts at you as a constant reproof, striking a jarring chord in your head—*idiot, idiot, idiot*!

After all, it sucks to wake up the next morning with a beer pull tab on your left ring finger and a lad you've never seen snoring on the pillow beside you. It sucks, but it will be the best fun you've ever had.

Spelling Lessons

It's whisky with a Y not whiskey with an E, cuz whiskey with an E goes ick not yum!" This was a simple theme song I picked up along the way—courtesy of an irritating Liza Minnelli identity crisis put to music—which initially helped me spot the difference between the whisky from Scotland and everything else claiming some ancestral link to the world of fermented grain mash. Although, years later, I now know that it is not simply Scotland, but Canada, Australia, Japan, and some countries in Europe that embrace that spelling. Still, it was an innocently naive life raft I clung to in the early days that guided my hand when reaching for a bottle. Today, thank God, I have broadened my palate and no longer whistle that song unless I'm determined to painfully remind myself what an ignoramus sounds like.

Pinning this cruel and callous show tune of a ditty onto the profit-sharing sect of all things not born of rebellious clans and illicit stills emerged strictly from a matter of taste. Okay, and maybe I was cruel and callous. But it was nearly thirty years ago and happened with good reason. Partially because I do not like sweet drinks, and I'd found—at least in my early days of taste testing—many American and Canadian whiskies presenting an ample measure of sugared notes. The other part of the blame falls squarely on the shoulders of Michael Pollan who, in 2006, wrote *The Omnivore's Dilemma*.

Shortly after reading his opinion and convincing proofs—that a good majority of Americans are basically "walking corn"—I banished

all things maize-derived from my pantry and fridge. At the time, I felt
hugely smug, except for the fact that those clever, well-paid marketing
directors hired by the corn industry were usually one step ahead of
me and continued to rename the plant's abundant products. One must
be part chemist to fully realize all its forms and labels. Corn seemed
to show up everywhere—almost as much as my mother's favorite
additive to all my childhood meals, Campbell's cream of mushroom
soup. I could not escape it. I continue to have a prolific fear of fungi
in general and can hear the opening hiss of a can from one county
over. It's the same with corn—and since numerous whiskies are made
with the grain as its primary cereal, it lends sweeter notes to the finished product. Also, in my defense, at this time in the 1990s, rye and
wheat grain mashes were rather challenging to come by in the liquor
stores I frequented.

Therefore, for numerous years, I flat-out refused to sip anything not
falling into the strictly outlined and highly enforced definition of uisge
beatha—or Scotland's "water of life." The classification of this beverage
can be a complicated maze to maneuver through and come out the other
side with a clear understanding of what means what, because there are
more rules and regulations to define this drink than laws that now
govern the operation of a cup of hot coffee. Much of the interpretation
is dependent upon the individual explaining. And since this is my tale,
we use my definitions. Okay, and we'll use the official Scotch Whisky
Regulations of 2009 just for absolute clarity. Plus, all the extra clauses
tacked on by Her Majesty's Revenue and Customs. Because some people
are super picky. Like Her Royal Majesty.

"Single Malt Scotch Whisky" is made up of only three ingredients:
water, malted barley, and yeast. It is made in Scotland, aged in Scotland,
and hugged by oak barrels for no fewer than three years. Many people
refer to this official description merely as *scotch*, but I might advise you to
be extra prudent with the word when visiting the land of molten magic. I
say this only by quoting the previously mentioned heavily bearded, dyspeptic distiller I worked with years ago, who said to me, "No Scotsman
worth his weight in hair would call it that. We dinna need any new-
fangled term to distinguish the stuff made in our land versus the draff
made anywhere else in the world. Mostly because ye'll not find much of

anything else available. Everyone drinks whisky—unless you work in a distillery—in which case you're so desperate to get away from work, ye just drink beer."

At the time, I'd say the old geezer was right, that few pubs held special shelves for Japanese, or Indian, or American spirits. And I've had more than a huge handful of barkeeps look at me as if I'd nearly committed a crime when asking if they kept any other country's whiskies behind the bar. Not like I craved anything apart from scotch, but I was growing curious.

I'm going to go out on a limb and say that most Scots I've worked with are wholly fine with the term *scotch*—as long as you use it when referring to the drink and *not* the people. They are Scots or Scottish, not Scotch. But occasionally, I've come across a fellow like that highly opinionated double for Sean Connery—who probably didn't give a flying fig that Scotland has spent thirty years of expensive and dogged marketing in an attempt to separate Scotland's spirits from her competitors. I simply thought it was worth bringing up, if for no other reason than Sean Connery is an entirely believable actor, and why should I question someone so marvelously well-favored and handsome?

Now, it's true that since I first stuck my toe into the pond of spirits, it has grown exponentially around the world; that is, the depth and breadth of spirits—not my toe. There are artisans out there who are continually finding new ways to attract attention and win accolades with their ingenuity, distilling liquids with intriguing combinations of grains and fruits, herbs, and God knows what else. My liver and my pocketbook cannot keep up with advertisements for everything that comes across my desk, begging to be added to my already overflowing inventory. And even though there are the occasions where I will vary my routine, stray from my biweekly drams, and delve into the arena of grappas, eau-de-vies, or *Shōchūs*, it is usually followed by a long bout of guilt for not choosing a single malt and is further enhanced by the noises coming from the depths of my pantry.

I have been assured that those noises I hear—the blazing battle cries uttered in the rough tongue of Gaelic—are all in my head. But just passing by the pantry door I'd swear I can make out the soft burr of incensed Speysides, Islays, and Campbeltowns, all my boys whose names begin with Glen or Mac or Ben. I feel a traitor, tested and proven weak. And who could blame their grumbling? At one point over the years, I had nearly two hundred of them vying for space on the shelves that used to hold things like dried beans, flours, and olive oils. They had to find new ways of grabbing my attention as I scanned past their labels humming the melodic lines of "Time in a Bottle," Rescue Me," or—I admit with great embarrassment—Barry Manilow's "Can't Smile Without You."

But to this day, I push the guilt aside, as I do truly prefer a single malt from Scotland to any other spirit. The soul-ingrained taste of that sweet biscuit-like grain reminds me of what I cut my teeth on. And I am nothing if not loyal to the bone—er . . . the barley.

PART TWO

You Can Take the Lass Out of Scotland . . .

Pipers on Sale,
Aisle Three

When you think about giving someone a gift, I'd bet most of you don't entertain the idea of gifting a *person*. It seems a horrible, archaic bestowal, one reserved for history's long-dead plantation owners, increasing their enslaved workforce, or a pharaoh choosing who will accompany him into the *world to come*, except when you consider who is bestowing the gift. My English then-husband, Sir Sackier, considered himself—if the fates cooperated—the future royalty of reclaimed land (that would be America). Therefore, granting a human endowment would not make him pause, believing the token curious, or even perhaps illegal. But regardless, it is among one of the nicest things Jonathan ever did for me, however problematic.

It happened on the day we moved into our newly built house on top of a mountain. A place we'd spent close to five years building. Five years later, we *still* had workmen at the house daily. It seemed it would never be done. We'd gotten every variation of Murphy Brown's permanent painter, Eldin, working whenever it suited their schedule. This usually meant whenever they'd run out of ammunition, beer, or the cash to replenish that ammunition and beer—and usually in this order.

The day we finally got the okay to claim occupancy was a gloomy, misty December morning. Both my folks had come to help unpack boxes and direct the crews of moving men. Shortly after they'd left, and as I was in the kitchen buried in a box of newspaper-wrapped crockery, I thought I'd heard somebody shout. I pulled my head out of the four-foot-deep carton, thinking maybe someone had finally discovered my favorite chocolate chip cookie platter that had gone missing two moves ago.

I heard both Jonathan calling from outside and my mom rushing into the kitchen, all a twitter, saying I'd better hightail it out to where he was. I expected the worst. Surely the man had fallen into an undiscovered well, or maybe he'd come upon a civil war burial site and disturbed a pine box of old bones that now meant we'd be haunted for the rest of our lives here. When it came to Jonathan, my mind whirled with all the usual suspects.

I stepped out onto the deck off the kitchen—the one I'd dubbed "The Whisky Porch"—because it faced the mountains to the west—where we'd undoubtedly be spending many an evening watching the sun go down on the Old Dominion. Jonathan stood there with a ridiculous grin spread across his face. He looked like he was eight and had found his first frog.

"Do you hear something?" he asked, cocking an ear toward the mountains.

I leaned forward and scanned the horizon. What should I be listening for? The scream of a bobcat? The cry of an eagle? The sound of a bullfrog being squished behind his back?

"No," I said and stopped. Because just then I did. I heard the magical sound my heart had suctioned itself to, years earlier, when I first went to Scotland.

Bagpipes.

I looked out into the midday murk, across the tree-covered slopes of the mountains, wondering how in the world I had gotten so lucky as to pick a plot of land to build upon that was within earshot of a practicing piper. Then I saw him coming up our driveway. *Wheezing* up our driveway. Our driveway, which is one mile long and one thousand feet straight up.

"What do you think?" Jonathan asked as both my parents joined us, a video camera now in his hands and pointed at my face.

"Oh my God, the poor man!" I said, positive the piper was going to have a cardiac arrest before he made it to the top. "Did you do this?" I pointed at the gasping musician in full Gaelic getup.

He nodded proudly. "Yes. Happy moving-in day, darling."

"Did you tell him beforehand that he was going to need a Sherpa to make it up here?" I bit my lip envisioning an eventual lawsuit, but hearing that beautiful sound in the most perfect setting made tears come to my eyes. A piper! To christen our new home.

After fifteen more blissful and painful minutes, the piper finally came through the front door, without pausing for breath, and into the hallway—where I thought he'd surely collapse. Instead, he stood bellowing in the hollowed-out foyer, perfectly centered beneath a space that rose to the tower a full forty feet above him. The blast of pipes exploded through the house, puncturing the walls, and paralyzing my parents, which is oftentimes the sneaky tactic of a military piper, who then signals the rest of the highlanders to sneak up behind their stunned victims and slice off their heads with a clean sweep of their broadswords.

Although this probably wasn't intended, it was the by-product of my husband's housewarming gift.

Even if everyone else listened to the performance because they were too polite—or too stupefied—to put their fingers in their ears, I stood there, rooted to the ground, thrilled with the marrow-piercing, razor-sharp melody.

It was this man, whom I will call Donald for the sake of anonymity, who later performed at our first ever Burns Night. An event I will save for chapters further afield. A night when it usually takes more than a horse's trough full of liquor for any piper to give the airbag a rest.

"What do you think of your gift? Are you pleased with him? He's ours whenever we'd like," Jonathan shouted at me.

It was then that I realized, like a restaurant that chose a *house wine*, or my mother-in-law, who refused—until it was time to dress for dinner—to shed her *housecoat*, that Jonathan had appointed a *house piper*.

"He's wonderful. And we should invite him here often—to play OUTSIDE. I feel we owe the poor man—not *own* the poor man, as he's nearly done himself in while climbing the mountain to get up here."

And we did owe him, despite the fact he was idiotic enough to pick up the phone when harkened by this aspiring new monarch. But I doubt Sir Sackier heard what I'd said. He had his fingers in his ears.

Ernest Shackleton:

The Women, the World, the Whisky

W ho doesn't love Ernest Shackleton? Adventurer, explorer, commander, womanizer.

Wait.

Forget that last part.

Ernest Shackleton had an appetite for discovery, for fame, and for hard liquor.

Hold on.

Maybe skip that last bit.

Let's concentrate on the fact that this was a daringly brave man with an optimistic sense of determination and a dicey cocaine habit.

Dammit.

I'm really trying to write an interesting mini-biography here, while attempting to capture the magnitude of the man. Except what if that which made him great also pulled him down? Or might we liken it to the debate of the chicken and the egg? Perhaps his foibles propelled him to bold, portentous escapades.

Whatever the timeline of vice and virtue, making history was Shackleton's goal, breeding fame and fortune, if possible. He wanted to taste life while standing at the edge of it. Literally. And I wanted to taste the whisky he forced a few sled dogs to pull around with him so he could have a drink when his frostbitten digits stopped responding, or when he finally planted his flag of triumph and needed to celebrate. Thankfully, someone made that possible.

Shackleton attempted to reach the South Pole twice with no success.

The four members of the party that set out to become the first to reach the South Pole were defeated just ninety-seven miles from their destination, a point they reached on January 9, 1909.

The first undertaking brought him a fractured friendship and the unjust, heavy blame of defeat to shoulder. His second venture illuminated what did and did not work—like replacing food with "Forced March" cocaine tablets.

It must have sliced him to the core to hear of Roald Amundsen's victory, and the planting of a Norwegian flag—but Shackleton never gave up. His spirit was strong and his determination unbeatable. He planned one more Antarctic expedition to beat all others, wishing to triumphantly cross the entire continent from one coast to the other.

Bad luck continued to dash the hopes of those attempting the Imperial Trans-Antarctic Expedition. After the Weddell Sea swallowed his ship, the ironically named and freshly unearthed *Endurance*, Shackleton's new goal was simply crew survival. Personally, I'm thinking the fuzziness of hard liquor might have helped with the whole "keep calm and carry on" bit.

Making the onerous decision to leave most of his men behind, Shackleton and five others sailed on toward South Georgia Island and its whaling stations, fully determined to find a ship that would return to rescue the remaining twenty-two crew members he'd stranded on Elephant Island.

After reaching South Georgia, Shackleton again halved his ailing company and left to cross the twenty-two miles of mountains, ice, and snow to eventually reach the opposite side, where the whaling stations stood.

From May 23 through August 30, 1916, sailing attempts with four separate ships and the help of several South American countries finally brought Shackleton back to Elephant Island, where the remainder of his nearly two dozen marooned men still lived and now breathed a sigh of relief.

Sir Ernest Shackleton's last voyage brought him back not only to his favorite destination but also to his final one. After suffering and succumbing to a heart attack on South Georgia Island, he was buried there, close to the frozen continent that had claimed his heart from the beginning.

What does this have to do with whisky? Surely, you want to know why one of the world's leading master blenders found himself handcuffed to an ice chest, don't you?

Nearly one hundred years after Ernest Shackleton's death, restoration workers from New Zealand's Antarctic Heritage Trust discovered three crates of whisky (and two of brandy) frozen beneath the adventurer's home base on Cape Royds of Ross Island. This caught the attention of whisky lovers around the globe.

And it came as no surprise to find a few key individuals scratching their noggins while debating the logistics and potential profitability. In the end, three bottles of "Rare Old Highland Malt Whisky, blended and bottled by Charles Mackinlay & Co." were permitted to return to Scotland for analysis by Whyte & Mackay's master blender, Richard Paterson, and the company's chief chemist, James Pryde. Keen thespian that he is, Paterson handcuffed himself to the two coolers that housed the three bottles, allowing no room for James Bond–like espionage to take place while flying home to the motherland. And it's a good thing, too, because most of us know—whether from personal experience, or from simply watching Daniel Craig on film—that the bulk of crimes take place on billionaires' high-security jets. I've seen it countless times. Thus, many thanks to Mr. Paterson for his painstaking care.

Now, everyone waited with bated breath for the results. Was it a single malt? A blended whisky? Would this reveal further truths about our intrepid and complicated Shackleton?

After working their way through meticulous—and I'm sure delectable—scrutiny, it was determined that the whisky was likely a single malt from the now silent Glen Mhor, that it was aged in American casks previously housing sherry, that the water came from Loch Ness and the peat that smoked the barley originated from the Orkney Islands. Yes, they were thorough.

Most of us might have simply popped the cork, taken a sip, and declared it worthy. Most of us do not have instruction on how to handle rare malt whisky.

And luckily for some, Whyte & Mackay has allowed Richard Paterson to reproduce, to the best of his ability, a blend of whiskies to resemble, almost identically, old Shackleton's preferred tipple.

A door to the past has been unlocked, and for those hoping to connect with this famous explorer, it's almost like seeing Shackleton wave to you from the other side, beckoning you to join him.

For a more authentic experience, you might stop eating for three days, walk a dozen miles on your treadmill while pulling one hundred pounds behind you, down four cans of Red Bull, wrap yourself in one of your reindeer pelts from the basement, and stand for an hour in front of your open freezer, sipping a dram of the newly made malt.

It might not be exactly the same, but that's not really the point.

The world has changed in the last century. The same challenges no longer exist. Even as the New Zealand Antarctic Heritage Trust diligently works to preserve the truth of those polar voyages, and the miraculous mix of science and art has been able to replicate the now celebrated whisky, no one will ever duplicate Ernest Shackleton. The giant ambition, the legendary man. Someone worth toasting.

Go Fetch Me a Pint

There is nothing more attractive to me than a big burly Scotsman dressed in a kilt.

Scratch that.

There is nothing more attractive to me than a big burly Scotsman dressed in a kilt and holding a glass of single malt scotch.

Oops. One more go at this.

There is nothing more attractive to me than a big burly Scotsman dressed in a kilt, holding a glass of single malt scotch, *and offering it to ME.*

BINGO.

And the great thing about every January 25 is that my chances of seeing this attractive vision unfold increases monumentally, all because of one charming fellow.

Who happens to be dead.

Nonetheless, Robert "Rabbie" Burns is still remembered, admired, and hailed around the world. His birthday is celebrated in ways that likely have him both wishing he could be there and glad that he is not. It all depends upon what party you attend.

Let me explain . . .

Ole Rabbie Burns was born on January 25, 1759, in the southwestern part of Scotland, in the village of Alloway. His folks were farmers, and as most farmers rarely have two farthings to rub together, they rubbed together that which they did have—each other. Robert had six siblings—plenty of hands to lighten the load—which might have been the reason he had time to read and write.

And chase girls.

Lots of them.

After his father's death, Rabbie and his brother took over the family farm. At this point it seems he may have asked himself some questions about the direction he wanted to take with his life.

"Would I prefer to be writing up the yearly farm accounts, or writing down poetry? Better yet, would I rather be watering the land, or down at the local watering hole?" And finally, *"Should I choose to sow seeds into the soil, or into all of the bonnie women I can catch?"*

It was clear Rabbie excelled with whatever was behind door number two—which was usually him and some lass.

His poetry was oftentimes meant to impress the fairer sex, in order to *have* sex.

And lest you think I'm pulling your chain, let me provide some proof. Our lustful lyricist had a total of *twelve* children by *four* women. Seven were illegitimate, because, well . . .

It seems the old bard knew how to make his quill sing.

Despite his evident zeal for life, Burns died at the tender age of thirty-seven from what was apparently reported as "heart disease," although there were plenty of folks who stated that whisky and women contributed to his demise—his cronies decided to carry on the tradition of celebrating his birthday with a yearly tribute: booze, women, food, and yes, poetry.

If you were to cast a wide net, chances are you'd find a Burns Supper happening somewhere within spitting distance. If you're a champion spitter. Thankfully, the circle grows smaller each year.

Here are the few necessary ingredients for the success of any worthwhile Burns Night:

1. FOOD: The evening's fare must be Scottish—at least if you're attempting to be authentic. Staples should include neeps and tatties (smushed turnips and potatoes), cock-a-leekie soup (chicken and leeks, not leaking roosters!), haggis (most of you do *not* want to know), and cranachan or cream clowdie (this is just a hot mess of oatmeal,

cream, sugar, and whisky—a true and hearty highland breakfast).

2. MUSIC: Make friends with a bagpiper. Tell him to bring an extra lung or a tank of O2 because it'll be a long night. If there isn't a piper, you might as well call it a nice little dinner party, because without Mungo MacBugle blowing the cobwebs out your ears, it's just a slightly Celtic book club meeting with weird snacks. If you're looking for a proper playlist, Spotify has a bazillion, but at least make sure your piper can play a few tunes like "Lord Lovat's Lament," "Auld Lang Syne" (written by the deceased birthday boy), and "Amazing Grace." Sure, throw in "I'm Gonna Be (500 Miles)" by the Proclaimers because you're just a bit hip, right?

3. POETRY: Bring your favorite dusty tome of rhymes or any good storytelling material. The guest list is also crucial for this endeavor. Have a gathering of wall-flowers or self-indulgent bores who are certain they're channeling Laurence Olivier and your evening feels like watching your computer do critical updates with dial-up internet: it will never end. As far as poetry choices, "The Selkirk Grace" is a must, "Address to a Haggis" will doom anyone trying to recite it who *isna a Scot*, so search for one to attend, as it's worth it, and toss in a few dirty limericks to make sure everyone's awake and paying attention.

4. WHISKY: The liquor is simple. Only the best. Famous Grouse need not apply. Let's stick to a few bottles that highlight Scotland's regions, like Glenkinchie from the Lowlands, Dalwhinnie from Speyside, Oban from the Highlands, and Lagavulin from Islay. The more you imbibe, the better the food becomes, the more appealing the music grows, and everyone becomes a balladeer capable of reciting rhapsodic soliloquies (insert eyeroll here).

The point is to enjoy a night of all the things that delight our senses, but unlike any other holiday, you may bring your broadsword and claymore to the dinner table.

Burns Night Suppers are usually long and lewd, reeling and risqué, and require myriad aspirin and a taxi at their completion.

They are worthy and memorable events. Source out a local shindig. Or be brave and throw the dinner together yourself. After all, attending a Burns Night is your best chance for running into a big burly Scotsman dressed in a kilt and holding a glass of single malt scotch. Whether or not he's going to offer it up to you is something you may have to negotiate. My advice? Hum a few bars of "Auld Lang Syne" and see if he warms to you.

Old Pulteney:

The Demon's Drink

I f I were asked the question "What makes you really thirsty?" chances are I'd have several answers—eating popcorn, bacon, toast with Marmite, or nibbling on that old salt lick in the backyard I put out for the deer come wintertime. I would most likely not answer "Going fishing."

Yet, it turns out herring hunting is a withering affair. Five hundred gallons a day of thirst-quenching liquid was needed for the fishermen of one Scottish town back in the middle of the 19th century. This might not be such an eyebrow-raiser if the requested liquid were something like water, or iced tea, or Florida orange juice. Instead, much to the dismay of the local minister of Wick, the chosen beverage was whisky. Thank goodness James Henderson's distillery, Old Pulteney, was up for the challenge of slaking the thirst of all those dehydrated salty sea dogs.

Not surprisingly, plenty of folks on the vicar's side were determined to save Pulteneytown from Beelzebub's attempt to transfer Wick into *Wicked*. The year 1922 amplified those voices who were resolved to see the town go dry. The chief flag-waver in support of the ban was the leader of the Wick Salvation Army group, the most felicitously named Captain Dry.

Perhaps those in favor of a tipple or two after work may have had a chance to continue enjoying the privilege had they shown up at the town hall to vote. Instead, they stayed in the pubs to show support of their local branch of the License Trade Defense Association, which collectively made the mistake of slashing the cost of drinks that day—a fine marketing plan that left many scratching their heads and, later, crying in their tankards, now empty of beer.

Of course, the landslide victory for the prohibitionists was doubtless met with much backslapping and the comely phrase, "We rock! Now, let's go celebrate with a glass of water."

So, Wick's days of silver and gold were halved to include only the silver bits. It was still legal to fish for herring, but the bullion-colored whisky was shipped and sold elsewhere. Pickle a herring and you're doing a fine day's work. Pickle a fisherman and you'll be strung up by *yer wee toesies.*

With the ban on alcohol sales in place until 1939, the distillery closed its magic gates and went silent for the next twenty years. Several attempts by hopeful hands were made to bring the Maritime Malt back into production, and the distillery experienced many openings and closings, remodelings and expansions.

Currently the distillery is owned and operated by Inver House Distillers. Their ample line of offerings includes their historical nod to one of Wick Harbour's last remaining drifter boats (*The Isabella Fortuna* [WK499]) and a whisky liqueur.

By ticking off the boxes in the flavor camps—everything from fruit and spice to smoke and brine—there's surely something that will tickle your fancy.

With a catch like this, the Old Pulteney distillery can tempt even the strongest of teetotalers.

What to Wear for Burns Night: Getting Your Plaid to Work for You

I remember my first Burns Night. I'd never heard of the celebration and was thoroughly embarrassed when I asked, "Who's Robert Burns?" to Jonathan, who promptly replied with a look of astonishment and disapproving incredulity (one of his most perfected visages).

He raised his brows further when the look did nothing to jog my memory. "*Auld Lang Syne?*"

Ah, yes. I knew the song. "What about it?" I asked, feeling my automatic shrinking reflex whenever finding myself put up against his six billion years of private English schooling.

"He's the poet."

"I thought it was a song."

He rolled his eyes. "It is a piece of poetry *put* to music, Shelley."

It was at times like this when I wished some giant Monty Python cartoon foot would swoop down from the sky and squish him flat. Clearly, it was my feelings of inadequacy flaring up, but part of that was due to the fact that he was eleven years my senior and, also, he could just be a pure pompous asshole at times. A messy combination of all three, I'd wager.

"Well, if you know nothing of him currently, you'll soon be an expert by the end of the evening. We've been invited to attend—"

And here is where my memory is a teensy bit foggy. I'm fairly sure he said *The Royal College of Surgeons* but it could have been any puffed up "learned society of the United Kingdom," as we visited a great number of them. Jonathan was always lecturing, always on some panel, and thereafter, always invited to some dinner.

I have never been particularly drawn to slideshows on the anatomy of the common bile duct and the importance of always—*always*—employing a cholangiogram, but I can confidently say that, I could probably guide an unfamiliar and undereducated surgeon through the whole process if called upon. Sort of like landing a 757 if both pilots have passed out in the cockpit and two hundred passengers are counting on you to locate the runway. We may not all make it, but there's a chance a couple will survive.

Anyway, despite lack of surety, let's just say it *was* The Royal College of Surgeons that held my first Burns Supper. With no idea how to dress, or what to expect, I wore my best *I'm a humble American and please speak slowly so that I can understand you* outfit, bracing myself for a night of deciphering the dialect and being asked to repeat myself (with my Midwestern, *Fargo*-ish, vowel-splatting variant), as well.

It was especially difficult for me to understand certain dialects that had been perfected in British boarding schools, illuminating innumerable ways to warp and twirl vowel and consonant sounds. I, on the other hand, spent umpteen years mimicking barnyard animals while growing up in Wisconsin.

As memory serves, I can recall only a few scattered details from the dinner:

- I may have been one of only a handful of women attending the evening and could have easily been mistaken for one of the all-female staff.
- Nearly every man I met had a name that sounded almost as important as they deemed themselves to be: Sir Christopher Cheselden, or Lord Royston Pinfield Headington, or First Baronet Henry Savory Brimble.
- The food was fantastic, and the waitstaff were always caught off guard whenever I turned and made eye contact to offer a "thank you" for the dish they'd placed in front of me.
- The speeches were god-awful and boring. I'm quite sure this was the night I perfected sleeping with my eyes open.

- The whisky was copious, which made the speeches longer, but at least more bearable.
- There was a display somewhere—a series of cases—that held wonderfully horrific and fascinating things in jars. I revisited this strange and probably forbidden hallway often.
- I have never seen so many men toast the good health of a woman in my life and, in the end, began wondering just how healthy they all wished their queen to be when, in between toasts, they openly criticized everything she and her parliament were doing.

The other indelible mark left upon my hippocampus was the men's evening uniform. I viewed countless aging, learned men who likely wished they were the fairy-tale image of great Scottish warriors from centuries ago, and not just playing dress-up with all the fancy frills and fluffy bits of adornment their family—with some filament of ancestral linkage from long ago—threw onto a costume that grew more festooned with each passing year.

But they knew what each little badge, button, and medal meant. From wearable academic awards to proof of one's posh schooling, they were plastered head to knee, proudly displayed, a lavish story behind each.

Most Scotsmen I've met in slightly polished-up plaids would have looked at all the puffed-up insignia and howled. Then point at a few spots on their own weathered apparel and say, "That's where McGuffin's blood wilna come out. Here's just a bonnie bit of thistle I came cross whilst walkin' the five miles to this shindig. Pierced my thumb right wicked as I picked it tho. And this here is a wee bit of kidney pie the missus made for the lunch I was eatin' as I stood whilst she mended a rift in this here kilt."

Not fancy shmancy. Just plain and truthfully unapologetic.

I know how overwhelmed I felt with all the pomp and circumstance I was introduced to with that initial experience, but I also know that if you *look* the part, it can become much easier to *play* the part. This point was becoming clearer to me with every passing hour and with every royal surgeon. Sometimes you have to fake it to make it. I kept my fingers crossed their surgical skill acquisition had been put through a much more rigorous rehearsal.

So, with folks around the world preparing their poetry, sharpening their dirks, and hunting the haggis, you'd best get on the ball and get your kilt cleaned if you find yourself accepting an invitation to *your* first Burns Supper. As January 25 always feels just around the corner, one needs time to prepare a costume that can make a statement. An authentic declaration that speaks "true to self" will bring you the greatest of pleasure. If you've grown a few inches widthwise or found the family colors have been reassigned to other duties in the rag bin, now might be the time to do some shopping for that brand-new beauty.

First, ask yourself how it is you'd like to be interpreted. Many might believe that "a kilt is a kilt is a kilt." But I say, put those preconceived notions to rest and embrace your full-fledged and flavorful self with a plaid expression of who you really are.

Before we begin, one note: plaid, tartan, and flannel are not as interchangeable as most of us believe—if we want to get into the particulars. Flannel is a fabric, tartan is a pattern, and plaid is typically reserved (although now somewhat synonymous with tartan) to describe the long and large piece of cloth that makes up a fully outfitted Scot. If you possess any Scottish ancestral bloodlines, look up your family's clan colors. If you're an *outlander*, find a pattern that brings out the mischief in your eyes.

Below is a list of what one would typically see on a Highlander in his glory. Pick and choose from the list when cobbling together your outfit and planning for the big day, but understand, you can't buy attitude, and that's much more relevant for the evening than authenticity. So have fun with it.

1. The Belted Plaid (the *féileadh-mór*): It's the great kilt—a bit like a giant, loose tartan blanket perfectly pleated and hella impressive. As it typically requires one to lie down on the ground in order to appropriately put on and gather it around one's waist and shoulders, I'd suggest moving on to choice number two, which is much more manageable.

2. The Little Wrap (the *féileadh beag*): Still authentic, but with the ease and convenience of making a cake from a box rather than from scratch. It's basically the bottom half of the full kit and kaboodle, only with the pleats all sewn in for you and no need of staff to help stitch you into it.

3. Hose and Garters (*cath dath* and *garten/gairtéar*): If you're shooting for full-fledged indigenous, go barefoot and bare-legged. For a more updated look (and a warmer evening), any checkered stockings that rise to the thickest part of the calf is perfect. The garters are now more for show than for keeping your socks from pooling round your ankles, but if you're striving for the earthy agrarian effect, skip the cloth and braid some hay to wrap around that part of your gams.

4. Footwear: If you're skipping the barefoot route, and you have some spare deerskin hanging around in the garage, just be sure to put the hair side outward and punch a few holes in your moccasin-like slippers to drain out any water you may puddle through. Otherwise, ballet flats or brogues are fashionable and pay respect to the costumes of old.

5. Sporran (*sporran molach*): Your purse. Uber important. Hung in the front from the waist, and often made of animal skins with the fur still intact. Where else would you keep all the lead balls for your musket and coins to pay for the damage your lead balls will produce? An essential accessory.

6. Bonnet (*boineid*): Tis your Tam o' Shanter. Nuff said.

7. Knife (*sgian dubh*): Call it a dagger, call it a dirk, it's typically hidden if you're heading into a skirmish, or sheathed within your stocking if it's a night of merriment and the mayhem comes much later.

8. Jewelry: brooches, clan badges, silver pendants, bejeweled cloak pins, buttons, or buckles—whatever you choose, the most essential purpose is to make sure you've got enough wealth on you to cover your funeral and a decent headstone if the mayhem does not work in your favor.

Whatever you decide to wear and from wherever you raise your glass, I hope you'll be in good company from sea to shining sea.

And if you are not, I sincerely hope you'll find some strange and wildly entertaining hallway filled with jars of indescribable treasures. (Or maybe just the whisky bottle trolley.)

Men in Plaid,
aka Highland Games

The demands of "real life" prevent me from traveling to Scotland on my preferred weekly basis. Yet every time the strains of a bagpipe seep past me, I spot a flash of tartan, or I walk into my pantry—overrun with single malt scotch—I am transported back, if only for just a moment.

Absent getting on an airplane or strapping some whopping big horns onto my dog and begging him to release his inner Heeland coo, I realized I could go to one of Virginia's many Highland Games.

Just before the world's spreading scourge occurred, I went with door number three.

A few thousand others did, too.

What is an outpouring of Scottish culture doing in the Old Dominion you ask? Well, thankfully, when the second George of England requested that the Scots kindly exit the United Kingdom for a permanent vacation, they (at gunpoint) willingly agreed and took one of the original cruise ships over the pond to set up a few tents in Canada and America. I say *thankfully* simply because one of their campground sites turned out to be near my neck of the woods, and apparently, her welcome was warm enough to encourage putting down a taproot.

And since the crabby English didn't like seeing the Scots in their party clothes, or hearing their party music, or following their party leaders, the

Scots took all of that with them, and dumped it on the front lawn of the Blue Ridge Mountains. Celtic riffraff but really lyrical riffraff.

Even having spent the last couple of centuries sliding away from a Scottish burr and into a Southern drawl, these folks have held tight to their customs, if not their castles.

The Virginia Highland games, while not as raucous and cutthroat as those I've breathlessly watched in Scotland, still retain one thing that binds them no matter which land you're visiting.

PRIDE.

The clan system is strong.

And they keep reminding each other of just how strong *their* clan system is. The Camerons are stronger than the McDonalds. The McDonalds are mightier than the Fraziers. The Fraziers kick the butts of the Buchanans. And the Buchanans think the only thing the Camerons show superior strength in is body odor. So, there you have it. Clan competition.

Pipers piping.

Caber throwers cabering.

Archers arching.

Leaping lassies leaping.

Stone putters putting.

Sheep herders picking out the prettiest sheep.

Cattle smugglers pointing up at a fascinating cloud formation to throw you off the fact that you've just lost half your herd.

Fun and games.

And whisky.

And haggis.

And then more whisky.

Gun and fames.

You're never as thunk as you drink you are, but the drinker you sit there, the longer you get. *Hic*

Although seeing someone toss their caber is an absolute thrill, the highlight for me is hearing the electrifying, heart-quickening rush of one hundred pipers pouring every ounce of their spirits into music that will shred your soul. It's an addictive experience—and one that will leave a tiny tattoo on your heart (sorry, Mom).

The first Burns Supper I hosted is burned into my cerebral cortex like a cattle rancher's ID butt brand. I can picture myself the moment Sir Sackier uttered the innocent question, "What about doing a Burns Night this year? Would that be fun?"

I should have remembered who I was. I should have recalled the unavoidable fact that I hate parties. And more remarkable than that, I hate people at parties. I am *not* a party person and I avoid people, in general, at all costs. Especially ones who are dressed up and ready to have a good time. And now I had just spread a big fat smile across my face and accompanied it with a resounding shriek that unmistakably meant *yes*. What the hell just happened? How did I lose all sense of self?

Now I was stuck because I was married to a man who adored parties. Telling him I changed my mind after a quick stop in the bathroom, where I splashed cold water on my face and banged my head against the wall half a dozen times, would undoubtedly bring a change in mood. It would be a little like telling a five-year-old boy he'd won a flying dragon, that he could keep in his room like a pet, and then after he's run around the room, bouncing off all four walls, and has finally collapsed to the floor, totally spent, you tell him the store just ran out of dragons, and they sold the last one they'll ever have in stock to his best friend, who gets everything before he does. Kinda sucks to do that to a person.

The event went from conception to planning, and with each passing day it grew closer to a frightening reality. We sent out invitations, received responses, and started talking menu. My brother, a Culinary Institute of America (CIA) alum, was coerced to be head chef.

"What's on the bill of fare?" Steve asked over the phone from his home in Wisconsin.

I nibbled on a fingernail, thinking about how to word it so he wouldn't put the phone down on me. "Uh . . . It's kind of traditional."

"Traditional English? You mean like the food from where Doc grew up?"

"No. Robert Burns was Scottish. And from the 18th century."

"Hmm," he said, tapping something on the other side of the phone. "I must have been absent that day at school. We'll have to think this one through. Do some research."

"Well, I sort of have a general menu planned out."

"Great. Let's hear it."

"Usually the dinner starts with cock-a-leekie soup."

Steve snorted. "That sounds like a medical problem. And I'm not sure I want to know any of the ingredients."

"It's not what you think. It's something akin to chicken soup with leeks."

"Whew," he said. "Much more appealing. Next?"

I looked at the scribbles on the notepad in front of me. "There's a sweet course called Clootie Dumplin'. That's just a steamed pudding. And cheese and bannocks—those are sort of like bread rolls or biscuits."

"Okay, everything sounds fairly simple. Except I didn't hear a main course."

I took a deep breath. "Right. Well, there is one, but it's a little out of the ordinary."

"Shell, I've been cooking for close to twenty years now. I can handle most challenges."

"It's called haggis."

"Haggis?"

"Yup. And you can't have a proper Burns Night without one."

"Is it a meat?"

I swallowed uncomfortably. "Not entirely. But I suppose some of it is considered meat-like."

"Which parts?"

"The sheep pluck parts." I listened to a few moments of silence and then that tapping on the other side of the line again. Was it a pencil? His fingers? His teeth grinding down to a powder?

"You expect your hoity-toity guests to eat sheep pluck? How many of them regularly make a habit of that? And where do you expect we'll find sheep's heart, liver, and lungs? Planning to raid a local farm in the dead of night?"

I heard him sigh.

"It's not just sheep's pluck. There are other things in haggis, as well."

"Oh, goody," he said.

"Now just wait a second. There's also minced onion, oatmeal, spices and suet."

"Suet? Will there be a table of wintering birds at the party? Wow."
He groaned. "And what do I do with all these singular ingredients? Is
this like a meatloaf?"

"Not a meatloaf. A sausage. Everything gets minced and put into a
special container."

"What kind of container? I need something to cook it in."

"There is. It's a sheep's stomach. It gets boiled."

"Of course it does."

"I'm serious."

"You're crazy. This is the worst party food ever. And it's not like I
can't cook this, but why would anyone want to? Unless you're hoping to
sever ties with all your party guests."

I bristled. "No, but I want this to be authentic—and I've tasted decent
haggis before."

"You see, Shelley, this is where you and I differ. I don't want my name
to be attached to a menu that whimpers *decent*. If I'm cooking, I want
the reviews to be stellar."

"Well, I haven't exactly finished. I know the basic recipe sounds a
little odd for most appetites and I don't want to turn anyone's stomach.
Back in Burns's lifetime, this was what was available to them. They didn't
waste anything. I'm a fairly adventurous diner, and I know what kind of
courage it takes to dig into some unidentifiable steaming pile of mystery
meat, but I'm also fairly certain that most everyone at the party may not
be so keen. Therefore, I've had to think this through. Let's play with
the original recipes for some of these dishes, update them, and maybe
reconstruct them. What do you think?"

"I think this will be a challenge. I think you will owe me, and I may
have to change my name if it doesn't work out."

I smiled and put the phone down. It would work out. Because at this
point, I was putting my own heart, liver, and lungs into the endeavor.
With my ass on the line.

Bottoms Up for Burns

In honor of Scotland's beloved bard, I wanted to mention a single malt that I can weakly connect to Robert Burns but confidently recommend for any Burns Night.

Glen Garioch, pronounced *Glen Geery*, is one of Scotland's oldest distilleries and is also the most easterly, about eighteen miles northwest of Aberdeen. Oldmeldrum is the distillery's hometown, renowned for its beautiful barley. The distillery was founded in 1797, mere months after Burns's death, hence my threadlike connection.

One of the stories I love sharing about Glen Garioch is when the distillery went dry and then silent, as they ran short of the one thing a distillery can never afford to exhaust: water.

In 1968 the shop experienced chronic water shortages, so Glen Garioch was sold in '71 when the hunt for a new source was employed. Success came from a neighboring farm where an unseen, unheard spring had been discovered. "The Silent Spring of Coutens Farm" was a godsend and more than made up for the insufficiencies of the past, boosting production tenfold.

Clearly, this would have reassured Burns, as he was a man who relied upon his whisky, and some said claimed it as his muse, crediting it for "fueling his creativity."

After reading his ode to Ferintosh (apparently his preferred dram of the times) from the poem "Scotch Drink," one might conclude it also "blurred his vision," except I have been reassured the poem made sense to those one barstool over.

Still, I'll let you be the judge, because I'm sure most folks have seen plenty of modern-day examples posted on YouTube, where after one round too many, the guy standing on the bar suddenly thinks he's Patrick Henry, or Cicero . . . Or Rick Perry.

You don't see a lot of poetry like that scribed by Robert Burns of late. Maybe we've all learned our lesson and have stopped putting together bound volumes of the one hundred greatest slurred sentences by drunken people we admire.

Here's a taste of his words, taken from the poem "Scotch Drink."

Thee, Ferintosh! O sadly lost!
Scotland lament frae coast to coast!
Now colic grips, an barkin hoast
May kill us a';
For loyal Forbes' charter'd boast
Is taen awa!
Thae curst horse-leeches o th' Excise,
Wha mak the whisky stells their prize!
Haud up thy han', Deil! ance, twice, thrice!
There, seize the blinkers!
An' bake them up in brunstane pies
For poor damn'd drinkers.

Umm . . . "seize the blinkers?" Maybe we should seize the bottle, hey Rabbie?

All kidding aside, the man wrote a great deal of laudable poetry. Whether scathing, satirical, humorous, or beautiful, they are worthy words for an appreciative audience. And if you cannot find Glen Garioch, then a gorgeous bottle of Aberfeldy, Dalwhinnie, or Edradour will be a fine substitute. Ultimately, I think many a flask of any of these beauties—had they been present with Burns and in a hand not grasping a woman or pen—would have been repeatedly emptied and maybe even the next focus of homage.

The Calamity, Chaos, and Conclusion of Burns Night

T onight's the night. The guests begin arriving—and I don't want to see them. Stupid, isn't it? I'd much prefer if I could hide from view and watch the night unfold from someplace backstage. A fly on a wall. A faceless member of waitstaff, an elf on a shelf someone forgot to bring down after Christmas.

Thankfully, there were so many things to attend to that there wasn't more than the need to warmly embrace and usher guests inside.

My two children were already hard at work, one of their friends charitably lending a hand. One child was stationed at the highest point of our house—a four-wall windowed tower reached via a head-spinning spiral staircase—and could see cars winding their way up the serpentine driveway, reporting upcoming traffic, via a walkie-talkie, to the sibling in the courtyard, who would direct them as to where to park.

No one was getting out tonight until *every*one was ready to go. Thirty-five cars and sixty-some people all had to agree the night was set to end.

"Donald," our beloved friend and piper, greeted the guests in the courtyard once they finally had the courage to come out from the noise-canceling comfort of their cars. Then, upon entering the house, they were handed two small glasses. One was a soup shot of Cullen skink—a quick, thick gulp of smoked haddock, potatoes, onions, and cream. Knock it back and replace it on the tray the kind waitstaff is offering for your discard. The second was a choice of two small glasses for carrying around: warm ginger wine or a few sips of Drambuie—a Scottish liqueur made from whisky, honey, herbs, and spices.

The message was one of welcome and playfulness: *one of these two will warm the cockles of your heart, the other the heart of your cockles.*

Steve and I, having spent two full days in the kitchen, were quietly, quickly moving. Words barely passed between us, as I had worked with my brother before and knew what each hand gesture, nod of the chin, or glance meant. He was a serious and professional chef—and always impressed the hell out of me when I saw him in his element. But he also had a temper, and if someone was about to fuck up the meal service, it sure as hell wasn't going to be me.

People milled about in the kitchen—a large, multi-countered, airy room that had open access to hallways, porches, and the large room serving as the dining hall for the event.

I so wanted them to vanish.

Yes, they were mostly friends of mine, but they wanted to talk, and I had absolutely no time for talking. I wanted to shout, "I invited a million other guests for you to chatter with. Leave me alone while I work on feeding you, dammit!"

I would pass on a pleading, desperate look to one of the hired waitstaff who knew that translated to, "Please, oh please, move these people to anywhere, but far from here!"

Then, feeling guilty for having given even the smallest version of a stink eye to someone who truly didn't deserve it, I'd rush out of the kitchen and into the butler's pantry, or the large staging room from which the staff would be scurrying back and forth, refilling appetizer trays, or getting fresh glasses for the cocktail hour, and I'd stuff something delicious into his or her gob and say a quick, "I'm sorry. I'm stressed. Here's food."

Waitstaff can be so forgiving if you give them rock-star chef food for free. Well, I used to be anyway. It seemed to work on others, as well.

Steve had created stunning appetizers that disappeared down the gullets of all guests in record time: duck and white bean confit with black truffle oil, buttermilk fried oysters with crème fraiche, and King Island Roaring Forties blue cheese rolled in smoked almonds. Wheeling a large trolley behind the snaking line of crisply dressed waiters was another well-trained server, offering people drams of whisky from every corner of Scotland, his explanations of region, history, flavor, and aroma profiles enhanced by a large poster board I had him direct people to if truly wanting to research their dram in more detail.

I had spent days creating that trolley and every description that spelled out the flavor profiles that were typically attached to each province. I'd carefully secured what I felt was the perfect whisky for each uniquely represented area of Scotland: Lowlands, Speysides, Highlands, Islands, and Campbeltown. I thought I was *all that* with my dozen years of traversing that countryside in search of knowledge and scholarship on whisky.

But then, a much more familiar theme crept in, crushing my wobbling confidence. No . . . I really didn't know shit, because although I'd been raised on a stage, I'd achieved only mediocre talent in a world saturated with brilliant artists. I had learned early on how to pretend to be someone else, or amplify and appear to have more expertise on most things simply by talking a good game.

Talking a good game was what landed you gigs. And gigs provided a paycheck. And a paycheck paid for food and electricity.

Some people call it confidence, but in my industry, we nailed it as *swagger*. Glancing around at all the people who had come to see my show, I tried burying the fact that my swagger was skidding toward a tumble into the ditch.

I felt compelled to step away from the vast amounts of food prep, with the endless plate-filled counters needing immediate attention, to answer any quick question about a whisky that someone had chosen to sample from the trolley.

"Yep, it's a gorgeous bottle, but I'm fairly sure that if this is your first taste of whisky, something that steeped in peat reek is going to scrape the tartar off your teeth. And that's fine if you decide you never wish to see a dentist again, but chances are you'll never want to try another single malt, either. I'd go with a Speyside."

Or—

"I specifically chose that bottle from the Orkney Islands because I think the presence of iodine—that sweet smell of maritime air that comes through when you draw it to your nose—is a perfect match to highlight the oyster apps."

I'd march back to the kitchen, feeling comfortably surefooted, but with each step I'd lose a tiny bit of faith in myself, weirdly wishing I could press rewind. The last thing I wanted was to come across as if I possessed some baseless authority I was dishing out with as much enthusiasm as Steve's food.

I hoped that to most people I was simply part of the entertainment, and most people do want to be entertained.

"Shell!"

That's usually all I needed to hear before I'd rush back to the kitchen and reclaim my space at Steve's elbow. One sharp bark.

People were seated, waitstaff were loaded, and Jonathan paraded around the tables pouring wine—or more whisky, if people preferred to keep sampling along with the dinner we were now serving.

Cock-a-Leekie Consommé with a 2006 Esporao Branco Reserva.

Then Scallops with Gravlax in a Virginia Malvaxia Passito Broth.

With great flare and precision, Steve held high the main dish and walked through the dining hall as Donald the piper followed him, "piping in the haggis."

And it *was* haggis—of a sort: Haggis Wellington—venison, lamb, juniper berries, oats, morel and porcini mushrooms wrapped in puff pastry and served with a lingonberry-citrus chutney and perigueux sauce. The Wellington was accompanied by neeps n' tatties a la "chef's whim." It was all guzzled down with a 2005 Borsao Tres Picos Garnacha.

Burp.

This was one sound I heard a lot following the main course. The other sounds were those of pure delight because, yes, my brah can sling food like nobody's business.

The two of us scurried to finish the finals on dessert: Sticky Toffee Pudding with MitiCrema Sheep's Cream. This was served with a miniature glass of Bell's Special Double Cream Stout.

People thought I was crazy. People ate and drank what I put in front of them. People offered me a kidney after the first bite and said it was there should I ever need one and thank you for being crazy.

The talk throughout dinner was interrupted several times by the master of ceremonies—Sir Sackier—as he guided the gathered crowd through a proper Burns Supper ritual. The stories, the poetry, the jokes, and quick speeches.

I wanted no part of that stage but had agreed to give the "Reply to the Toast to the Lassies"—a rather coveted response to all the lads in the room that many women have found to be an honor to deliver, especially if they can insert a jab or two of "thank you for all the years of mansplaining" into their quip.

I did not pass up the opportunity. I chose some witty Dorothy Parker quote to add to the milieu of raucous, ribald poems and speeches.

> *"By the time you swear you're his,*
> *Shivering and sighing,*
> *And he vows his passion is*
> *Infinite, undying—*
> *Lady, make a note of this:*
> *One of you is lying."*

Back to the kitchen I fled—back to Steve—where the two of us finally took a break outside on a porch, with no people, no heat, and only a bottle of whisky.

"I much prefer it out here," I admitted.

"Bullshit," he said. "You're ignoring your fans."

"People keep touching me," I whined like a child celebrity.

He rolled his eyes. "I didn't think it was going to work. I thought at first this might be one to run from, but hey"—he thrust a chin out toward the kitchen—"it didn't suck."

"Yup. It didn't suck. Which is so surprising because the more I learn about whisky, the more I realize I know dick all about whisky."

He snorted. "And I know dick all about cooking."

We listened for a minute to the piper playing a lung-busting rendition of some jig somewhere inside the house—maybe he'd been put in a closet.

Steve swallowed the last of his whisky and said, "Hey, do you know the one thing you never hear people say?"

I shook my head.

He looked out toward one car heading away from the party, down the sinuous one-mile driveway and away from the sound, and then chuckled. "People never say, 'Oh, that's the bagpiper's Porsche.'"

PART THREE

An Apprentice of the Motherland

FAMOUS SINGLE MALTS: "GLENLIVID"

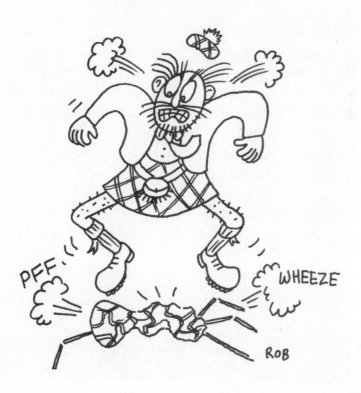

PFF

WHEEZE

ROB

Ardbeg's Whirlpool Whisky

Most folks remember turning toward a parent at some point in their youth and begging, "Tell me the story of you and Mommy/Daddy."

A large portion of the answers are wistful and romantic, including flowers, courting, stolen moments, and an earth-shattering occasion of someone down on one knee.

Several may incorporate the loading of a shotgun.

But not many will involve a Scottish island chieftain announcing to his potential son-in-law—the Scandinavian prince, Breakana—that the only way this out-of-town barbarian was going to join the family tree was if he could spend three nights in a boat surviving one of the world's seven most dangerous whirlpools.

Easy-peasy.

According to legend—or to the "half in his cups" fella on the Islay barstool next to me on my second night at the Harbour Inn—our visiting Viking warrior consulted the island's wise woman, who must have gazed into a reflective pool of water, a crystal ball, or a blazing fire (the boozehound couldn't recall which) to find the tidbit of advice that would help him succeed with his quest.

The diviner advised the young hero to fashion three ropes—one for each of the deadly nights of seething seas. These would anchor his small boat back from the bloodthirsty hug of the whirlpool.

The rules were thus: the first rope should be fashioned of wool and the second of hemp, but the third would involve finding a maiden of pure virtue, telling her she'd look fabulous with a pageboy cut, and using her leftover tresses to make a cable. Strongest stuff ever, apparently.

Our strapping soldier did as counseled, managing to convince his dewy damsel to part with her hair and plait her sheared filaments.

Night one—treacherous, but survivable. Thumbs up to the lads on shore.

Night two—the hemp just held, probably a bit better than the suitor's bladder. Shaky but resolute, he signaled his willingness to persist and follow through.

Night three—armed with his desire, his determination, and the locks of his beloved, he set out to prove his worth, pitting his competence against the brute forces of swelling seas and mighty magic. Confident he had what he needed to sustain his life, secure in the knowledge that his betrothed was as uncharted as the seabed beneath him, it came as a jarring shock when the rope of her hair snapped and the vortex engulfed him.

From the shore, his fellow Vikings watched in horror as the sea swallowed their leader. Turning to the fair lass, one warrior, eyes wide with understanding, clutched his heart and asked, "Did you falsely tell him you were a pure and untouched maid?"

The girl looked aghast. "I thought he asked if I was sure that I could braid!"

And so goes the story (which I may have fleshed out a little) about the "untamed spirit of Islay," Ardbeg's Corryvreckan. Described as powerful and dangerous, it's an undeniable magnet to anyone in search of something out of the ordinary—a precarious flavor profile, a journey only a few will dare.

I did.

And I'm living to tell of it.

Apprenticeship 101

If someone had asked me at age twenty-two, after my first sip from a Glencairn glass, whether I believed I'd one day find myself participating in a tiny internship at one of the most prestigious distilleries in the world, I would have likely made an incredibly unattractive face and then asked if that person had had one too many drug-laced gummy bears. Then, I would have led them to a couch to lie down.

No. What kind of ludicrous, dope-induced question was that?

Only, it happened. And not only were there no narcotics involved in the arrangement and implementation of this internship, but it also ended up being one of the most profound and independence-creating experiences of my life. Looking back, I see Fate grabbing me by the collar and dragging my ass across the stage of Life.

After having visited the island of Islay, Jonathan apparently did some research and surprised me on my fortieth birthday with a gift. A piece of paper that declared I was to pack my bags with work clothes and a sturdy raincoat, as I was off to learn the art of making a single malt scotch. If my recollection is correct, this announcement was followed with something like, "Once you come back, you can set up your own distillery and make us all wealthy."

Not sure if my eyes have ever swiveled so far back and skyward. It actually hurt.

I panicked. For a couple of days. Then, not one to take a challenge in any half-assed manner, I buckled down and filled my desk space with every whisky magazine, technical textbook, and personal memoir of spirit-making I could get my hands on. I was set on the task of wholly preparing myself for an education I had not signed up for, and an experience I would never have enrolled in.

Whisky *tasting*—oh, how I loved it.

Whisky *touring*—oh, how I craved seeing every inch of the process, hearing every unique tale, all so I could love tasting it more.

Whisky *science*? Oh, good God, please don't let there be math. Even if math is disguised as whisky tasting and touring—it's still goddamn math.

My work up to this point had not been "hands on." Yes, I studied enough to write about it—and I did so with the enthusiasm of a deranged six-year-old taking her turn at whacking the piñata at a birthday party. And I was continuously asked to speak about it, which I frequently declined because I still felt a bit wobbly with the occasional worry that I did not possess the necessary credentials for eloquent, factual lectures, aside from that which could sufficiently satiate the appetites of large dinner party gatherings where the guests, already glassy-eyed, believed I was learned.

I wasn't. At least I didn't think so, as there was still so much I did not know.

It often reminded me of fruitless conversations I'd had with Jonathan, where when approaching him with questions of minor skin conditions for myself or the kids (rashes abound when you live in a forest), his answer was typically, "I haven't the faintest. I'd skipped that chapter in medical school as it held no interest."

But it wasn't like I was skipping insipid chapters of whisky education; it's just that I hadn't unearthed them yet and feared being found with a deficit of expected knowledge.

I soothed my feelings of self-doubt with a quote from Arthur C. Clarke, who said, "Now I'm a scientific expert; that means I know nothing about absolutely everything." The relief came with the notion emphasizing that the more one learns about a subject, the more one realizes just how much there is to learn about the subject. I was not wholly deterred. To me, this was a scalable mountain I could surmount with enough effort.

But right now, I was going to have to rise to an occasion that I wanted, but also didn't want. Pointless fear really gets in the way of sought-after accomplishment.

I can only remember swallowing the large rock that had lodged itself in my throat and looking at that paper—that "gift"—and seriously wondering if I could "gift" it back. There was an incalculable number of times Jonathan had taken the steering wheel from my hands and redirected me toward some other destination, as if he possessed some unseen set of blueprints for the scaffolding of my life, and this invisible architecture kept shaping my choices.

My new plan was to think of a million ways that I could sabotage my ability to participate in the experience. Come down with a disease that was temporarily disabling, but that I could fully recover from? Initiate an airline strike? Win a literary prize whose ceremony would happen to fall on the same day as my apprenticeship was slated to start?

I know, they were all brilliant, but I was unable to make any occur. Instead, I tried to focus on the things that pushed me to go forth, the siren song that both enchanted me and convinced me I would soon be facing my doom:

1. Scotland.
2. I'd never hear the end of it from Jonathan if I allowed my fear to override my enthusiasm—I'd be a major disappointment as the perfect wife he was attempting to cultivate.
3. Yeah . . . Scotland.
4. I *sooo* wanted to learn with a hands-on experience, as in my mind it would be like becoming friends with the guy who makes all the David Copperfield illusions and seeing how they work from backstage.
5. *Sigh* . . . Scotland.

I closed my eyes, made a mental nod of acknowledgment to the fear in my heart, hip kicked it over to the side to make room for courage, and turned to embrace my fate.

Barley

A distilled spirit, by definition, is an alcoholic beverage containing ethanol. It is produced by fermenting fruits, grains, vegetables, or other forms of sugar, and then distilling the resulting solution. In my research, and in meeting innumerable people involved or interested in the spirits world, I have come to find there is precious little that mankind has not tried to ferment.

Everything—including beans, grains, vegetables, fruits, honey, dairy, fish, meats, and teas—has at some point been transformed from its original state into something wild, wonderful and, oftentimes, truly god-awful. Let's put it this way—though much can be fermented, not everything *should;* but if your chosen material can have its sugars converted into ethanol, then you've got yourself a whopper of a science project.

For centuries, folks have been using fermentation as a method to both enhance the nutritive value of foods and preserve crops for winter and droughts. It's an ancient practice that came about most likely by accident or happenstance, as one of the first "chemical reactions" man happened to witness was likely observing good food go bad. Spoilage resulted in a few (but by no means all) things becoming just as pleasant to consume as the original form, if not more so—though one must wonder who drew the short straw and stepped forward to try the slop.

A member of the grass family, barley is among the three powerhouse ingredients in Scotch whisky. Until the combine harvester made its way to the United Kingdom, the reaping of barley was a tad more time-intensive.

You could liken it to raising a barn with nothing more than wood planks and a glue stick instead of ordering one online, prefabbed, and having it delivered the next day via Amazon Prime.

Nowadays, distillers spend a lot more time on the science of barley than the scything of barley. Issues such as nitrogen levels in the grains, the climate and soil where it's grown, and the length of the growing cycle are at the top of the barley "worry" list. The key is starch levels, but just like yeast biochemistry, the agricultural secrets of what makes the perfect grain are not what's keeping most whisky imbibers up at night—so we'll skip on to simpler science.

In barley's freshly harvested state, it's not of much use to anyone trying to bottle its potential. That beautiful little bud, like many living things having been just rudely ripped from the ground, hesitates to show its sweet side to a guy with a 26" blade in his hand.

Long ago, as I was just developing a taste for the spirit, I first toured the striking Campbeltown distillery of Springbank. The local tour guide was truly memorable, as no well-honed docent's script was going to supplant his personal take on the actual operation of this hooch house, although he surely raised eyebrows with his colorful explanation of the process of making whisky.

How do they extract sugar from the raw grain? came a question from the group.

A wicked gleam flashed across his face.

"We trick the wee buggers," he said. "Sugar must be coaxed from the grain, so just like ye court a bonnie lass, ye make them think it's all flowers and springtime. They open their little hearts to us and then *BAM*! We toast their tiny arses."

As poetic as this man's verse was, I still lacked understanding. After a few more years of autodidactic whisky research, and the chance to see it done firsthand, enlightenment ensued. Once you and your farmer have made a firm handshake deal, and you have your new supply of the perfect barley variety delivered to your distillery doorstep, you pop those puppies into a lovely bath. It's a big, oxygenated Jacuzzi called a steep. Here, the grain swims in the convincing rains of a "springtime shower" for approximately two days. They float for a few hours and then get some airtime as the bathwater is drained and the process is repeated with warmer tub water until the grains have a 45–55 percent water content. Ask any woman what a day of bloating feels like, and she'll probably give you an earful. If barley could talk, it would likely have the same script.

Here our plump grains, now referred to as *green malt*, leave the vessel for a trip to the malting floor. We know the barley is ready for the next step because they're sporting tiny rootlets, as their starches and proteins have sufficiently broken down to sprout. You may have heard the expression *chitted barley*, but I doubt it was explained the same way my ladies' man guide from Campbeltown put it:

"Now the lass has unbuttoned her blouse!"

I don't know which creeps me out more: the fact that he's such a cad with women, or that he's a sexual predator of barley.

Spread across a malting floor or placed inside Saladin boxes—vessels with a mechanical means to turn the grain—the germination phase begins. The differences between the two methods are numerous, one being traditional and time-consuming and the other having economical value. Being one who is rigidly fixed in time-honored tradition, I love arriving at a distillery that still operates their own malting floor; for me, it's part of the wand-waving magic. Understandably, the charm of the malting floor may detract from the bottom line when the finicky controls of temperature and humidity refuse to cooperate, but perhaps that's where I appreciate the masters of craft at work (and not a series of machine-driven settings put in motion with the push of a button).

If the Saladin box is the distillery's preference, the green malt is aerated in lengthy troughs where long and twisted screws—likely used in a previous James Bond film as torture devices—coil through the grains, methodically introducing oxygen to the malt and allowing unwanted gases to pass.

If it's a malting floor, the grains are spread on the concrete while a couple of fellas with rakes work in eight-hour shifts for several days to churn the grain by hand, perhaps wondering why they're the last distillery on earth living in the Middle Ages and when it might be time for tea.

Either way, the process of modification is the result.

To be clear, the ideal outcome is one where your grains have sprouted evenly and perfectly. If you've hired yourself a naff crew who have been surfing their iPhones for game applications and mindlessly watching

TikToks rather than deftly wielding their shovels, the distillery is now the proud owner of a barley carpet, where the rootlets have intertwined, knotting themselves together in pure solidarity.

For my little lecture's sake, let's just say things go flawlessly. Now the enzymes have been released, causing the breakdown of carbohydrates and proteins. This allows the kernel to release its store of starches. If you were on the Campbeltown tour, Don Juan would have told you, "Right here is where we've coaxed the wee flower to open her petals. We've bathed, massaged, and convinced her to give us what we've all been after the whole time . . . her sweet sugar!"

As lyrically picturesque as that description was, it was no surprise that folks were beginning to look for the exit signs. And a makeshift weapon.

The next milestone in the life of our grains is death. Tragic? Perhaps. Necessary? Absolutely. Our barley now realizes, if barley were truly cognizant, that it has been tricked. Believing it was experiencing the first encouraging signs of spring and coming out of its winter kernel dormancy, the grain reached out with tentative tentacles, and those very tiny toes received a most ruthless welcome. Death by desiccation.

Kilning is a word that when placed into a Google search, is most often replaced with *killing*. It's easy to see why. When our green malt is kilned—that is, dried with forced air at low temperatures to arrest further germination—its future hopes and dreams are brought to a halt along with it. As our perverted distillery guide (whose sanity was now being questioned) gleefully hissed, "Now that we've gotten her to her most vulnerable position, we kill her!"

It was here that I ultimately departed the tour to ask for directions to the local post office, convinced I'd find his face plastered on a "Wanted" poster there. Once assured that local authorities weren't in pursuit of the strange character, I concluded I might be better off getting the rest of the story from much more trusted sources. Like Wikipedia.

Okay, for your sake, I also consulted my whisky chemistry books, which, as I referenced before, are not written in language a sixteen-year-old could comprehend. This proves to be a problem of major proportions, as I have not sought the explanation of anything chemistry-related since I *was* sixteen. It leaves me the ambitious task of attempting to simplify the kilning process through my own interpretation. Not that anyone reading this has asked me to dumb it down, but I'd rather this essay not serve as a replacement for Ambien.

From *my* perspective, one of the most important roles of kilning is to remove disagreeable flavor elements and find pleasing ones to replace them with. There's also that other added necessity, which allows the grain to be stored and used when needed.

Lacking a silo in my backyard, I still must recognize the importance of drying out our grains to a moisture content of somewhere between 4 and 6 percent, but achieving that result seems to require a doctorate in potions and herbology. There are terms tossed around from paragraph to paragraph of my chemistry chapters that assume I understand: "enzymatic activity," "fermentability percentages," and "predicted spirit yield." I could hardly imagine then that they'd ever become a part of my daily vocabulary.

It is equally frustrating when my daughter leans over my shoulder, reads a few lines of barley chemistry, and says, "Oh yeah, I remember the Maillard reaction. We studied that along with the Strecker degradation. Aldehydes, furans, and pyrroles are so cool."

I give her a look that suggests I'm about to turn her into a toad and, thankfully, she leaves. I would hardly enjoy the necessity of dedicating my acknowledgment section to my daughter, expressing my gratitude for her explaining all the "big words" to me.

The one thing I remember repeatedly striking me, as I pored over books and periodicals addressing aspects of the kilning process, was that it was at this stage my favorite flavor component was introduced. Unfortunately, somebody other than a poetic wordsmith dubbed it "peat reek." If it had been a little less ham-fisted, it would have been my first choice for my son's name. Ah well, cooler heads prevailed.

But back to kilning. Now that our malt has been *elevatored* up to the kilning floor, it's again spread out. If you're a distiller wanting to offer up the experience of what it's like to be barbecued from inside your digestive tract, you'll then fill one kiln with as much dead Scottish vegetation as possible (primarily for that delightful "peat reek" flavor) and another with something that will effectively dry the grains—high-carbon fuels like anthracite or coke. Years ago, other options were oil, natural gas, or coal, decisions often based on cost-efficient economics.

Interestingly, I came across a supposed opinion of Sir Robert Moray of the 17th century, who suggested "local peat and faggots of heather" were appropriate fuel for malting barley, but "faggots of broom" were discouraged because of the resulting unpleasant aroma; so, apparently, broom did not make it into the flavor profile of any whiskies I've come to find, but I'll keep looking.

There are many ways in which a whisky gets its flavors, and many arguments as to the veracity of each. Some believe the distillery's source of water is a major contributor. Others are certain the air where the barrels are stored plays a more important role. Just think of the difference between the briny, oceanic hints in a glass from any barrel stored on the Isle of Islay compared to a barrel warehoused just off one of Glasgow's congested motorways.

Regardless, the thing about peat is that without its physical presence during the kilning phase, there is no other way to obtain its tantalizing taste and aroma. That can't be said for other flavor components like butterscotch, biscuits, citrus, or pear. I've yet to come across a master distiller who throws the odd lemon zest into a barrel or crumbles a few pieces of shortbread into the mash. Those scents and traces are the results of multiple factors, my favorite being the congeners kept or included at the end of the distillation process—the cuts from the distillate, called the foreshots and feints (or in my neck of the woods, heads and tails). This is where it pays to have yourself a competent master distiller.

But peat is different. When burned, peat creates an abundance of smoke, and the volatile oils—or the phenols—within this smoke are then absorbed by (or *coat*) the grains. Of course, the intensity of this flavor is dependent upon other factors: for example, the dryer the malt and the later it is in the drying process means less smoke will adhere to the barley. But you've also got to consider the temperature of the peat fire, the amount of smoke directed to make contact with the grain—and, of course, whether the guy in charge of the kiln even remembered to turn it on.

One other sidenote on peat is that it likely carries the compound that gives certain whiskies their "briny" or "iodine" notes. Ocean waves and kelp release bromine into the atmosphere, winds push that chemical element far on land, and rain pulls the compound with it into the peat bogs.

The water filters through, but the bromine instead combines with the phenols within the bog, and together they create bromophenols (which, as above, coat the grains and make it through the processes of fermentation and distillation and finally into your cup). Fascinating, eh?

For many, the drive to create a whisky with the most peat reek—or ppms (parts per million)—has grown into a contest of epic proportions. In some cases, you might as well just pull a piece of smoldering peat out of the embers and spread it on some toast; I expect this might be a tasting note soon found on the backs of a few labels.

So now that our barley has been tricked, tortured and, from some Campbeltown perspectives, thoroughly "taken advantage of," we finish off any dreams the sweet, crunchy grain might still be clinging to by crushing them. Literally. A fearful future, to be sure, but before we address grain angst, I face my own.

Fear Realized

I cannot count how many times during those following weeks I woke up in a heart-palpitating panic.

What the hell am I about to do?

Yes, I had grown a fierce passion for this spirit and everything related. I wrote about all of it, and oftentimes to warm and receptive reviews. I knew about the stories behind each distillery, the people responsible for their successes and failures, and the basic steps involved in whisky's production; but the problem lay with that last bit. I was a writer. I knew about storytelling and had a fairly good handle on all things that benefit from a beginning, a middle, and an end. You know, stories that started with *Once upon a time* and ended with a *Whew! That was a close one!* The issue was the lack of a meat and potatoes middle of my story. A part of me knew that I'd never stitch together all the fascinating bits without spending time on the production room floor up to my elbows in sausage making. Until I filled in those gaping holes, it would be clear to just about anyone that there wasn't enough knowledge in my bucket to draw up a full pail.

Certainly not enough to tag me as a likely candidate for future work. Despite the mountains of research I'd already done—or climbed over many years, and usually with a dram in hand whilst doing it—I still felt like I knew basically nothing. Let me rephrase: I felt like that basically meant nothing.

My textbook studies and distillery visits would fail on the prerequisite checkbox list, and worse, I believed I'd recall next to nothing of what would be needed when entering one of the sanctums I held in such high esteem.

I remember experiencing a near–death spiral of terror when the extraordinarily well-educated and highly cultured English headmaster of my children's school suggested I attend his British Men's Club one evening and give a jolly speech on all things spirit related.

Nuh uh.

I'd come to know of a phrase—much later—one my daughter began using with great frequency once she'd left for college. It's called imposter syndrome. She had it and didn't deserve to suffer it. I also had it, and boy, oh boy, it was fiercely present within me. Graver still, I erroneously believed it to be true with every molecule of my body.

I had donned the familiar smudgy spectacles through which I viewed my education and accomplishments, and its ocular evidence suggested that perhaps I'd simply been using enough of the subject's lingo where people were crediting me for more than I deserved. I dreaded the thought that when asked any pertinent questions at the distillery my only recourse would be to point skyward and shout, "Look! An eagle!"

Via a distorted lens of self-assessment, I'd sharpened a poisonous blade, used by endless women and minorities, and meekly carved my name into a tree identifying the unqualified.

My plan—and as every college student knows this is a stupid plan—was to cram. Cram ten years' worth of info I'd already learned (and believed I'd callously tossed to the side) back into my brain and see if maybe two years' worth of it would stick.

I was not terribly hopeful.

I was not terribly comfortable.

I was just terribly terrible. And time was running out.

There's Trouble at t'Mill

Every year on the Fourth of July, I used to watch my British husband become as giddy as a five-year-old in anticipation of the big night. He claims he wasn't, and that the holiday held no meaning for him apart from the painful reminder that we Americans had wreaked havoc with this country—he was simply here to reclaim the colonies and become King of America. Charming.

We would spend a chunk of the summer at my parents' home, where he could enjoy his favorite Independence Day activity. He'd stand at the end of the old dock, with two sparklers in hand, singing "God Save the Queen" at the top of his lungs across the lake to the old fishermen puttering about in their bass boats. For the month leading up to that moment, you could find him periodically visiting the front hall coat closet, where he kept his supply of amateur fireworks. It's also where we stored our recycling bins, so he often claimed he was simply making trips there with a plastic container or an empty wine bottle—but I knew him. That gleam in his eye was not a reflection of his hunger to save the planet, but rather to strike a match. He was about as green as our front lawn come a heat-scorched August.

Everybody likes fireworks. Except dogs, of course, who would also like to see thunder banned. Still, for a guy who was awfully sore about being on the losing side of the battle, he sure didn't mind celebrating with the winners. And yet, with the many years of practice he now had under his belt, and even watching the careful instruction he had put into practice in teaching our son the basic safety procedures, I still stood teetering many yards back. Half of me wanted to spring over and yank them back to safety, admonishing each for playing with explosives, while the other half watched with wide-eyed anticipation. It's not that I had some beef with pop rockets and the lot; it was rather that I have a basic knowledge of combustion. And a healthy fear of it, thanks to whisky.

When learning how to operate the old 1913 "Boby" mill at a distillery I'd recently visited, my teacher explained in no uncertain terms that grinding was a risky affair and not everyone could live to tell of it. With a grizzled face that looked as if it had been through the rollers itself, he narrowed his cloudy eyes and raised three gnarled fingers. "'Tis not much of a thing if ye've only the fire triangle: dust, air, and stones, but if ye have the fearsome five." He stopped to shake his gray head. "Best say yer prayers before work."

I was expecting the final two to be something apocalyptic, something ungodly that only Wiccans would have access to on a full moon in October. But I was wrong.

Father Fun continued, piercing the air with a finger. "If that dust can be suspended in the air and that cloud be confined, then ye have the makings of an explosion none the likes of you have seen." Apparently, he's not been privy to any Bruce Willis movies—or maybe the cinema in general.

Regardless, the process of milling in distilleries these days sports a safer track record, but the gloom-and-doom prophesies still excite the tourists, and the thought that someone risked their life to bring you that sip of nectar makes the taste that much sweeter.

It's a simple procedure with a keen eye kept on the moisture content of the malted barley. Too high and you've got gunk on the rollers, too little and you're making barley flour. Neither is appealing.

The malt first passes through a revolving drum with a wire mesh—a dresser. This simply catches any straw or small stones present, and often it also passes by a series of magnets, which helps the "de-stoning" process.

The first set of rollers (one of usually four, but sometimes six) pinches the grains, spitting them right out of their husks. The grains are then ground, and the remnants—the *grist*—pass through three screens. Ultimately, you're hoping for a specific balance in your grist makeup. Husks are somewhere around 20 percent, grits or middles are 70 percent, and the flours or fines make up the last 10 percent.

The magic that comes from each distillery's mill is essential to the finished product, and every distillery has their utopian numbers. I could break down the machine further to its true nuts and bolts, but there really is no need to in this book. At least you now get the general gist of the grist. The mechanical malt mill is an historical "boombox" worth seeing; just leave your sparklers at home.

A Messy Return

After a roller coaster of anticipation, nerves, and ironic dread, those six weeks flew by. Before I knew it, it was time to board my plane to Scotland. Dammit.

The afternoon was sticky and rainy, ratcheting my discomfort skyward to where all that sticky and rainy came from. Hair pulled back into a ponytail, clothing plastered to me from the spray of cars as I unloaded my heavy suitcase and carry-on from the trunk, and thunder rumbling overhead as I tried to shush the inner voice of reason and snotty-nosed-know-it-all-ness that screamed this portended a very bad adventure.

But my kids were in front of me, bubbling with excitement for something they couldn't really grasp. Yet they did possess a vague understanding that *Mom was headed off to the place she gets all swoony over.*

I *so* wasn't feeling swoony.

More woozy. Queasy. Bilious. Maybe dyspeptic.

None of it could be attributed to anything fun like whisky. Just a big mess of twisting intestines, intent upon making a mockery of the art of pretzel puzzling.

Airports and all things airport-related were, by this point, reaching the highest point on the scale of my "*Things I would be okay replacing with toenail removal with no anesthesia*" list.

I hated airports. Jonathan had made me hate airports. He'd always get us there at the last possible second, then the rush at fevered pitch would begin with me sprinting, lunging, leaping, and generally hauling ass behind him toting two small children, a violin, a guitar, a diaper bag, and usually a livid expression. That last item was the heaviest to cart around, but I was rarely without it, so its weight was at least wholly familiar.

It was rocking horse–manure rare when our family had a scheduled flight and we found ourselves not screaming, "Hold the gate!" as we bowling-balled our way toward flight attendants who'd already done a firm head count and were bolting the plane's latches.

Did I mention I hated airports? Going there on my own was by no means some sort of balm. The damage had long been done. And the feelings of anxiety started usually somewhere around the moment he uttered the words, "I've booked us a flight."

I got myself through check-in, through security—which never, ever went well with our family. Jonathan was always pulled aside for having sixteen pieces of technical equipment that he felt should be exempt from *his* personal security checks, or he was pulled aside for being surly and affronted at security officers just doing their jobs.

We were always pulled aside. Period.

I made my way to one of the airport lounges Jonathan had membership to—which, if you have never been fortunate enough to experience, is worth giving up a kidney for. At least once in your life, as you only have one to spare. And in this lounge, I managed to find a quiet enough corner to begin taping myself as part of an audio-visual series of camera footage for the kids (and myself) once I'd arrived home, to show proof that I'd actually gone through with it.

Don't think for one second that I did not contemplate switching flights and heading to somewhere like Hawaii for some sun and surf, or St. Barts for some sun and surf, or Detroit because it was a place planes flew to.

Quite frankly, everyone knows I would have chosen Detroit because I weirdly hate sun and surf in tandem.

But there was a part of me that felt the familiar tug, the tiny skip of heart, and the flittering butterflies that signaled I was likely thinking about Scotland, or sipping on Scotland, or I just shook hands with a guy named Scott, which was close enough to flush a crimson surge of heat through my body because my soul sighed the phrase *My beloved Scotland*. I needed to focus on the fact that "my beloved Scotland" was hours away.

I glanced around the posh lounge, believing every person there was likely staring at me as I whispered into a handheld video camera with my Susie Sunshine personality radiating for my children. I soon gave up and was grateful when an overhead announcement stated it was time to board.

Settling into my seat, I instantly realized that someone had either freshly laundered this one with a garden hose or they'd accidentally left all the airplane windows down and forgotten to roll them up before the rainstorm had unleashed a near–Niagara Falls spectacular.

It didn't matter. The flight was full, and I was stuck. I put my coat down on the chair and got to work studying. For the next eight hours. Until I got to Heathrow. Then I studied all the way from Heathrow to Glasgow, then Glasgow to Islay. Actually, that's a lie.

I tried to study from Glasgow to Islay, but the woman next to me was having a panic attack the entire way.

It is so hard to focus when someone else is puking into a bag.

I don't blame her. When we'd finally boarded the aircraft in Glasgow, the pilot came on to say that our little puddle jumper was in for a doozy of a drive, and we'd all best buckle up so our wee heads wouldn't crack off the top of the plane from bumping into it.

I turned to her from where I'd been staring at the pelting rain outside my tiny window and laughed—thinking she'd have chuckled at the pilot's humor, too—but she had that wide-eyed, oh-my-god-where's-my-barf-bag kind of a look on her face and I resignedly turned back to the gray bucket of water outside my window. So now, the storm outside had a soundtrack. And smellovision.

I quickly pulled out an embarrassingly large bag of Mentos I'd pilfered from the airport lounge and handed them over. Here's some mints. Maybe they'll help?

More puke. Maybe they wouldn't.

It was a long thirty minutes. And bumpy. And ugh, whenever someone else starts puking, I nearly always start puking, too. Or at least gagging. Which is probably worse than puking because it's all the mechanisms of puking without the after-relief of the actual event.

When we finally landed, there was a polite smattering of applause from the flight attendants and then the quick realization that we were not going to be afforded the oft-taken-for-granted protection of a covered walkway into the terminal.

In fact, there were no gates here at all. Just the front door.

Guess what? It was raining. Maybe raining isn't the right word. Maybe sheeting is. It was sheeting water outside.

I popped on my still soaked raincoat, grabbed my backpack, headed down the gangplank and straight into a truly massive pond of water. I was ankle deep. Looking up I could see, between sheets, dry people inside the terminal laughing at all the passengers who fell for "that ol' trick" that apparently the pilot loved to prank his passengers with.

Noting it had been at least a year or two since my last visit, I took a deep, wistful breath and reminded myself that despite Scotland's propensity for keeping me cold and wet a good chunk of the time, I could not love her any less.

Once inside, I stood dripping on the slick linoleum floor and watched my soft-covered luggage sit on the tarmac, soaking up more of Islay's sodden sky.

Ten minutes later, I dragged my dripping bag toward the car rental counter, and just before I took the last step up to officially greet the woman behind it, whose eyes were locked expectantly with mine, a man slid in front of me from the side.

I stopped. Abruptly. Mostly from surprise at his effrontery, but also because we would have collided.

I knew he saw me. Knew it.

I'd seen this man in Glasgow, pacing the floor at our tiny gate before the flight. He'd given me the once-over, like a butcher might quickly inspect one of fifty cow carcasses on a mechanical conveyor. I took no real notice of him there, as I was familiar with those looks, and had long ago learned to dismiss them as quickly as the individuals dishing them out.

I waited. And fumed. Actually steamed. He got his car keys, and I secretly sent out a wish to the universe that his car would not start and mine would be the last one on the lot, so he'd have to choose between going back to the mainland, calling the one taxicab available on the island, which sadly didn't work today anyway, or renting the dilapidated golf cart they used for transporting the contents of each airplane's toilet holding tanks out to the disposal trucks. I tried mentally pressing my odious desire onto his back—like a tiny spell—and hoped it stuck to him like toilet paper on a shoe as one walks up to enter Air Force One with everyone looking on.

When it was finally my turn, and after the woman apologized for the rude American, I tried extremely hard not to sound like a rude American. Or any American, for that matter. And that's not a big ask. Raised in the Midwest, having lived in countless regions, and being married a dozen years to an Englishman had granted me a mishmash of speech quirks that befuddled most any linguist. I mumbled my way successfully through that exchange.

Once inside my car, I reacquainted myself with the always shocking fact that it is possible for many people to flip their brains like a mirror. Or drive on the opposite side of the car, on the opposite side of the road, and still come out alive at the opposite side of their place of origination.

I was going to be one of those people. Eventually.

The Bugs in Your Bourbon, the Growth in Your Grog, the Spores in Your Spirits

Folks who know me understand that most available brain space I've been loaned is taken up by purple prose and melodic lines of mismatching music. Although it was crammed full of numbers and formulas during my formative school years, many things science and math–related were shoved out when margins reached capacity and I needed more room for things like Monty Python ditties.

And yet, I still, with each passing year, found myself drawn to the science of whisky making. Most of what I've learned provided a thirty-second "aha" moment, which I attempted to recall when next holding a dram. Occasionally, the info faded into the amorphous background of hazy-edged knowledge I struggled to lug back toward the surface.

Therefore, writing about it has always provided me with a threefold benefit:

1. Sometimes putting the science into laymen's terms allows me to understand the concept more fully and then present it to another interested party.
2. There is info ready at my fingertips for a quick refresher, should I need it (and I always seem to need it).

3. There is documented proof I did not spend all day
watching YouTube videos.

And even though my family regularly stands amazed at my lack of
science recall, I am not as daft in the subject as they would have most
folks believe.

I am not a backward-thinking, dubious troglodyte who still insists
that illness is caused by evil spirits.

It's caused by evil spirits who have a score to settle with you.

Okay, and by bacteria.

Tiny as they are, it's easy to see why these nearly invisible beings are
confused with the unseen undead. And they are prolific, existing virtu-
ally everywhere, and in numbers rivaling the stars.

But not all bacteria need to be scrubbed away with a bucket of bleach
and a strong wire brush. Some we invite onboard our bodies for sound
reasons. Many are beneficial to our digestion, others are key ingredients
in making dairy delectable, and scores act as cleanup crew to the world's
newly departed.

As spirit drinkers (not the evil, but the liquid kind), most of us know
the ingredient list. I shall remind you once again, because I am nothing
if not a huge fan of sticky yellow Post-it notes scribbled with reminders.
The ingredients in whisky include grain, yeast, and water.

The end.

Occasionally, the odd boot is thrown in, but that is purely for natural
coloring.

But what many are beginning to realize is not only that bacteria are
clamoring for recognition via a spot in that seemingly minimalist contents
catalog, but they play a more important role influencing flavor profiles
than they were once credited for having. Maybe not Oscar-worthy, but
significant, nonetheless. I once came across comic Steven Wright's quote:
"Support bacteria—they are the only culture some people have!" It's
beginning to make more and more sense.

So how do these hints of life find their way into the mix?

Various factors affect their presence and population. They—the lactic
acid bacteria, or LAB, which contain different types of bacteria—hitch
a ride with the barley when it first gets shipped to the distillery. The

LAB resident numbers are often determined by harvest factors. Additionally, there is an impressive head count of bacteria on the distillery's equipment—the mash tuns (think massive stock pots), the pipe moving wort to the washbacks (wort is like weak beer), the washbacks themselves (yet more colossal buckets, either wooden or made of stainless steel, that hold the now fermented wort before it heads off to the stills), and even a few crumbs from the cheese sandwich the mashman dropped into the wort while on lunch break. Mashing is a slightly dicey part of production, in that some bacterial strains are more impervious to heat than others, and will withstand the mashing process, and then carry on reproducing to make up for lost brethren.

Another consideration is just how clean the operational staff keep their equipment. Bacteria will happily hide in all cracks and crevices of pipes, pots, pails, and pumps. Some distilleries are a bit lax, but others clean with a fervor as if their mothers were hovering over them and judging the results.

Lastly, the length of fermentation is also a key component in the final tallying numbers. A lengthier fermentation equals higher bacteria figures because once the yeast dies off, they often leave a little present behind for the resident bacteria—food. Happy, well-fed bacteria make more bacteria. Colonization under primo conditions.

So, what do we make of all this?

The bacteria are capable of contributing flavor compounds—or altering other existing compounds and the conditions they exist in—within the new-make spirit, and can increase the notes of sweet, sour, fatty, fruity (estery), sulfury, tobacco-like, and meaty essences.

Research is still ongoing as to exactly how these little fellas are putting their unique fingerprints on the product, so for now we'll have to sit tight and let the lab coats unravel more of the magic.

But embracing and understanding bacteria sure beats lighting a smudge stick to rid your room of any spirit other than the one you hold in your glass.

Attagirl

Thank God Islay was an island with mostly one-track roads. Part of me was super happy about that, but then another part, the part that said, *just sit back and think about that scenario for a second, and walk it fully through with all its possibilities,* convinced me that maybe the golf cart was a better choice after all.

I'm sure everyone remaining in the tiny airport was wondering why the hell I was still sitting in my car half an hour after I first got into it, and in fact, a man eventually came out and tapped on my window.

"All okay in there? Car wilna start? Or are ye in need of assistance wi' your map?"

I had it spread out in front of me—one of those colorful children's book illustration maps. I'd been studying the entire island.

And of course, delaying the inevitable: putting the car into drive.

"All's good. Thanks a million," I said, now slightly shivering from the nerves of airports, bad weather, rude and retching people, and nearly fourteen hours of being wet and only getting wetter. Oh, this was such a good idea, right?

I rolled up the window, waited for him to go inside, and put the car into drive. Now I just had to get up the nerve to take my foot off the brake.

Remember how much you love Scotland.

Remember how much you love Scotland.

I do. I do. I do love Scotland. I do love Scotland.

I turned slowly out of the airport onto the main road (Ha! The *only* road.) and rolled along for all of ten seconds before I remembered that windscreens need to be wiped down to be effective. I fumbled, searching for the right controls, ultimately pulling off the road to start pressing buttons. I'd soon figured out how to operate the emergency lights, the turn signals, the radio, the trunk and gas hatch latches, and the fog lights.

The closest I found to windshield wipers was the button that squirted cleaning fluid out of it and then automatically engaged the wipers for three swipes across the glass before calling it quits.

Good enough. I'd just keep pressing the button and apologize for using up all the fluid when I returned it. But at least I had access to a function that increased my visual skills. And I needed visual skills for a whopping nine miles.

I know. I can hear you. And try to keep your eyeballs from rolling so far back into your head that you can't read text any longer. But nine miles for me was mentally like nine hundred miles. On top of a particularly exhausting trip—the beginning of one that was going to "help" mold me into the perfect vision my husband and I *surely* both shared—it had been more than a decade since I'd been daring and adventuresome enough to step out from beneath the monolithic shadow of a man who had long taken charge of everything.

Having control thrown right back into your lap is akin to being thrown off a cliff with a parachute you'd only used a couple times before and could not quite remember if you'd rerolled and repackaged expertly enough for its next use, or if you'd intended to redo it when you finally had time.

Didn't matter. Off the cliff I was thrown. But no way in hell was I going down without actually pulling the rip cord.

I rumbled slowly down the A846, or whatever vegetable-soup name these folks had given the single-track road, and prayed—literally prayed with a few hastily mouthed Hail Marys—that no one would decide that today would be an awesome day for a stroll toward the southern tip of the island to see its miles and miles of peat bogs. Because that's all I could see on either side of me. Surely, they all had work to do, right?

Hopefully not mining peat from the bogs.

I made it to mile seven, and since the road was straight, I could see the oncoming car for what felt like the distance from me to the moon. I slowed down. Way down. Like walking would be faster. I looked around desperately for a passing place—a small half circle of extra tarmac where vehicles could pull over and wait for oncoming cars to pass and then feel benevolent as the other driver waves in gratitude for your exceptional politeness.

There was no passing place. In fact, I'd not seen *one* passing place the entire length of the past seven miles.

"What is this fresh hell?" I shouted up at the rain.

I pulled off the road and waited. I wasn't going to take a chance that the other driver maybe had a passing place on his side farther down the road.

The other car came upon me—not going terribly fast—and seemed to slow down with curiosity.

In fact, he was so curious, he stopped and rolled down his window.

I mirrored his action and got a face full of sideways rain.

"Ye all right there, lass?"

I nodded. "Yes, thank you."

"Ye stuck? Car trouble?" The man's face was as quizzically arranged as could be without forming a question mark with his features.

"No, I was just pulling off so you could pass."

His whole face brightened.

"Oh! A tourist!" he bellowed. "No need on this stretch, lass. This is one of our best roads! Wide as the smile on a fat, drunken Scot." He continued chuckling. "This here's a two-lane motorway. No worries. We all fit fine."

"We do?" I looked at the road with doubt.

"Oh aye. But I'd warn ye agin pulling off to the side like that, as the whole road, ye see, actually floats on the peat bog, and once ye get yer wheels in some spots, there's no reclaiming ye. The bog'll swallow you whole."

"What?" My heart leaped with anxiety.

He waved it all away. "Oh, not for a thousand years, mind ye. It'll take some time. But the de'il holds tight to what the de'il wants. Good luck to ye and enjoy your stay. It might be longer than ye wished for!"

Yes, good luck to me, I thought as I stared resolutely at the track in front of me. Basically, as best I could remember, from both having visited the year before, and from having just spent half an hour in my car poring over a map, my destination was nearly a straight line from airport parking lot to hotel parking lot. Easy peasy.

I followed the road round just one steep bend, keeping my eye on the signs posting my road name—or number, if you will. The Harbour Inn was dead end of that road's pavement. After that was seawater.

I pulled into the hotel's parking lot and saw a familiar whitewashed building outlined in black, and a tiny sign, hanging above a doorway, that sported a picture of a sailing ship and the name of the establishment.

I'd made it. I was here. I was an idiot for wanting to just sit in my car and blubber with pitiful, self-congratulatory hugs, but I excised the absurd notion by saying out loud, "No one gets whisky if they're gonna lose their shit for driving nine fucking straight miles. Get your ass inside, Sackier."

Clearly, I was tired. Clearly, I was emotional. Clearly, I was sick and tired of being emotional.

Yeast

A re you trying to write a science text?" my then fifteen-year-old daughter asked. Chloe is a science and math guru. I am not.

"Huh?" I answered, whipping my head up from where it was resting.

She peered at me and walked closer, her eyes narrowing in at something above my own. A snort escaped from her nose. "Studying hard, are you?"

"Why?" I asked, stifling a yawn. I stretched my eyes wide, thinking maybe the surface of my eyeballs could use some extra oxygen for energy.

"Cuz you've tattooed some of the materials onto your forehead. Is this a new study method you're researching?"

I put my fingers up to feel the words.

"It's not in braille, Mom."

I'm an idiot. Yes, I know that. But I really wish she wouldn't point it out so often. "What does it say?"

Chloe leaned in to inspect the artwork. "Well, it's backward for one, but I think it says . . . *Yeast biochemistry.*"

I sighed. I couldn't believe I was still on this chapter. Granted, yeast is an integral part of the whisky-making experience, a subject anyone interested in whisky *might* be interested in knowing about. Except that most of what's to know is all in Latin.

I sat there struggling to think of yeast's most important elements to share, since its presence is so crucial. It is, after all, one of only three ingredients in whisky. Without it, you have barley water—something the

British have tried convincing themselves and others tastes good, when in fact, the name should send you running. Seriously, even the wards of Mary Poppins told her in song that the perfect nanny should never smell of it. And they were looking out for her best interests.

So, after hours, no *days* of research trying to find crucial things to relay, I've decided to go with yeast data that might be most memorable, if not entirely useless:

- Yeast are single-celled fungi.
- The word "yeast" is Sanskrit for, "to seethe or boil."
- Yeast cells are minute. One cell is somewhere close to the size of a human red blood cell. If you're in need of around one gram of compressed baker's yeast, then you'll have to gather thirty billion of these guys.
- Yeast eat. (Just like us.) But if you refuse yeast its food, it doesn't die, it simply goes into sleep mode. Give it a drink of water, and that H2O acts like an alarm clock. (I agree. A bucket of water dumped on my body would be a surefire way of wrenching me out of my stupor, as well.)
- Yeast fart CO2. (Again, just like us.) I'm sure at one point, years ago, I owned a Weimaraner that was made up entirely of yeast.
- Yeast are all around us. The microorganism is in the air, on the skin of fruits, and even on flowers in your garden. In fact, wild yeast propagules are continuously floating in the air and landing on your uncovered food and beverages. So, in essence, you're never really eating alone.
- There are more than 1500 recognized species of yeast (and according to the general scientific community, that may be only about 1 percent of what we have yet to discover).
- The species of yeast that we use in food is called *Saccharomyces cerevisiae*, which is Latin for "sugar fungus."
- Brewer's yeast has a spherical shape. The distilling hybrid is elliptical. Believe it or not, yeast cells are heterogeneous in size and physical form. Scientists have identified them

morphing into categories that, apart from the above, include globose, pointed at one end, tetrahedral, cylindrical with rounded ends, rectangular, pear-shaped, or lemon-shaped. I'm going to guess that a fair number of women can wholly identify with yeast and their many silhouettes.

- Yeast is probably one of the earliest domesticated organisms. Yeast would make a great pet if we could create a small enough collar for it.

- Reading about and viewing diagrams of yeast cell "budding"—the birthing of new cells and the detachment of daughter cell from the mother and then seeing them both "bud" again—may interest those who are either massive chemistry fans, or women who can't seem to get past reading the first couple chapters of *A Child Is Born*. For me, when they start using terms like cell membrane and cytoplasmic material, or even budding, for that matter, I get a little squeamish and find I'm peering inside my whisky glass wondering if I should set it down and walk away.

- Beer was found aboard a sunken ship off the coast of Finland recently and determined by scientists to be somewhere around two hunded years old. Because yeast reproduces so quickly, the strains we use today have evolved into something totally different from what was available two centuries ago. The plan is to recreate the "Wreck beer," allowing folks to either get a taste of the 18th century or be thankful they don't live in it.

- Good distiller's yeast (by Scottish law) should have a lack of flocculence. I'd say I was a little stumped on this one, but after comparing every dictionary definition I could get my hands on, it does not mean what I at first thought—which was that the yeast should not be at all like sheep. It basically means the yeast shouldn't aggregate into wooly cloudlike masses. That comes from the *World English Dictionary*, and they rarely get it wrong.

Of course, the further I read about flocculence, the less I snicker. It turns out that brewers are somewhat partial to the flocculence of yeast as it helps with clarification of the beer when the fermentation process has ended. Distillers, on the other hand, want nothing of it because the clumped yeast cells settle onto heating surfaces thereby toasting themselves to an objectionable charred mass. This, as you can imagine, imparts the oh-so-special flavor every cook wants from the bottom of their pan: burnt bits.

- Congeners are by-products of fermentation—the process where yeast turns sugar into alcohol. Congeners are the *flavors* (both scent and taste) in alcohol. Therefore, congeners are our friends. Although if you were to see a table listing all the products of yeast fermentation (congeners) that contribute "flavor metabolites" to beer, wine, and spirits, you'd see something akin to the periodic table of elements. There will be no lovely descriptive terms of *butterscotch, heather,* or *carburetor oil from a '57 Chevy.* Instead, you'll see terms like ethanol, butanol, succinic, ethyl hexanoate, and hydrogen sulfide. Anyone who knows what ethyl hexanoate tastes like, raise your hand. You may skip this course because you're way ahead of the rest of us. (In other words, if you answered fruity-like or apple-ish—you're excused.)

- Yeast is a leavening agent, just like baking powder. It makes bread rise and biscuits fluffy. My ex-mother-in-law refused to use leavening agents because, on their own, they taste awful, and why in God's name would anyone put something that tastes horrific into their cooking? The resulting hockey-puck biscuits were always, "Something's the matter with the oven."

- Nutritional yeast will never make bread rise because the fungus is killed during processing.

- Baker's yeast is not the same as brewer's yeast, distiller's yeast, or nutritional yeast, although they are all the same species—part of *Saccharomyces cerevisiae.* Brewer's yeast is grown on hops, which is used in beer making, and has a bitter flavor. Nutritional yeast is grown on molasses and has a sweeter flavor. And I once read in a research paper that distiller's yeast grew quite capably despite the presence of arsenic, therefore, I'm quite certain distiller's yeast would win in any yeast-on-yeast battle because being raised on baby bottles full of arsenic gives you an edge when attempting to resist all other forms of death.

- There is ongoing research on the role of baker's yeast in the treatment of cancer. Apparently, when cancer cells are exposed to yeast, they eat them and self-destruct. Just further evidence of how amazing the seemingly humble world of yeast can be. It would seem plausible that cancer cells are gluten intolerant and should not sign up for patron punch cards at Panera.

- Just to clarify, it's fine to eat baked bread (unless you're a cancer cell), but never eat raw active yeast, because these fungi are still alive and will ferment in your digestive tract, where they will scavenge for your body's B-vitamins and produce gas.

- And speaking of bread, each American consumes an average of 53 pounds of it per year. That's a lot of yeast!

- It takes nine seconds for a combine to harvest enough wheat to make about seventy loaves of bread. It takes one eighth-grade class of thirteen-year-old boys the same amount of time to demolish them.

- Early Egyptian writings urged mothers to send their children to school with plenty of bread and beer for their lunch. Most thirteen-year-old boys wish they had early Egyptians for mothers.

- Marmite, a yeast extract paste eaten in vast quantities around the world and a by-product of brewing beer, is a wonderful example of how the yeast-using industry is a *waste not want not* business. Distillers (and Diageo in particular, who must win first prize at absolutely everything) are taking the whole by-product/new product idea even further. In an upcoming chapter, I'll illustrate how they are well on their way to utilizing whisky-making leftovers for providing homes and businesses with power and creating biofuels to power cars and aircraft. Pretty soon the pump choices will be unleaded, diesel, ethanol, or the dregs from pot ale.

- Just like a person's genetic makeup affects the way you look, behave, and function, yeast strains all perform differently during fermentation, and therefore can change the flavor of the finished product.

Seriously, I've just summed up about fifty pages worth of text, tables, and graphs on yeast biochemistry. Remember my ink-tattooed forehead? You can thank me later. I hope it was worth it.

Chicken and Clapshot

After finally leaving the car and checking in at the Harbour Inn, I dumped my soggy bags in an adorable attic room with whitewashed walls and six variations of everything plaid. Following the rumblings of chuckling chatter and soft Celtic music, I made my way downstairs to the lounge outside the restaurant. A young, gangly barman in a crisp white shirt and tartan vest stood behind the thick horizontal slab of polished wood. Well, not so much stood as leaned over on one elbow and nattered with one of the barmaids. Dressed in a near-matching outfit and holding an armful of dishes from the kitchen, it was clear work was the last thing on the barmaid's mind. He growled, she giggled, and I made a slight cough of arrival.

They separated like fingers from a hot stove.

"Just hoping for a dram to warm up," I said, looking skyward and slightly apologetic.

The flustered barmaid scampered, and the lanky young lad stood slightly taller than the space above his head allowed, banging it on the overhanging shelf holding a long line of whiskies from which to choose.

Rubbing his head and probably his pride, he gave me a sheepish grin and said, "An American? Lovely."

I wasn't sure if he meant how lovely to have an American in his little pub, or what a lovely example of an American, but not wanting to find out, I pointed at a beautiful bottle behind him and said, "How about the Renaissance?"

"How 'bout it?" he answered, one eyebrow cocked.

"How 'bout it gets poured into a nosing glass and I leave so that she can return?" I nodded my head toward the swinging kitchen door.

Dram in hand, I climbed the stairs to my little room under the eaves. I turned on the spigots in the large cast-iron tub and whispered a quiet request for water hot enough to boil a dozen lobsters in. Then, while waiting for the bath to fill, I pulled a barrel-shaped chair to the windows, tucked my feet up beneath me, and sipped as I watched the drizzle outside through the panes facing the gray and frothy sea.

I followed the whisky's warmth as it seemed to touch upon all the frazzled, damp, and tightly twisted emotions that had somehow lodged themselves in the lining from my esophagus to my stomach. The loosening came with each deep breath, my nose hovering over the lip of the glass as I drew in its aromatic hug.

The scent and taste were reminiscent of my grandmother's attic—a bit dusty, the ancient floorboards emanating lemony polish, the tobacco pipe smoke clinging to old tweed. It comforted me like that memory-filled loft as well, in that no matter the mischief of accidentally breaking a carefully stored tiny porcelain figurine or creating a small tear in someone's yellowing decades-old wedding gown while impermissibly trying it on, everything would be just fine because people were cooking downstairs and that meant I was safe, loved, and occasionally overfed.

When perched snugly inside a hefty dwelling and fueled by the heat of potent alcohol, one paradoxically plans to conquer the world. One becomes king, one builds a castle, one delivers momentous speeches to the plebeian crowds that now gratefully fill your coffers with half of what they reap yearly. The whole practical planning and implementation bits are irrelevant and seamlessly dismissible. It's a strange but beckoning world. In the new matrix that, surely, some teenaged techno prodigy will one day produce, I would like to briefly sample this world and try to glean how someone like Jonathan could see it as plausible reality.

It does not feel realistic—nor appealing, no matter how compelling an argument Jonathan makes. His Fourth of July "act" of aiming to recapture Britain's loss and put himself forward as America's royal successor is often cloaked in his typical wry humor so that he could snatch back any suggestion of verisimilitude. I pondered how it is that people change from when you first met them, and then pondered further the uncomfortable fact that our family was being forced to change with him—despite mounting discomfort with his direction.

His expectations for all of us were impossibly high, his demands for attention frustratingly unquenchable, his displeasure with the status quo alarming and sobering—despite the soft, fuzzy-headed reverie I found myself swimming in. I stared at the warming liquid clinging to the sides of my glass, its slow drizzle from rim to bowl echoing the leggy path of drops upon the windowpane.

"I don't want to come home and make us all wealthy. That's not the point. That's not why I love this." I pulled the glass in toward my chest, cradling it. "Why can't I just love something because it's worth loving? Must you monetize everything? Must you conquer it—claim it—exploit it all? Do I have to come home and make you proud or can I just come home—maybe with no plan at all but maybe enlightened, maybe strengthened? Would that be okay?"

The voice inside my head said *no*.

Do you know how much it cost me to send you to Scotland? To give you this opportunity?

I would know. At some point soon. The burdensome, unrelenting echoing words reminded me that Jonathan would expect a return on his investment. Because he was forever "Eliza Doolittling" me from a before into an after.

And then, with an alarming about-face, I felt a huge wave of guilt gush through my veins even faster than the effects of the whisky. I *should* be grateful. He knew I loved Scotland, knew I loved whisky, and likely knew I would benefit from a challenge such as this.

With a disheartening sigh, I trudged to the full bath and slipped beneath the blanket of hot water, blissfully relishing the whole "before and after" transition that leads to great gratitude for the tiniest of things we typically brush off. I reminded myself that I should never ever again display signs of hubris or an effrontery of nerve that reveals a lack of compassion because, at that very moment, I knew warmth and protection and abundance—and I *was* grateful.

And then, two tiny hours later, I was fuming with all that shit I promised I would never again demonstrate simply because I was hungry and things weren't going my way.

Ugh, God, sometimes I seriously face-palm myself on behalf of myself.

As I sat in that same lounge from earlier, I looked about and wondered for the umpteenth time where the staff was and whether I'd gone invisible. Should I knock something over? Send a table crashing to the floor to see who came running? Maybe just walk up to the bar and pour myself another dram to see if anyone was truly paying attention?

But I didn't. I sat with my menu, a dinner choice made fifty full minutes ago, and waited for someone, anyone, to return and ask me to follow them into the dining room. Or into the kitchen for a free-for-all ravage of the fridge. I'd have been totally fine with that, too. All would have been forgiven.

I got up and headed toward the tiny front hall and its tinier front desk, but someone stepped inside just as I was getting up all my nerve and dander.

"Madam? Your table is ready."

I didn't look like a madam. But maybe I looked like I was *damn mad*, and the waiter was just being polite.

The pretty Scottish lass had left—probably absconded with their barman while I was in the bath—and I followed another young lad, who'd earlier checked me into my room. He led me toward a small table by a fireplace and a window. The table was set for one.

"And no one will be joining you? No one at all?"

I looked at the young man, gauging his questioning visage of pity. "Happily, no. I will finally get to eat every scrap of food off my own plate and am forced to share it with no one."

He dusted some nonexistent crumbs off the empty side and made a quick nod to depart.

"And speaking of," I added quickly. "I already know what I'd like to order."

He turned back and looked at me expectantly.

I held out the menu and said, "Grilled salmon, please. No need to fancy it up. Just salmon grilled."

He made another nod. "I'll tell chef, shall I then?"

"You betcha," I added, guessing that was the first time he'd ever heard that word.

I pulled out my journal and started penning a few notes for thirteen-year-old Chloe, who had made me promise to write in the gift of her tiny travel journal: here's what I saw, here's how wet I got, here's what I'm doing now. *Blah, blah, blah.* She'd be happy. I was happy. And hungry. And hangry. But a little bit closer to at least not being two of them any longer.

I waited. And wrote. And stared out the window. Then stared at the fire. Rinse and repeat. For another hour. I was the only person in the small dining room. In fact, looking around at the other tables, I saw they were all set for breakfast, not dinner.

I looked at my watch. Ten after nine. This did not bode well. Apparently, Scotland closes down at 8:00 P.M., and no one slipped the memo under my door.

Again, I got up to hunt for someone, and an older woman came rushing across the plush navy-blue carpeting of the dining room. She held a plate and a wide-eyed expression of haste. Which was nearly unrecognizable, as swift speed was something I was beginning to understand had not been bred into these islanders.

"Here we are, love. Enjoy."

The plate in front of me was definitely not glistening with grilled salmon. Or even salmon at all. But it was food. I'm pretty sure. I thought it best to ask for reassurance.

"Grilled salmon?"

The woman squinted. "Oh, no, lass. We've no salmon today. That's chicken. Or haddock." She leaned in to look closer. "I'm not sure, but it's definitely one of the two. And rumbledethumps, as well."

I eyed the other pile on the plate. "It's what?"

She leaned farther in. "Could be clapshot. They're both similar. But ye'll like it nonetheless." She gave me a matronly smile. "Eat up, lass. We're closin' soon. We dinna usually allow guests to come down so late to dinner."

I swallowed the words that rushed up and were barely stopped by some wiser part of my brain that instinctively made my lips press inward. I forced out a smile and a nod of thanks.

And proceeded to eat the most delicious chicken-or-haddock and rumbledethumps-or-clapshot I'd had in a long time. Or ever, I suppose.

Burn, Baby, Burn

I love old wives' tales. Mythology, folklore, and stories spun from ancient wisdom make me giddy with the magic of history's possibilities. I know there are plenty of people out there who are sticklers for truth, and it certainly has its place—namely in a court of law, on my credit card statement and, wishfully at the time, behind every word my fourteen-year-old son would utter.

When it comes to whisky and all things spirit-related, I do enjoy the slog through historical documents (yawn)—but I much prefer to be sitting on a barstool beside a gnarly-knuckled bloke who happens to have firsthand knowledge of what he's talking about from cutting his teeth on the industry, or because his grandpappy was the guy who'd made it all legend. Tall tales and just-so stories often contain the real emotional truths.

One dry summer Friday, whilst perched on the edge of my porch steps, I looked out across the mountains and saw the billowing smoke of blazing wildfire. Certainly, when I was first thirsty for learning about every angle of *all things involved in the art of making whisky*, wildfires around my home were not as common as they've become today. As worrisome, yes, but as frequent, no.

But it got me thinking about all those lovely trees going up in flames. And whether folks at the time explained away the event by saying it was good for the health of the forest, and Mother Nature knew what she was doing, or that all things were related to climate change, and Mother

Nature's nature was wholly fed up with those of us who treaded heavily and irresponsibly across her domain, my thoughts remained with the loss of life. Namely, the life of a tree turned into a barrel.

And that, mixed with all the drifting smoke mingling with my dram, had me itching to learn more about the art of *charring*.

Who was the clever clog who decided some alcohols might benefit from a rub up against scorched lumber? And was it the same guy who chose to keep it there, or was it merely luck of the draw?

Responses to these questions were abundant. Many insisted their answer was the right one, the only one, and that their answer could beat up your answer. So be it. Choose one you like and stick with it.

Here's what I've sussed out thus far.

1. Elijah Craig, Baptist preacher from the Old Dominion and a distiller in what eventually became Kentucky, found that the overly rank taste of whisky stored in old fish barrels might not appeal to everyone. It has been said he discovered an inexpensive method to remove the previous inhabitants' perfume by burning it away. And that charring unleashed a helluva host of gluttonously good flavors (sorry, Reverend!).

2. A story from another camp suggests it was a giant whoopsie, as several of Reverend Craig's barrels received an accidental charring in a barn fire. Apparently possessing a penny-pinching personality, the man refused to kick them to the curb. After he filled them with spirit, the barrels were then shipped either downriver or via horse and buggy on a multi-month trip. The product had altered to a most preferable state, according to the receiving-end patrons of Craig's products. Imagine the barrel acting like a giant, unwieldy water pitcher with a carbon filter, smoothing out some of the spirit's rougher edges and contributing vanillin and tannic acids. You already know that vanilla is pretty lip-smacking, but tannins can punt the less savory sulfury notes, add some color, affect the whisky's mouthfeel, and break down lignin, which can add truly

applause-worthy aromatic compounds. While the language of wood science wasn't available to the reverend's clients at the time, reverent requests for his tasty whiskey piled up nonetheless.

3. Or maybe it was as simple an explanation as a cooper heating his staves to make them pliable enough to bend to his will. A little over-toasting might have been an unavoidable result.

4. Some believe cognac was the pivotal piece in this puzzle. According to records, brandy has been placed in toasted barrels since 1440. New Orleanians liked their brandy, and when bourbon distillers of the 1800s put their marketing teams together for some brainstorming, it's possible someone raised a hand to suggest the idea of coloring their new-make spirit, allowing it to compete in the marketplace with the deeply hued local favorite. Since the guys in France found their spirits had colored after aging in toasted wood, why not jump on that bandwagon? Furthermore, since the French took their time and let their product hang around in the containers for several years, why not speed up the process by burning the bejeebies out of the barrel? That'll teach the French a thing or two about early birds and worms, right?

Or maybe the bourbon men truly were seeking a light toast but sent a young minion with no experience to hatch a fire in each barrel, and things got out of control. Give a boy permission to light a fire, and he'll do his best to make sure it's newsworthy. With modern technology, barrel charring is precisely controlled: a burst of natural gas, an impressive but guarded fireball, and there you have it! Bob's your uncle, Charlie's your aunt.

5. There is the possibility that because many of the new American distillers were old Scots-Irish distillers, they longed for the flavors of home. Smoke and peat were part of that connection. Is it likely they charred the barrels to imitate that flavor profile? There are more opinions on the matter than I can shake a stick at.

6. A couple of sources threw out a scenario envisioning the quickly buried stock of one's spirit with the intention of keeping it out of offensive hands—whether enemies of war, gluttonous lairds and landowners, or excisemen. Continuing with that thread, the burning down of one's buildings was the occasional result of those feudal disagreements. But I have a hard time connecting the consequential charring of a barrel's outside with the aftereffect of altering its content's flavor. Then again, cooperage chemistry is a complex science.

   As an aside, returning—either months or years after the coast was clear to reclaim your booty—and finding one's harsh liquor was suddenly ambrosia is a viable explanation for how barrel aging might have been a serendipitous discovery. But that is another discussion entirely.

7. One explanation I must pin as anachronistic is that charring was performed to purify the barrels from disease. While I can't find any written documentation of this practice early on in America, one could imagine the act might have been performed to rid the barrel of certain pests and fungi—which, of course, *can* cause disease. The Japanese utilized the surface charring of wood (known as *shou sugi ban* or *yakisugi*) to preserve and protect it from insect and moisture damage. It basically strips the surface of any nutrients that would provide measurable value to wood bugs and molds. So, if our friends across the globe discovered this technique back in the 18th century, who's to say a similar aha moment was not experienced elsewhere? What I *could* conceive to be true and more apropos to a few hamlets and remote back country areas would be the act of fire purification to exorcise any remaining evil spirits in the barrel before refilling it with a welcome one.

There you have it: a nighttime tale to ponder while sipping your dram. Sweet dreams—sweet, smoky, peaty, heathery dreams.

Solving the Mystery of Oysters

I had a day. And a map. And a car. Two of them I was super excited about. The other one . . . ugh. But still, if I could just grow a pair—no, I take that back, if I could just remember the fact that I was a fierce Lady-Dragon who breathes fire upon trolls, haters, and mansplainers—I could have the time of my life in my favorite place in the world. And I would do my damndest to banish the feelings of impending doom that hovered over my head and murmured, *Tomorrow is the day you will suffer for all your life's collective wrongdoings. You will face deep humiliation and be humbled to lie prostrate on the floor. Remember how awful you were in third grade? Yeah, payback time, baby.*

Yeah, I should stick with the Lady-Dragon bit.

I pushed the guilty thoughts of "You should be studying!" right to the back of my head, as the only thing I knew I must now competently focus on was the act of driving, and not crashing and burning.

I was on an island. It's not even a big island. And there were only a few roads. Surely if I just pulled out of the parking lot onto the first one available, I'd find great things of interest sooner or later. And then, eventually, find myself right back here in this parking lot. All roads lead to Rome, right?

I wanted to see the place I was going to be working, come tomorrow afternoon. Or at least acquaint myself with how to get there, so I'd not show up late and give anyone a reason to see my lack of punctuality as a reflection of my interest. I'd rather it simply state that when it comes to automobiles, I'm not terribly ambidextrous.

Now if there was one thing I was utterly capable of, it was guidance and navigation. I'd learned how to fly an airplane, getting my pilot's license for no other reason than because Jonathan had a horrible sense of direction, and on more than one occasion when flying with him as aviator, I was quite certain we'd be landing on some unwelcoming military tarmac rather than at the general aviation port where we'd been instructed to set down our wheels.

I also wanted to make my way to Portnahaven to seek out the selkies I'd seen on a previous trip. Of course, when I say selkies, I mean seals. But to me, they were likely one and the same, as I was neck-deep in writing a middle-grade novel all about them and had studied those part-animal, part-humans for the last couple of years.

A selkie, for the unacquainted, are said to be mythical creatures from the sea. They wear their sealskins when at home within the depths of the ocean but can just as easily strip themselves of their coverings and make their way onto land, appearing as your average Joe or plain Jane. Only, maybe a little better looking, as in the old tales, real humans are always falling in love with selkies and then, once the slighted human discovers their lover has another family, life, and probably hidden bank account at the bottom of the Atlantic, they hide their lover's seal skin to punish them with a stint on land until they die.

It's awful. I feel for them. They're just terrible at hiding stuff. Like their seal skins, or their other lives, or the fact that they're part fish.

Anyway, as I drove, I found the perfect radio station to accompany me on my seaward travels. It was also the only radio station, but in my mind, I was super lucky because it was blaring out my favorite instrument—bagpipes.

Bagpipes aren't for everyone, sure, but after stopping on the side of the road, I felt like either Jack or Rose from *Titanic* as I stood on the roof of my car with the wind rushing past, the mist falling about like tiny wisps of ghosts, and the bagpipes blasting out at a caterwauling volume from the speakers beneath me.

Yeah, top of the world, for sure.

It's just all the looks one gets from grazing cows that can be unnerving, as adorable as they are.

Along with my bovine friends, I had my spiffy little video camera, circa 19—totally nerd-fest—92, and I continually pulled my itty-bitty car off the one-track road to press "record," taking in the gray sky, the gray water, the gray seagulls, and the gray rocks. So many shades of lead can really open your eyes to a lack of appreciation we, who live in sunny climates, are not usually privy to. Fifty shades of gray, you aren't kidding.

Farther down the road, I pulled off again to stare with slightly knocking knees at the distillery, whose doors I would shortly be rapping upon. It was like requesting entrance onto the hallowed grounds of Willy Wonka's Chocolate Factory. Surely my golden ticket had been forged.

I stepped out of the car and stood to look over the roof of it, staring at the collection of buildings that created this sacred compound. I swallowed, closed my eyes, and rested my forehead on the car's wet rooftop.

The fundamental fear of *fear* is unspeakably debilitating. It can tether us to the ground, clench our throats, squeeze the breath from our lungs, and paralyze our movement, numbing our feet so they cannot travel in any direction. The events of the future were piercing this hallowed blissful bubble of now. I heard a part of me so faint, so far away, asking why I was smothering my right-now joy. I also heard my yoga teacher quote the great Roman Stoic philosopher Seneca: *There are more things likely to frighten us than there are to crush us; we suffer more often in imagination than in reality.*

My yoga teacher was right. Or rather she was well-read enough to read profound literature and quote it to our class.

I took one of her cleansing breaths, got back in the car, and sped off.

Well, not so much sped off as moved slightly faster than if I were jogging away rapidly. My car was not much more powerful than a slightly jacked-up scooter with four wheels and a windshield with no remaining cleaning fluid. But to compensate for the lack of speed that communicated strength and resolve, I donned my best Maria von Trapp attitude and belted out all the lyrics to "I Have Confidence." Apart from the section where she says—

A captain with seven children
What's so fearsome about that?

—this song was obviously written for me. Or maybe we should all just thank Rodgers and Hammerstein for tapping into global consciousness.

Suddenly, I was forced to alter my route. The road was blocked. A spray of orange cones—the only splash of color within the landscape—stood hip to hip beside a large diamond-shaped orange sign that shouted in black letters, *DETOUR*. Also, a hand, pointing with a finger in the direction I should move.

Not like there was another one. It was drive right, or swim left. Since I wasn't a selkie, I chose right and headed upward, over a dirt track that cut through farm fields filled with the hairiest, most pointy-horned Highland cows I've ever seen. I've seen a lot, and I adore them. I have never met a person who has not immediately fallen in love at the sight of these creatures. They come in a variety of hues: black, brown, and a beautiful creamy beige. This island sports a whole spectrum of colored cows that we do not keep in our fields in the U.S.

The best part of them are their faces. Giant swaths of hair fall like unwieldy bangs across their eyes, rendering them nearly blind, and highlighting the fact that these animals still haven't moved on from hair stylings of the many UK 1960s boy bands. Thankfully, they sport super sharp pointy horns that protect them from their hair-blindness. When they bump into things, the horns give them first warning before their noses smash into any surrounding trees.

Frankly, this part of the island was wholly treeless; therefore, the only things these guys would be bumping into would be one another.

Again, I pulled off the side of the track and went to stand at the fencing to practice bovine babble. Having grown up in Wisconsin, I have become extraordinarily adept at all things cow. Cow tipping, cow milking, cow shooing, cow *GET OFF GET OFF GET OFF MY FUCKING FOOT*-ing. Yeah, just about everything. But I wasn't sure if Highland cow-speak could be understood with my Midwestern twang.

We practiced. I told them a good chunk of my life story—some parts of it were even true, but those were mostly bits in the beginning because I could see they were feigning interest. Within minutes I was spicing it up with a ton of sex and a few misdemeanors—even hinting at espionage. After about ten minutes of balancing on a thick old wooden fence, waving my arms around to keep their bulgy eyeballs trained on me—or at least their faces pointed in my direction, as, like I said before, so much hair—I realized there were two other eyeballs centered on me, too.

A farmer had apparently been working the back forty, repairing a fence on the other side of the pasture, and was now staring, mallet in hand, watching. Fixedly. Probably gauging whether I was more a danger to myself or to his livestock.

I slunk off the fence, wincing at the sliver of wood I wedged beneath my palm, and then skedaddled to the car. Back in the safety of my tiny tin can, I putted off down the track toward . . . well, I had no idea, really. This road wasn't on my map, but my map was mostly full of hand-drawn pictures of sheep, red stag, and spots to see birds. It is likely that Islay was, at this time, far more populated by furred and feathered faces than those with only whiskers—and by that, I mean those that become present because no one feels confident enough to hold a morning razor to their necks when their blood is still singing with the juice from the pub last night.

Enough of the cows. It was time to revisit some other old friends. I pointed my nose and that of my tin steed toward the direction of cupola-shaped roofs. An architectural oddity compared to elsewhere in Scotland thanks to a geezer named Charles Doig. He designed a boatload of distilleries—inside and out*—during the late 19th and early 20th centuries and became famously known for his kiln chimneys. It was a ventilation thing. In fact, for a long time they were simply referred to as Doig ventilators. His chimneys, installed for distilleries that had their own malting floors, simply allowed the kilning fuel—peat, or wood, or other bits and bobs—to escape the malthouse roofs in a swath of 360 degrees.

Plus, they were pretty.

So pretty, I put two on top of my house as well, in a desperate attempt to fool people into thinking I had a swanky way with architecture and also in preparation for the eventual day I would clear out the living room of furniture and spread the floor thickly with six-to-eight inches of freshly steeped barley. (It will still happen one day, dammit.)

I drove. Tossed the map out the window—okay, actually into the backseat, cuz I just can't quite *Thelma and Louise* the whole *do not litter* rule—and simply drove on the road in front of me. There was no other choice apart from the odd driveway and tractor path.

I stopped at the first interesting thing I found: the Kildalton Cross at an old kirk. According to the ancient stone carvings and symbols, this was the earliest Christian cross etched by travelers from Iona—a 9th-century man-made, ring-headed "high cross" carved from a local piece of stone. Filled with Pictish art. A masterpiece.

It stated on the tiny placard on a stick right next to the cross, but I'm fairly certain I would have figured nearly all that info out on my own eventually. Like the parts about it being a cross, made from stone, and super old. The rest is pure filler.

A few feet from the old church and graveyard was a sizeable pile of oyster shells. There was no placard for visiting tourists next to this phenomenon, so I had to create my own outdoor docent dialogue.

Here, ladies and gentlemen, lay the remains of a grave robbing beach party. Or,

The ancient Christians had nothing but oyster shells to use as carving devices and discarded the dulled instruments in a pile, right here, like so, way back when. Or,

Unexplainably, oysters, for years, come here to die.

I don't know. I'm not sure. But I hate leaving any possibilities unexplored.

I'm back in the car. I have now probably a good two or three collective hours under my belt of driving on this island. I am now an expert. I have now found a way to drive on the wrong side of the car, the wrong side of the road, and film whilst doing it. I am driver, cameraman, director, and star of this stupid drama. The scriptwriter must be fired, as I find the more I speak in front of it or behind it, the more I realize just how much I am not an "off the cuff funny" kind of a person. I'm not even an "off, off the cuff funny" kind. My humor for these segments is so far down the road from "off the cuff" that it's still not found a cuff to fall off of.

I spot a sign pointing toward Laphroaig, Lagavulin, and Ardbeg—distilleries with so much beautiful peat in some of their whiskies that it's a bit like discovering what liquid peat might taste like. Liquid peat with a kick-ass proof and an aftertaste of well-worn cowboy saddle stored in an empty canister of gasoline.

I know, lip-smacking delicious, I can hear you murmuring.

Don't be judgy. I would donate an organ for a few of their specialty bottles. I'm guessing part of my liver has already signed off in that regard.

I pull into Ardbeg's driveway and draw in a huge breath of admiration, and quite possibly a potent lungful of alcoholic air. It's not like it's the first time I've seen Ardbeg. It's just that I forget what things look like the moment they're no longer within my field of vision. Same thing happens with my kids. Although struggling to give a description of one's children is probably a tad more forgivable than not recalling the grandeur of this fine spirit-making establishment, as kids' faces and bodies change in the hours they lie prone in bed at night. You send them to their rooms and say goodnight and, the next morning, someone new sits down at the breakfast table. Oftentimes, someone you'd like to uninvite.

But Ardbeg has looked the same for over two hundred years. I should be able to remember all the whitewashed buildings, the cupolas, the crashing sea behind it, the ferry in the distance. In fact, they all look this way on Islay and have for decades. Maybe the owners have shifted around a few picnic tables here and there, but it's all dependably unchangeable.

The tour through Ardbeg's distillery is led by a young man who is clearly speaking another language. Or who's speaking English but by no means clearly. I understand none of what he says. But I recognize everything he points to. I fill in his foreign tongue wording with the last few weeks of my study and feel my heart quicken and my stomach sicken with the notion that by this time tomorrow I, too, will be tested on this equipment. To see how much I know, or to expose how much I don't.

An hour later, I'm staring out a window in Ardbeg's café, a bowl of haggis and lentil soup cooling in front of me.

I know "haggis and lentil" is not a combo flavor that immediately would make a kid do somersaults with joy, but I think if blindfolded and really hungry, and maybe threatened with losing all access to technology for a week, then yes, they'd likely report back that it was not the vomit on a spoon that it looks like.

Seriously, I cannot do this savory potage justice with mere words.

But it was enough to make me all broody about my love for Scotland and settled my jittery nerves a bit before heading back to the hotel for an early night. Okay, and studying.

Once settled in, I sat on the floor, a dram of Port Ellen in my hand, and my notes circling me on the plaid carpeting. I leaned back against an old and also plaid-covered chair and took a sip of what was becoming an often yearned-for spirit. I'd wager it was for two reasons: one, it was a damn great whisky, and two, the distillery (also on Islay) held my favorite mound of dirt, which was actually a giant heap of peat. And I think by now it is clear to anyone reading this tale that the scent, taste, and sight of peat absurdly makes me as giddy as a schoolgirl seeing her first crush. It is both calming and exhilarating. It is an aromatherapy massage, but with flavor. It says to me, *you are home*. I was just hoping I'd still feel that way tomorrow.

Breathing Room:
Whisky's Wooden Lung

S ure, there are plenty of words that live arm in arm and are seated side by side through thick and thin, but it's a bit of a headscratcher when pairing these next two. What could whisky possibly have to do with the word *headspace*?

If you do what I do a thousand times a day, you'll Google it and find out that the term is attached to musical albums, rock groups, a horror film, firearms, and—the empty space inside the fuel tank of a liquid rocket booster, located above the liquid propellant.

In whisky terms, NASA's definition fits best.

Fascinating as the parallelism may be, I doubt any master distiller would want a patron likening his product to rocket fuel—unless you happen to work for Ardbeg, the first distillery to get their spirit into space . . . for some—ahem—*research*.

Having ditched repeated efforts to understand the baffling alchemy taking place beneath a barrel lid, I thought I was done with it. Until my mother handed me a book revealing exactly what she thought I needed a dose of. It's called *Get Some Headspace: How Mindfulness Can Change Your Life*.

Apparently, it was also a message from the Distillery Deities I worship: clear your head and don't give up.

Coincidentally, headspace also changes a *spirit*—and I'm not referring to the essence of life, but rather the *water* of life. At the risk of repeating myself, it's magic.

And by magic, I mean much of the "oohing and ahhing" we utter is a result of the effect of those hidden spaces, invisible to us within a cask. In keeping with my theme, I'll not explain things like you're reading a lab report, rather I'll attempt, in slightly elevated Harry Potter terms, to explain the bewitchery of a barrel.

I've always liked the analogy of seeing a barrel as a lung. And since I cannot go five minutes without using a metaphor, it works for me.

Lungs expand and contract with the intake and exhalation of air. So does a barrel—but you'd probably need sorcerous eyes to truly see the movement. Regardless, once a whisky barrel is filled, it breathes, although much depends upon the climate surrounding it. Here, climate refers to temperature, humidity, and barometric pressure.

Heat will expand the cask's wood, which allows the spirit to seep into its pores, whereas a colder climate will force the wood to contract and will squeeze the fluid out, reversing its direction. Inside the fibrous makeup of the cask are wood-derived congeners—myriad beautiful compounds that contribute flavors of butter, caramel, vanilla, clove, smoke, and nuts. When the spirit soaks into the wood, it has access to the wood's flavorful elements. When the liquid is forced back out, it pulls those elements out with it and shares all those lovely congeners with the rest of the spirit it has rejoined.

Another fascinating note when speaking of climate is how it affects evaporation within the cask. Perhaps a more interesting question is *what is evaporating?* And the answer to this lies within a barrel's storage conditions. Both alcohol *and* water are evaporating over time, but depending upon where the casks are aging within the warehouse (at the top, where it's drier and hotter, or on the floors, where it may be cool and moist) and what type of warehouse they're stored within (racked, dunnage, or palletized), they will evaporate at different rates of speed.

—Damp conditions = a speedier loss of alcohol (ethanol)

—Dry conditions = a quicker loss of water

—Cool environment = slower aging

—Hot/warm environments = faster aging; though according to some, often at the cost of the product. Much has to do with the size of the barrel and the wood's surface-to-spirit ratio.

This explains how some spirits increase in potency during maturation while others decrease. Don't forget that alcohol has a lower evaporation point than water, so what is pumped into the barrel at 56 percent alcohol by volume (ABV) can be poured out at 58 percent. Like I said, magic.

What is not magic, but rather some basic middle-school science many of us learned and then promptly forgot, is how a liquid can evaporate without boiling, because of course, there is no boiling taking place within the casks inside the warehouse. Let's make the explanation as easy as possible. Although alcohol evaporates at 172° F and water at 212° F, warehouse temps do not achieve these thermic heights, right? Instead, we must recall that evaporation is simply a slow process where liquid changes to gas and can occur at all temperatures, whereas boiling requires heat. Evaporation is also a surface phenomenon, while boiling is a bulk phenomenon.

But evaporation rates also depend on airflow around the cask. I remember my internet whisky feed blowing up with discussions and debates over the Diageo "experiment" in 2008, when they dabbled with wrapping casks in cling film. My smart-alecky guess was that idea came from someone in accounting looking to squeeze the most out of every effort. But there were a few others who defended the company, stating they were doing some worthy science, attempting to discover how much spirit is held hostage within the cask by eliminating an influencing factor: evaporation.

(Snort) Okay, sure. Despite the high opinions of many in the whisky world, I'd bet it was a nifty science experiment regardless.

But interaction with air is something distilleries are still researching. Where the warehouses are located (by the sea, in a cave, just off the M8 or Route 66 on the side of the road), the types of warehouses (again, dunnage, racked, or palletized—therefore impacting the airflow around the barrels and the heights one can stack them to), the environment inside the warehouses (temperature, humidity, and barometric pressure), and ventilation within those warehouses are all variables in the quest for answers regarding air's effects on a spirit's quality.

Even the act of filling a cask or rolling it creates a meshing of air and spirit; the oxidation process. There's a wealth of science that can explain how oxidation and evaporation are heavy hitters in maturation reactions, both additive and subtractive, and how they eliminate or modify the components of the spirit.

Of course, there are other agents that participate in altering the flavor profile. In reference to our Japanese friends and their philosophy of the five elements—Earth, Water, Fire, Wind, and Void—I think we've touched on them all if wind and air could be interchangeable and headspace could stand in for void.

Suffice it to say, finding the perfect balance is a worthy quest—both in this world of whisky and in our way of thinking. The spirit needs room to breathe, to experience an ebb and flow of variables, and we need an opportunity to review the cause and effect of each influence.

Do yourself and the whisky world a favor; create a little headspace in either your literal or metaphorical barrel. Scoop in and have a dram.

Give your spirit a little room to breathe.

Squeaky Clean

The next morning, before showing up for duty, I decided to make a quick swing over to Port Ellen for a swift starry-eyed gaze at my favorite pile of peat. At this time, Port Ellen—a malt mill established in 1825 and then a distillery starting around 1833—was an on-again, off-again facility: acquired, closed, rebuilt, opened, and closed again. The remaining stocks had been purchased by Diageo and word on the street was that, although currently it was being used simply as a malting and peating facility, soon her mighty wheels would be turning again, and Port Ellen would be brought back to life as an operational distillery once more.

I'd read that her stills—equipment wholly precious and, in some minds, irreplaceable if one wanted to recreate the whisky's distinctive flavor profile—had been destroyed. I drove slowly by the old buildings, the warehouses, and the massive peat heap with a slightly heavy heart.

The smell was undeniably heady, and I thought about the few old bottles I had remaining in my cellar, and the disheartening notion that I'd never find replacements. The mountain of chocolate-brown bricks made me think of a giant woolly mammoth, slowly sinking into the earth, melting toward extinction.

I drove back to Bowmore and passed by Kilarrow Parish—better known as "that wonky round church at the top of the road." I love it. For two reasons:

1. It's stunning to view. The design is so unusual with its two-and-a-half-foot-thick whitewashed silo walls and black funnel-shaped roof, eight thick radiating beams spreading the load above them.

2. It boasts an explanation for its shape that thoroughly appeals to me (and is an example of the joys of historical research): the walls are round—corner-less, so the devil has no place to hide.

One side of the church faces the town, observing it, and maintaining a firm reminder that "God is always watching." The other side holds the grassy graveyard, providing protection from the frothy foamy sea at the bottom of the hill, and possibly serves as a reminder to the townsfolk that *God is always watching—and these guys are now meeting him face-to-face.*

It is beyond romantic. And I become beyond tolerable in any scene that I deem romantic. People seriously want to kill me to end the gushing.

If that should happen, I hope my demise would take place near the graveyard at the Round Church, as this final resting place would suit me just fine.

My last stop—another favorite of mine on this tiny island—Spirited Soaps. A matchbox of a nook, this snuggery is tucked into the line of white stuccoed cottages and shops selling—you guessed it—soaps made from whisky. And gin, and flowers, and barley, and myrtle. Even something called whin, which is apparently coconut and honey. But it's all so heavenly, and the moment I step inside, I almost want to swap whisky for soap-making.

It would make for quite a modern fairy tale. Woman leaves America after unruly English husband thrust her children into Scottish boarding schools, where she is denied access to them because of some wicked parental kidnapping and their dual citizenship. (The perk of this yarn is that it has me leaving said English husband half a decade earlier than I did.) Despite the refusal of help from the American Consulate or any International Bureau of Consular Affairs, this woman hunts them down and now just needs to hatch a plan with some newly made and handily clever Scottish friends, who will help her reclaim them in the dead of night. Until then, she must work quietly and patiently as an innocent, creamy-skinned soap maker. Somewhere along the way, said woman, of course, falls in love with one of the distillers whose whisky she uses to make her fair and heady soaps. Together, along with her newfound clansmen family, she recaptures her children, he falls in love with them too, and together they open the world's most elite distillery/ soap shop/Amnesty International secret headquarters and live happily ever after.

It would be great, wouldn't it?

But back in the real world, at that moment, at least I still had soap.

After filling my nose with the dreamy scents of fresh Islay sea foam, malty roasted barley, and the aromas that saturate every Islay warehouse, I stepped out of the cottage shop and looked across the water of Lochindaal to where the Bruichladdich Distillery stood on the opposite end.

I got in my car and pulled up to the stop sign and took a second to gaze at the street marker that pointed toward the distillery and the one with the picture of an airplane on it. Making a right would bring me to my tiny apprenticeship and all its worrisome challenges. Turning left would take me back to the airport, where I could change my flight and head back home to Virginia, safe and sound, relieved and unburdened.

I turned left.

The Water of the Water of Life

T rying to get a straight answer from anyone intimately connected to the whisky-making process about whether water plays a part in the flavor profile of a spirit is like trying to get a teenager to tell you what they've been up to for the last hour in their bedroom. They will hem and haw, pointing out that maybe it wasn't exactly an hour, or they had left the room a couple of times to do other things, but the question will never truly be answered. Many mothers quickly realize this is a question we really do not want to know the answer to anyway. But as most master distillers I know were, at one point, teenagers, it comes as no surprise that they have mastered the art of diversion and deflection. And that is wholly frustrating.

Some distillers, if you are lucky enough to speak to one on a tour, emphatically answer *no,* and then spend copious minutes telling you why water cannot, under any circumstances, impart flavor to the finished product. There are phrases slung out about the filtration system, the heating/boiling regimens during distillation, and maybe even sterilization by magic lights—or more likely they said ultraviolet lights, as my note-taking was a little crummy from having too many sample drams too early in the day. Regardless, it's what many experts *start out* saying.

But perhaps we should back up and see the process from a 30,000-foot view, as when seeing the big picture, making whisky is simply a matter of adding and subtracting water repeatedly from the product, from the moment we start to the moment we finish.

1. Water is added to the mash
2. It's then subtracted through heating (evaporation within the mash tuns or tanks) and distillation (separating the components via boiling points in stills)
3. Water is added to the distillate when barreling
4. It's then subtracted from those barrels via evaporation in warehouses via climate
5. Then water is added to (most) bottles
6. And finally, it's added to (some) drams

Many distillers choose different water sources depending upon what stage of the above process they're in because the source of the water is influenced by further pivotal factors that will contribute to its aroma/flavor profile. Factors like:

1. The pH balance:
   a. Water used for the mash and fermentation must be of low alkalinity to achieve the correct pH balance, which allows the enzymes to be activated and extract what you are trying to get from your grains. This creates a healthy fermentation. Yeast also requires (apart from sugar) a few trace minerals for nutrients, and these affect the flavor of the end product.
   b. The water one adds to the distillate for aging should be considered, as it interacts with the wood compounds.
   c. And of course, the water one adds into the bottle for proofing is, without a doubt, of considerable weight. A distiller should identify the precise mineral content, as this water can add flavor (good and bad), aromas (good and bad), and viscosity or a weightiness to the finished product.
2. The water's source: Natural sources will have a mineral content from the air (rainwater absorbs gases, mineral crystals, dust, and other compounds), from the earth (groundwater absorbs minerals from the earth it's filtering through,

among other chemicals present like pesticides or herbicides), from the sea (even freshwater sources that are located inland from the seashore are known to contribute medicinal, iodine, or briny notes). And if a distillery chooses to use distilled water, they likely will be adding trace minerals their yeasts will need, but it creates a blank slate for them to first work with.

3. Taints: Any atypical flavor caused by an environmental contamination including water sources, molds, bacteria, or others that are often hard to detect are concerns for distillers. Geosmin and also methylisoborneol (MIB) are naturally occurring compounds that have an earthy or beet-like taste and odor. Seasonal increases in naturally occurring algae or bacteria in water sources can cause a rise in these bacteria and become perceptible to the human palate.

4. And what of your ice cubes (if that's how you take your spirit)? Freezer-burned ice cubes will ruin your drink.

From those first enchanting sips, it was hard to conceive that someone realized it was possible to sum up the parts of their country—all rugged mountains, bottomless lochs, frothy streams, plaid-covered pipers, mist-soaked sheep, and grisly warriors—and pop them into a bottle to serve up in the perfect nosing glass. In my mind, there was surely an element of sorcery within its process. Incantations, grimoires, and kettles filled with unmentionable ingredients presumably had to be a big part of making whisky come out of the heat-blasting copper pots like they do. Thus, seeing a distiller scratch his head before answering the "water influence" query is par for the course, as he is likely sifting through what he may reveal of the process that happens behind the curtain, and what remains as legerdemain—the illusion of faint wizardry too precious a bubble to pop with the sharp tools of the technical.

It's also common for each distillery to guard their water source, (and they have since time began) but they insist it's due to the unpredictable nature of rainfall. Huh. *Unpredictable* rainfall . . . in Scotland . . .

Occasionally, distilleries have had to shut down production due to drought. In 2010, part of Islay came to a screeching halt. Several Scots in the hills where I live actually came to their knees at the news and went to bed pacifying a bottle of Bunnahabhain, whispering reassuring words that the end was not nigh and all would be well again soon.

The fact that a distillery's need for production water is as great as a politician's desire for headlines makes it to the top of a distiller's worry list when tallying up how much water is needed for each batch of booze. It's a little like walking through New England and somebody pointing out that if they tapped all the trees in Vermont for a day, you might have just enough sap to make syrup for your morning pancakes. It's eye-opening for some, but more importantly, nerve-wracking for others.

So, with all this water contact and contribution, is it truly unrealistic to believe that each distillery's source may add a signature of sorts to the end result? It's probable.

The influence of minerals, vegetation, peat, sand, and pH levels in the water may one day appear at the top of a chemical analysis report. Maybe they already have. Maybe the reports have been buried or burned. For some sleuths, pursuing the results will leave them plotting. For the rest of us, we may just raise our glasses in thanks to the clouds over Clynelish.

Sage Words from the First Lady

Y es, I turned left, but only because the guy behind me suddenly honked his horn, and I panicked. Plus, he was turning right, so there was no way in hell I was going to have this guy on my tail all the way to the distillery.

It's not like I didn't give staying on the road heading south back home any serious consideration, but I am not a coward.

Well. That's a lie. I *am* a coward, but I just don't let being a coward direct my life. It's more like *because* I am a coward, I do things to really piss that part of me off.

Like making a career of singing on stage even though I suffered massive stage fright—I did that little beauty from age eight through twenty-three. And again, I made myself learn to fly—not because I had some grand urge to soar through clouds and rise like eagles. Nope. On the contrary. I liked the ground—and believed even most swing sets I'd come across as a child should have been cordoned off with yellow warning tape. It just made sense that if something went to hell in a handbasket in our little cockpit, I'd best know how to park this little puppy.

I was forever finding ways to live up to my hero, Eleanor Roosevelt, who said, "Do one thing every day that scares the shit out of you." Or close enough. The "face your fear" bit was the whole point, though.

So, I flipped that car around—doing Y-turns on a single-track road is clumsy at the best of times, as in when you're on your own country's roads and in your own country's cars. But finally, I was on my way, puttering toward destiny.

I pulled into the distillery's courtyard and parked, then stood outside my car, inhaling the heady scent of barley grains, yeast, and new-make spirit. I looked about the snuggling, whitewashed buildings. I closed my eyes. I felt my heart leap and skip as awkwardly as a maniacally wild toddler at her first day of dance class. Trying to remember all the wonderfully sage meditation techniques that quickly calm and focus my mind when I'm in a room with nothing but a summer breeze and two sleeping cats, I opened my eyes again and gave up on the yogi thing and went with maniacally wild toddler.

I scanned the courtyard looking for signs, keys jingling in my hand, until I saw a workman exit one of the many buildings surrounding the circle. I leapt into action—but quickly realized I'd closed the car door on part of my rain jacket. After fixing that little snag, I truly and freely did leap into action—but the guy was already gone.

Fine. I just picked a door that said, BE GONE WI' YE! or maybe it said, EMPLOYEES ONLY, but still, it was a door with a warning to reconsider entrance.

I'd entered the bottling hall. Small and clean and containing one person. A young guy looked over from where he stood, hunched over paperwork.

"I'm here for the uh . . ."

"Tour?" he said.

"No, the—"

"Gift shop?" He jerked his chin back toward the courtyard.

"Nope. Actually, the work. The job-internship-thingy." There. Totally eloquent. My inner toddler would be proud.

"Seriously?" Now the guy stood upright and gave me the once-over.

I shrugged. "Yup. Where do I check in?"

He pointed toward the back of the bottling hall. "All the guys are up at the distillery manager's house. That's where yer all stayin'." He squinted at me again. "Best drive your car up there if ye've luggage. It's a bit of a climb."

I thought about home. About the fact that I lived on a mountain where the driveway was a mile long and a thousand feet up. I thought about all the times during snow or ice storms I'd had to park the car at the bottom and trek, slog, trudge, and toil while heaving backpacks, groceries, cat carriers, or small exhausted children to the top. "A bit of a climb" was not a deterring phrase to me. "A bit of a climb" meant home was at the end of it. My heart lightened a little.

I drove up, found a sign pointing to the house, and parked. I knocked on the back door and was met by Fenella, one of the cooks. She looked me over with the same surprise on her face as Bottleman Bob, and I heard her murmur, "What is a wee lass doin' in such a place?" as we struggled up the narrow staircase to my room with my giant, still wet suitcase.

"I kinda like whisky," I replied, forcing a smile.

She turned back to me. "There's plenty of it down at the pub in Port Charlotte, love—and more than a few lads who'll buy it for ye."

"Well, I'm more interested in making it than drinking it."

That was a lie. But not a whopper of a whopper. Knowing how little I knew about *actually* making it made me pause to admit that I did not have a true position on that just yet. Sure, I'd been on a gazillion distillery tours, but what they say, memorized from a script, surely was not enough to go on.

"Suit yourself," she finished with a lopsided smile. "Dinner is at 6:30 down at the table. Dinna be late."

Fenella left, and I lowered myself onto my twin bed. The room was clean, with a tiny bathroom and a mirror, a small closet, and a window that faced up the hill toward the warehouses holding the barrels. "Work" clothes were laid across the bed—two exceptionally large, but labeled *medium,* thick men's T-shirts with the distillery's name and logo etched across the chest.

I was not here for the tour, nor the gift shop. I wasn't here to find a fella to buy me a dram and then tell me what they wanted me to make them for dinner Monday through Sunday. I was not that girl. Or maybe I wasn't that girl anymore.

And maybe I didn't exactly have the new definition of who I was becoming, but the tug toward that sense of change was strong, magnetic, and undeniable.

I studied my schedule. At 9:00 tonight, I would have my "safety and orientation" meeting. Work would begin at 6:00 A.M.

I looked outside toward the fields, speckled with a few cattle in the distance, remembering umpteen childhood days waking up at 4:30 A.M. to start milking cows. "Huh," I chuckled, glancing back at the schedule. "This would be a dairy farmer's dream day. I get to sleep in."

Well, Well, Well.
Aberlour's History Runs Deep

M ost folks are well acquainted with the phrase, *You reap what you sow.* It's relevant whether you're making a stew, knitting an afghan, or collecting a hank of golden fleece from a herd of hominid-devouring rams.

If you use last year's carrots and potatoes, dinner is going to taste like dirt. (I just call it *earthy.*)

If you weave a blanket made from strips of recycled milk jugs, chances are most folks at the office are going to keep their fingers crossed you didn't draw their name from the Secret Santa hat.

And as far as the whole Cupid and Psyche drama, well, I'd suggest you don't piss off Venus by bringing her a cheap skein from Woolworths. I think you get my point.

But just in case, the point is your *ingredients* matter.

I wrote earlier about the importance of water to each distillery, and how they guard their source more closely than Donald Trump hid his tax returns, even though some distillers may casually say the water doesn't make a difference. But in the end, it's essential that the water's flavor be supreme to begin with, because no amount of praying will make a miraculous change to your final product.

That is, unless you happen to be Aberlour Distillery and draw your source from St. Drostan's Well.

Drostan, a Scottish abbot, accompanied Columba, an Irish abbot, from Iona to Aberdeenshire in the 6th century, determined to give the Picts a taste from the Christian buffet table, and hoping to gather up a few more players for Team God. Apparently, Drostan was a likeable fellow. Maybe it was due to his gentle touch when baptizing converts, or perhaps his "alleged" restoration of sight to a blind fellow monk did the trick and brought him fame. Possibly, he shared the old Irish monastic recipe for making a little aqua vitae—and I think we all know firsthand how an individual can take on a "saintlike" quality simply for sharing his private stash, or how firewater can make magic and miraculous things appear before your eyes if you've had enough of it.

Whatever the reason, the saint's well is occasionally credited for its fine contribution to the whisky's flavor profile.

If not divine intervention, perhaps Aberlour's success was fiddled with by fairies, as behind the distillery, visitors will come across the Pictish standing stones of Fairy Knowe, whetting any appetite for more legend and lore.

It comes as no surprise that the name *Aberlour* translates from Gaelic as *"mouth of the chattering burn."* Might those prattling pixies have had a hand in transporting dram drinkers into another realm entirely?

Of course, there is the notion that practice makes perfect, and perhaps after nearly two hundred years of whisky making taking place within the village of Aberlour, these folks finally know what they're doing and have the recipe down pat.

As the majority of Aberlour's single malts are double matured, dividing their maturation time between ex-bourbon and ex-sherry casks, many of the available expressions (or single malt variations) are heavy with fruit flavors and seasoned with various shades of sherry—some, a veritable nectar of the gods.

One whisky that garners some well-deserved attention is Aberlour's expression, *A'bunadh*, which is Gaelic for *origin*, and one emulating what the distillers feel is representative of Aberlour's original spirit from the 19th century. Described as dark and dusty, spicy and dangerous, one may be confused as to whether we're describing a whisky or an antique pie safe. Rest assured, after a few moments with it lingering in the mouth, most folks are searching for a hand to shake.

And this brings us full circle to the argument of credit. Heavenly? Mystical? Earthly?

You decide. Personally, my experience with this dram is transcendental any way you look at it.

The Best and Worst of
The Wizard of Oz

T he voices I heard as I came down the stairs were boisterous. But more than that, I noticed they were all men. Of course, they would be all men. It was such a rare thing to find female companionship in this realm, and although I was used to it, I still held out hope that one day I'd not be such an odd duck.

There were looks of barely withheld surprise—and one of recognition. The man from the airport. The *rude* man from the airport. I knew it. I knew somehow that the pile of challenges on my plate was not nearly high enough for the gang of mythological tricksters that I swear direct my life's trajectory. I silently raised my fist to the sky and spat out my internal vitriol.

By the looks of it, the fellas were already well into their cups—all glassy-eyed and rosy-cheeked. One seat was still vacant, and I slipped into it with what I hoped was a confident, "Hey all, I'm Shelley."

"You're here for the academy?" the round-faced, ill-bred man from the airport asked, his eyebrows announcing incredulity.

"I am. And what are you here for?" *Academy*, I bristled. Apparently, Plato was going to be making an appearance at some point.

He pulled back a little. "Well, the academy, of course."

Of course. I shrugged. "Of course," I said. And the lanky, dark-haired man next to me made a tiny grunt of laughter, pushing his thick horn-rimmed glasses back up his nose. I gave him a quick glance and caught a nod of acknowledgment.

"Hey, Shelley. I'm Jim—and the fellow you've just chatted with is James," he said, with a jerk of his pointy chin across the table to the cad from the airport. "Don't confuse the two of us. One of us knows a helluva lot about whisky and the other just thinks he does. You be the judge." His smile was broad, stretching across his thin face. I dubbed him the Tin Man, as his gentle goodwill was exactly what Dorothy needed after her first run-in with the Wicked Witch—or in this case, Warlock.

"Arms away," Fenella cried, as she carried in hot platters of food, another woman following her from the tiny kitchen. "This here is Margaret—she's staff cook, too."

We all sat back from the table as Fenella and Margaret placed plates in front of us. "'Tis marrow 'n haggis sauce tonight. Wi' cabbage and veg of sorts. Eat up while it's hot. Enjoy, boys!"

"And girls!" Jim piped up.

Fenella glanced back from her exit toward the kitchen. "Oh aye. And girls."

I looked up to peek at James, the Warlock, and saw his face pucker in an oh-so-familiar manner, the same look I usually got from Jonathan any moment I erred by having a contrary opinion. Or perhaps the Warlock's sour expression had sprouted because of the food beneath him, and not from the woman across from him.

But seriously, he was just missing a green-paint complexion and candy-cane-striped socks.

———

Marrow turned out to be squash—or somewhat like squash. I'd say I've yet to come across this specific vegetable growing in anyone's American back garden, but clearly, I've not yet been in *everyone's*. It tastes similar to zucchini, and later when I mentioned that to Fenella, she insisted that no, it's much closer to *courgette*. I decided not to inform her that they were one and the same, as I was well-versed in just how much weight my knowledge of cooking had carried when having identical conversations with my mother-in-law.

A bit lead balloon-ish.

The haggis sauce is exactly as described. Haggis liquefied. But uber delicious—don't get me wrong. I've come to love haggis, and people who know how to make it well deserve a kidney for their efforts. Of course, I've also had awful haggis—truly, just awful, awful horrible.

But this sauce was more like a thin, yet flavorful chili. Imagine making a great pot of chili for a quick get-together of four friends, and then suddenly discovering they each decided to bring along an extra guest. You make it work.

And boy, did Fenella and Margaret know how to make their haggis sing. And the cabbage, peas, and potatoes were piled on every plate along with great heaps of syrupy sweet orange melon. It was a weird and undeniably memorable plate full of food. I ate it all and asked for seconds. Or just took them. It was family style.

Halfway through dinner, and midway through glass of wine number two, I was beginning to feel a smidge more comfortable. Mostly because I did not have to do any talking. Tin Man Jim had come with two best buddies from New England, and they provided a sense of ease at the table by boisterously chattering away companionably. They all had wonderful sounding jobs in science and technology, but the Tin Man's was the most interesting—*genome* building. Or gnome building, but I'm fairly sure I heard right the first go-round.

I was about to ask him to elaborate, with the caveat that I'd understand nearly nothing, but would still nod with great admiration, when one of his friends—a mirthful man with a round belly and sharp wit—shouted out, "So, Shelley, what is it that *you* do?"

"I'm a writer. And basically, in charge of full bellies and clean underwear." My heart skipped a beat. *Please don't ask, please don't ask, please don't ask.*

"My wife is a writer," the Wicked Warlock said.

Whew, I breathed out. "Can't swing a dead cat around by its tail without hitting a novelist these days."

"Are you published?" asked the third in the trio of the Tin Man's friends.

Damn. Damn. Damn.

"Nope. Not yet."

"My wife is published." The Wicked Warlock beamed.

Of course she is.

"What are you working on?" asked the Tin Man.

I really wanted to hug him. He was so kind and encouraging.

"I write middle-grade humor, and young adult historical fiction. A lot of stuff about Scotland."

The Warlock puffed. Apparently, he must have attended the same facial expression academy as Jonathan.

"And I write about whisky." I continued. "I have a blog—"

"My wife has a blog."

"—where I mostly tell the history and stories about old distilleries, the people who ran them, the ghosts who inhabit them, and sometimes about special releases that are unusually interesting. Occasionally, I throw in some easy science about craft, or pick one whisky topic and take a somewhat shallow dive into the subject. It's purely driven from enthusiasm and not expertise."

"Fascinating!" the mirthful one said loudly. "A children's writer with a wickedly saucy secret! Tell us more!"

The back door suddenly opened, and a tall man—weathered and hairy as a graying sea captain—beamed at us. "Good evening, all!"

We turned in our seats.

"I hope ye've enjoyed the fine talents of Fenella and Margaret. They're canny wee cooks! Saints at the stove!"

We all nodded enthusiastically.

"Good. For a full belly is what ye need for my scary safety talk. But dinna worry. We've got plenty of liquor in the sitting room to ease the fears I'll surely stir up. If ye'll just come wi' me. Oh, by the way, I'm Graham."

But I was worried. The twinkle in Graham's eye suggested he was either a terrific jokester or a madman who was waiting with delicious pleasure to inflict some pain. *Plenty of liquor* sounded like an advisable balm while I waited to find out which.

Tipping the Hip for a
Sip of the Tipple

Picture an unshaven, threadbare, teetering panhandler. Propped against a wall, he mutters something about a shopping cart and how a pack of homing pigeons made off with his car keys before he takes a long draw from the top end of a paper bag.

You give him a wide berth and finger your pocket for the reassuring bulge of keys and cash.

Now picture your office Christmas party where some folks are huddled, benumbed, around the punch bowl. A few are smoking in the break room or, more likely, passing out edibles, several are pitching after-hours proposals at management in an attempt to leverage brownie points, and one guy has scored the key to the boss's private liquor cabinet and is looking for a few willing and daring delinquents to join him.

Which person are you likely to make a beeline toward for comfort and succor?

Answer?

None of them.

The guy you want is the fellow leaning casually against a wall, just on the outskirts, the one with the Don Draper attitude—slick and dangerous with a doesn't-give-a-damn gaze. The one who sips from a polished hip flask, emitting a heavy layer of natty sophistication that remains inaccessible to the envious wannabes surrounding him.

What's the difference among the swillers?

Probably nothing more than a little savoir faire.

Okay, and maybe good luck, a healthy bank account, a wife who didn't cheat on him, that four-year stint at Harvard, a summer house in the Hamptons, parents with a yacht. Yeah, I get it. The guy looting the company chief's cabinet and old Donny are both outliers and both doing the same act. Yet one of them is a magnet and praised for his finesse.

And that ladies and gentlemen, is what a hip flask brings. STYLE.

Who do we have to thank for this touch of elegance? Ancient pilgrims and pioneers, trailblazing tourists who never lived to see the opening of the first 7-Eleven and the ready availability of the Big Gulp. They had to prepare for the road and a trot across the globe.

First drafts of these finely cut containers received reviews from the public that would have surely put manufacturers out of business had those with the "can do" attitude not gone back to the proverbial drawing board.

Pig's bladders were reliable, but persuading a pig to hand his over required a grace that many lacked, and usually, a fight ensued.

Glass was helpful in that you could see the amount of liquid you still possessed, but so could your traveling companions, and that left you out of luck in the "I don't think there's any left to share" fib one relies upon in a do-or-die desert situation when sightseeing across hot sand.

Eventually metal makers threw a Kmart Blue Light Special, and folks tested the gamut of available options. Copper tasted tangy, tin made everything blue, and if it were pewter, you had to take your chances with a little lead poisoning and could reduce your chances of arriving to your final destination.

The answer was sterling silver. The *Medieval Times* printed rave reviews, and suddenly, villagers across Europe knew what they'd be getting their friends for Saturnalia.

Still, the population was plagued with the slightly annoying problem of shape and form. Horses voted for a design that wouldn't leave them with an agitated flesh wound, the result of the flask swinging back and forth on their hide for hundreds of jaunty miles, and most men wanted something that was slimming and ultimately wouldn't add pounds onto their hips (because wayfarers know it's hard to make good food choices when eating on the bridle path).

Women were the easiest to please in that they knew petticoats hid a multitude of sins. They could hide their cake and drink it, too.

And over the years, whether strapped to the thigh of a thoroughly modern Millie, who's simply biding her time through Prohibition, securely stationed in the top left breast pockets of legions of soldiers who refer to engraved inscriptions for remembered love and the contents for liquid courage, or used by Mad-Eye Moody to store his Polyjuice Potion, the hip flask has retained a constant, but quiet, presence in the world of spirits.

Raise your glass in toast to a nip of the tipple. Hip, hip, hooray!

The Distillery's Source
of Confusion

Graham's sage and worrisome words of safety were thus: *Don't screw up.*

Don't screw up, what? I wondered. There was just so much to choose from. And I had been bred with the mindset of "embrace failure." It's what I preached to my children back home, it was how I practiced learning anything new. Botch-ups—from the minor to the major—was a song whose keys I sang in every day: a set of scales and arpeggios that highlighted what you knew and what you didn't, what was easy and what was difficult, where you could skate and where you needed undivided focus.

Telling me not to screw up was like telling me not to learn.

I went to bed and wrestled with the heavily starched—near to sleeping on paper—sheets, and 5:30 came early, but not fast. Work shirt, work pants, hefty boots, and a ponytail. I was as ready as I could be.

We met Monroe—the mashman—at 6:00 A.M. sharp. I learned about barley: *the grain, the ingredient, the great pearl of power.* Within the two hours of both barley adoration and equipment identification, I felt profound reverence for this little bud of beauty and was contemplating leaving a few dollars in my will to any building foundation that would create a museum in honor of the grain, and for the education of all soon-to-be scotch drinkers—likely fifth graders in need of a field trip.

At 8:30 A.M. we ran back up to the kitchen, where those saints at the stove, the Faithful Fenella and Sister Malvina-Margaret, had prepared breakfast for the hungry—and in most cases hungover—mashmen gathered round the table. The five of us ate with gusto and speed, as we had less than twenty minutes before we were due back with Monroe, where we would labor for the next four hours, putting our newfound barley adoration to work.

During those four hours, we not only repeatedly sang the barley anthem, but we added in a full-blown chorus about the bounty of the burn (a local linguistic term for "stream"). Then, Monroe showed us the distillery's water source—really three sources.

As noted in other areas of this book, a distillery's water is paramount. Again, and please forgive the repeated reference, it's a little like watching *The Wizard of Oz*, but this time without Dorothy. We know the whole cast of characters are wonderful, in and of themselves, but none of them can truly stand on their own and complete that film.

Except maybe Glinda. God, we all know that woman has an awesome backstory. She might be able to pull it off. She's like bacon. Awesome in a BLT, but you could absolutely make a meal of bacon and be wholly satisfied.

And just like Glinda—or bacon—each of the distillery's water sources is noteworthy on its own, but purposefully compatible with almost every pairing the spirit-making process will throw at it. One source—the Bruichladdich loch or *An Torran*—is the water they use for mashing. The soft, brown peaty water is about two miles up into the hills from the distillery, sitting quietly in a shallow pond and waiting for the moment it will be piped down into the mash tuns so that it can begin extracting all the vital sugars from the wee barley grains having their bath.

The second source is the Bruichladdich burn, running adjacent to the distillery as it heads down toward the gray, frothy sea. Water from the burn is used to run through the condensers, cooling the spirit vapors and turning them into distillate.

The third of their sources lives another two miles yonder, farther up the road. James Brown, farmer and proprietor of Octomore Farm, collects this water—which comes from a natural spring that used to be the main water supply for the tiny village of Port Charlotte—and transports it to the distillery. Here, it's used in the bottling hall, proofing down the spirit from cask strength to somewhere around 50 percent ABV.

Thank you, Farmer Brown. Thank you for your efforts.

I'm feeling more certain about that museum, but now thinking perhaps we ought to add on a wing about water.

At 12:30 P.M. we were released back to the house and told to make haste with lunch. The haloed ladies had left us on our own to fix sandwiches with a surplus of ingredients. I ate the surplus of ingredients with renewed vigor. Blame it on the sea air. Or blame it on the fact that I have the appetite of a ravenous field worker—minus all the field work.

Shortly thereafter, I met Hamish. Hamish is the kind of man who most old-fashioned parents would relish having as a child. He is only seen and not heard.

Hamish told us everything we needed to know about distillation for today as we had our orientation within the stillhouse. But no one heard a word of what he said, as he's a tall man, soft spoken, and the stillhouse is noisy as hell. I think he long ago deemed it futile to try speaking against the hiss and whirling wash of the two large copper pot stills and gave up somewhere after his first week of employment.

It didn't really matter to me, as every stillroom I've been in is considered the happiest place on earth in my eyes, and seeing all those giant copper pots belching away, making distillate, fills me with a thrill akin to discovering you've been named in someone's will. I'd hug each one of those stills, all fat and happy like a giant Buddha belly, if they weren't a scorching billion degrees.

Graham popped in while we were working in the stillhouse, just passing through to see how we were faring during the afternoon shift, and announced loudly, "Make sure you memorize every precise word Hamish tells ye, as it's all going to be on the final exam. Ye'll not get your certificate of internship wi'out the exam!" His eyes twinkled. With joy? With evil intent? Maybe with evil enjoyment.

I had a tiny panic attack right there. And watched Hamish wave farewell to us as his replacement, Colin, came in to fill the next shift.

Colin greeted us with a good-natured smile and then raised his brows as the Warlock raised his hand.

"Apparently, we're going to be tested on what Hamish just uhh . . . told us. Any chance we could ask some questions about this phase?"

He chuckled knowingly. "Ask away."

"Well, firstly, do you do anything significantly different here than the way Hamish does?"

Again, Colin gave a small snort. "Nah. I'll tell ye everythin' Hamish said. Just louder!"

Whisky Coproducts:
The Extra Bits and Bobs
Part 1 (Draff)

There is a lot that goes *into* the efforts resulting in the honey-colored glass of whisky that swirls like liquid sunshine in your hand. What many of us don't see is that there's a lot that comes *out* of these efforts, as well. Some of the more invisible results are happily snapped up by folks who see the benefit of a symbiotic relationship with any distillery. Others are a headache for the manufacturer of spirits, and their disposal must be dealt with in a manner that will please government officials, caring and concerned environmental agencies, and any chef serving fish that understands customers will likely not order *Fresh, local salmon infused with a lively hint of toxins.*

These extras that appear alongside the whisky-making process are what the industry refers to as *coproducts*. I'll walk you through the most notable, attempt to explain them in rough laymen's terms, and give you an idea as to what distilleries do with the additional output.

First, let's give a nod to our mashman. He makes up a batch of grist, adds hot water to dissolve the soluble sugars, and after draining that marvelous, sweet liquid portion of the mash—called wort—he's left with a boatload full of protein-rich food that farm animals are more than happy to take off his hands. They sort of "lick the bowl clean," from the proverbial cookie-making process.

This good-for-you gruel is called draff and is often carted away to grain plants so it can be sold to farmers as livestock food. In some places, farmers have relationships with distilleries and will arrange personal daily pickups to collect the fresh feed. I would imagine that my beloved highland cows are more than thrilled with their assigned roles in the whisky/distillery ecosystem.

Ultimately, the distillery benefits from this working relationship in a multitude of ways: not only are they getting rid of a pesky by-product—and at a profit!—but that product is then returned to the land in the form of farmyard manure that is ultimately added to the fields and used to grow the next shipment of grain for their spirits. Buy grain, use grain, eat grain, poop grain, grow grain. Okay, so it may never be used as a T-shirt slogan, but it's an admirable cycle.

Distilleries need farmers. In fact, if I owned a distillery, I'd probably paste a few stickers on my bottle that announced my true admiration for the farming industry writ large, like: MY OTHER VEHICLE IS A TRACTOR, or I DIG PIGS, or I'd draw a big heart with two cow's feet in the middle and use the slogan, HOOF-HEARTED. Go ahead and say that last one out loud a couple of times just for fun. Just do it.

Of course, farmers need distilleries as well—well, maybe *need* isn't the right word . . . maybe worship. Again, perhaps that's stretching it a bit far, but anyone who gets head-butted incessantly by ornery farm animals understands precisely what will ease aching muscles and top off a day of backbreaking work: a small glass of barley bree.

Feeding draff to livestock goes back to when distilleries were farm-based. It was logical and profitable to make the most of all you had.

Eventually, production levels of spirits increased, as did the draff quantity. Manufacturing plants designed to dry the draff and process it into pellet form sprung up around distilleries to service the industry, creating yet another mutually beneficial working relationship.

Numerous distilleries, like Tomatin—a Highland distillery not far from Inverness, for instance—were early adopters and many still participate in the sustainable and environmentally minded practice. And if their draff could taste anything like their typically sherry-heavy, richly toffeed whiskies, I'd imagine scores of blissful bovines waxing lyrically when the aromas of dinner start wafting their way.

In a day and age when we are all reminded of the importance of seeking out, participating in, and championing environmental steward-ship, there's a lovely bit of quid pro quo-*ing* taking place. In other words, it's nice to see so many backs free from itch.

Time to sit back, take a sip, and think about your draff . . . I mean *dram*.

Field Trips

When we'd finished the day's work at Hamish the Stillman's side, we were released into the wild and told to return to camp in time for dinner. The five of us, a fine sheen across our brows from time spent in the Turkish bath of a stillroom, stared at one another, the unanswered question—*what now?*

"We could take a field trip. To another distillery," one of the Tin Man's friends said. His eyes showed both apprehension for suggesting we spend another hour in a facility such as this one, and excitement for spending another hour in a facility such as this one.

We were all on board.

"How about Kilchoman?" I suggested. The Warlock clearly knew which distillery I was referring to, as his face seemed to darken with acrimony. My guess is that he wanted to be the first to offer that up.

"I didn't think it was open yet," the Tin Man said.

"It is. I've been following it for the last couple of years," the Warlock puffed.

"I visited last year," I said with a tiny grin to the Tin Man and friends.

"You visited. Already?"

"It's adorkable."

The Warlock kicked a stone at his feet. *"Adorkable* is not a word."

"I want to see what adorkable looks like," the Tin Man responded. "Everyone in my rental. Let's go!"

—

From Barley to Bottle. That's their theme. And one that always makes my heart thrum with happiness for some reason, as I'm a big fan of companies finding success making their entire product within their little footprint. Or even if a company can just keep all or most of their labor, materials, and any other bits and bobs necessary to the manufacturing of their product as locally sourced as possible.

Kilchoman does just that. It was built on Rockside Farm—not terribly far from Bruichladdich—and is generally referred to as a "farm distillery." Built in 2005, they were the first distillery to be bred from Islay soil in almost 125 years. They grow their barley, then floor malt, peat, mash, ferment, distill, barrel, and finally bottle their spirit—all in-house.

When I'd traveled to visit Kilchoman the year before, they weren't giving tours, but said we could mosey about and peek into buildings. It was a sweet little farm, where the equipment used in the facility looked like dollhouse versions in comparison to her massively run counterparts. Tiny mash tuns, itty bitty washbacks, miniature copper stills. Big dreams, huge effort, hoping for massive success.

Their gift shop had been built, but they weren't quite ready to sell their very first bottlings for another few months—their Inaugural 2009 Release. I did *not* share this with the group, as the Warlock would have danced a jig. Chances are, he'd already located and secured himself a bottle or two and knew exactly how it fared against the rest of the Islay malt clans.

Our tour was typical, the same script just modified slightly to impress upon us workaday Joes the importance of the difference between the rest of the world and them. No one else—*no one else*—does what they do. And although I didn't see a cooperage on the site as we toured it, I'd not be surprised to discover they'd wrangled some freshly apprenticed bloke from the Speyside Cooperage near Aberlour, on the mainland, and promised him a spot on the tour and his face on the website if he'd agree to work on the farm and in one of their little outbuildings.

Hell, I'd do it.

It was a quick tour, but this time it produced a taste of their lovely organic whisky. We spent a few minutes in the gift shop, where the

Warlock showed the other three boys every bottle he already possessed in his collection back home, and I wandered around tables filled with pottery, fudge, and bucketloads of things manufactured to resemble either a highland cow or a wooly mammoth sheep.

Obviously, I was going to have to bring home some souvenirs, but in truth, I would likely convince both kids to put their treasures on my desk "for safekeeping." To them the trinket would be a pile of white wool with a goofy face, or a pile of unruly orange hair with a goofy face, all on top of a hairy chunk of peat, with a tiny handwritten label saying ISLAY LIFE, or HEELAND COO, or TOURISTS ARE SUCKERS on the back. To me, the best trinket is realizing it's 5:27 P.M. Greenwich Mean Time, I'm on the island of Islay, standing dreamily in Kilchoman's gift shop, and already wishing I could stay longer.

Our next stop was in Finlaggan—the seat of the Lord of the Isles under the Clan Donald. This is where lands, power, and titles were challenged by other Vikings—or the new Gaelic team captains, as I like to call them—who raided and invaded, hoping to expel some existing posse of people from a spit of land so they could relocate to a slightly less rainy piece of real estate than that from whence they came.

I've now been here twice, but I sometimes grow weary reading historical placards; so instead, I chose to gaze over the landscape and plop myself into a Roman Polanski film costarring Liam Neeson and Mel Gibson, happily conjuring up the turgid battles and blaring bagpipes.

From there we scooted the tiny rental car to Bridgend, a village halfway between Bruichladdich and Bowmore, where we found our way to Islay Ales—the island's microbrewery. It was a quick gulping, as my schedule was to include studying today's teachings for tomorrow's trials and the eventual exam. (I know, total "Hermione.") But first, dinner.

For the fellas, the schedule was . . . just dinner.

Except maybe for the Warlock. Surely, he had to oil and twirl his mustache to be ready for the evening's mayhem.

The Feeding Fenella and Sister Margaret Mary Mother of Pearl had prepared chicken stuffed with haggis and a side dish of cabbage. I was beginning to realize that the smell of boiling cabbage was likely their finest solution to overcome the smell of four men in the house. It would be with us for every single meal apart from breakfast.

Following dinner, the five of us walked down the road to the pub in the Port Charlotte Hotel. We were told it was two miles there and three miles back.

A snuggery of an inn, and right on the water, the pub was the stuff of storybooks. If Hollywood wished to make some blockbuster Celtic romantic comedy, this would be the place where everything should unfold. Everyone from central casting showed up to play their parts.

- The rugged fishermen fresh off their boats.
- The musicians dressed in their evening kilts.
- The doe-eyed bar maiden, apron bulging with tips.
- And the village farmers in their shit-caked boots. Including the one who found me having a rousingly bois- terous one-sided conversation with his Highland cows.

We eyed one another, as warily as we had in the field. I made a small smile, and he made his chair scoot farther back. Clearly, I'd made a friend.

The boys and I ordered two drams each from the exhaustive list of single malts available on the shelves behind the great wooden bar. We took a sip and passed our glasses to the right. Mathematically speaking, we proved that a dram can be divided into five equal (or equalish) shares.

It was a marvelous way to spend the evening. The music, the merri- ment, the mordant glances from the friendly farmer in the corner. We sang and danced, drank, and told stories. We discovered how much and how little we all had in common.

And we also discovered who could hold their liquor.

It is not a game I play. As in ever. Because I'm usually kicked to the curb in this competition by the time round two has finished. But I've grown immune to surprise as to just how much other people's bodies can tolerate. I must imagine that they've all been born with an extra liver and bring it to the pubs with them—like a colostomy bag kept around their belt loops.

Maybe they have a super filter system. I'm not sure. But mine is slug- gish at best and responds to even the heavenly scent of whisky aromas with a slight woozy muddle-headedness.

I bowed out of the tasting game and simply participated in the nosing game from then on. No complaints from the rest of the fellas. More for them.

The pub grew livelier as each quarter of an hour passed, with the heart-pumping blend of the small indoor border pipes and the fiddle in the corner pulling people to their feet, most forgetting to leave their drinks at their tables. They gathered in the middle of the old wooden floor, scuffed with thousands of boots and shoes from countless generations of dancers.

Well past midnight, we spilled out of the pub and into the blackest blanket of darkness. There were no streetlamps, no porch lights, just the crunch of ground beneath your feet to inform you if you'd found the asphalt road or were still on the dirt path leading up to the side door of the pub.

The five of us walked through that sightless setting. Under cover of darkness one feels liberated, and words slip effortlessly from one's mouth with a false sense of anonymity. Did I share things in my hazy wooly-headed state? Did I talk about my fear of never being published? Did I speak of the bundle of nerves I carried because I was dipping a toe into a pool I felt might have a BOYS ONLY sign hanging from the entrance gate? Might I have let slip proof that I possessed less whiskey-making mastery than the rest of them?

And most concerning, did I reveal anything about a marriage I feared was doomed? That was information I wasn't even ready to declare to myself.

The sound of Loch Indaal—its briny waves crashing against the rocks beside us—was another lulling, sorcerous layer to the night. No head-lamps of other cars, no buzz of electricity, no confirmation of modern-day life revealed itself on those two miles back to our beds.

But there was great humanity. There was laughter, connection, joy, and acceptance. We five walked the road. In a bubble of bliss. A bubble we'd all cling to until the buzz of an alarm clock pierced the air in four hours' time.

Whisky Coproducts:
The Extra Bits and Bobs
Part 2 (Pot Ale and Spent Lees)

Draff is just one of the coproducts of malt distilleries. Now, we will dive back into the coproduct pot to learn a bit about two others. The first is *Pot ale*—which to me always sounds delicious. It's a residue from the inside of the stills and is also referred to as burnt ale (that part does *not* sound as delicious). These dregs contain the following:

- Yeast
- Yeast residue
- Soluble protein
- Carbohydrates
- Copper
- Other minerals

In the past, the pot ale was considered waste and spread over farmlands or dumped into neighboring rivers and piped into the sea. Eventually, an ever-vigilant environmental protection agency got wind of the effluent and laid down the law. Lots of them.

One method of pot ale disposal is the manufacturing of *pot ale syrup* through evaporation. The result is a sweet, thick, malty nectar, not unlike molasses, and like draff, another constant request among the bovine and porcine diners. Sadly, sheep get the shaft, as the high levels of copper in the syrup tended to have a negative effect on their ability to continue living.

Although used as a liquid feed and fertilizer, pot ale syrup is often combined with draff, dried, and then sold as barley dark grains (cubes or pellets). I tend to see it as something like barnyard granola, if that helps, as many animals in the pasture population give it a solid two thumbs up.

Another coproduct from the distillery, one that has no profit-making potential, is called *spent lees*. It's the washing-up water left over from making each magical batch of spirit. You'd think with all that alcohol swirling about, cleaning would be self-actuating. Alas, there's unending minutes spent scrubbing vessels and pipes, all in an effort to make sure your bottle of whisky arrives in your hands sludge-free. Now that's service and dedication.

This waste water's next stop for many, but certainly not all, distilleries is at a bio plant—a treatment facility that will effectively alter levels of biochemical oxygen demand (or BOD), chemical oxygen demand (or COD), and copper, creating safe options for disposal.

Of course, we know now that copper toxicity is an issue to our seafood and freshwater fish, and farmers aren't too pleased if the copper levels in the surrounding soil become poisonous. Copper is as toxic to marine life as it is to mutton life, and it's challenging to sell grocery goods that have been stamped with a giant warning by the EPA.

If you've the time and inclination to dive further into the tongue-twisting jargon, you might want to spend a few minutes looking up and reading about Chivas Brothers' GlenAllachie Distillery and their fancy, new "in-home" treatment facility. Either you'll be thoroughly enlightened on the subject, or you'll need to lie down and take a couple of aspirin.

But again, from a broad perspective, we're able to see a symbiotic relationship between distillery and land. This one, however, is a little trickier to precisely define. On the one hand, the distillery benefits by ridding itself of two substances considered both coproduct and waste. The coproduct has commercial value—both distillery and local farms benefit. The treatment of waste necessitates spending money to reach environmental quality standards and meet the criteria for disposal under current legislation—the distillery is out of pocket, but the land, water, and salmon are breathing easier.

This is a good thing, because we all like our salmon pink—not blue from holding their breath while we sort out solutions to the problems we've created.

Whisky Thieves
Are My Best Friends

Five-thirty A.M. is not a time of day. Five-thirty A.M. is a slap in the face. It is a rudeness that roughly shakes your body until the unseen hands of stubborn universal alertness find the edges of your consciousness and snap it into place where the lines were once euphorically blurry and obscure.

I do not like 5:30 A.M.

But I rose. And washed. And then, because it was Scotland in August, where the light shining on this patch of earth was more present than not, I looked outside and discovered a more typical day on Islay than the past several I had experienced.

Horizontal rain is nearly as bad as 5:30 A.M. No. I've changed my mind. They are on equal footing with all other evil and swarthy creatures that roam about this planet. Horizontal rain does not respond to large yellow slickers and thick rubber booting. Horizontal rain is stealthy and underhanded. Literally, Islay squalls have found a way to pour rain upward.

We were sent up to Warehouse #3. I was uncertain, at the time, as to how many they had, but as the phrase "*in another one of our warehouses*" was often uttered, I had to assume there were more than enough to make a grown man—or in this case, woman—cry tears of blubbering joy. Seeing that many barrels, sleeping peacefully, oozing languidly, and breathing deeply is a gift to the senses and the soul.

If I should ever marry again, I might insist the wedding be held in a whisky warehouse, as I believe when one is experiencing one of the supposedly happiest moments in one's life, one should take into account how much smell can shape an experience. Church incense burning from an altar has always filled me with childhood fear, guilt, and shame, but whisky fumes, cow-pie patties, and wet wool should be made into an option on any aromatherapy massage menu—at least, if I had any say in the selection.

We spent hours practicing the art of barrel filling, barrel rolling, and cask labeling. During quick breaks we were given leave to wander about the warehouse, where I was usually found sprawled over one of Bruichladdich's "first growth series" barrels, where their spirit now resided in an ex–Château d'Yquem, Margaux, Pauillac, or Sauternes cask.

I did a lot of weeping, a great deal of sighing, and likely confirmed to the men that I was slightly off-balance—except for the fact that I caught a few of them behaving exactly like me and was ready to call them out on it too if I felt my back was up against a wall.

I have video.

The warehouse manager, a six-foot-seven, wonderfully warm and engaging fellow whom I called Lurch (from the *Addams Family*) in my head, found me hugging a Château d'Yquem barrel at one point, and taking great pity on me, came back with his whisky thief, and suctioned up an abundant glassful of the elixir. I could've kissed him.

I wanted to scurry behind a row of barrels deep within the warehouse and sit, nursing the drink for the next hour, but instead, I found the other fellows and shared. It was the right thing to do. Plus, I would have never been able to get back off the floor after drinking all of it.

I was rewarded for my benevolence with a taste of the distillery's organic barley whisky—not even on sale yet—and one of the pioneering spirits dabbling with the whole idea of organic and biodynamic. And by taste, I mean another whole glassful.

Yes. I shared. Again. Because clearly, karma was watching.

We shuffled our way down to Warehouse #2, where Graham was waiting for us. Lessons and lectures awaited us there. And now I've decided that all schooling should be held in whisky warehouses, as well. When I think of how different my life might have been if some authority figure had taken the time to discover what aromas make me most receptive to doing any volume or manner of work, I'd likely be a frickin' genius.

Clearly, a missed opportunity and a result of the negligence of my elementary schoolteachers. I shall place the blame in their soft and welcoming laps. Although, to be fair, most kids in my neck of the woods in Wisconsin entered our classrooms with cow shit–caked boots, so the affable cow-pie patty smell was undoubtedly present and should have contributed something to my sad-sack math scores.

My recollection of Warehouse #2 is a teensy bit foggy, as Graham was firmly in the mood to alter what was likely supposed to be a schooling session of "show and tell" into "show and tell and drink, drink, drink."

"Ye'll like this one, Shelley, with your fancy-assed taste buds," was what I heard when handed another dram of the Château d'Yquem. There was no way I was going to tell him that Lurch had already figured that one out, one warehouse before him.

Then he grabbed my glass and filled it with Bruichladdich's quadruple distilled spirit—which, at the time, formulated a question I could not articulate, but could actually see floating in the air out in front of me, where the rest of my school chums were swimming.

The three whirling letters formed the question: *Why?*

Why distill a whisky four times?

This was an especially pressing question as it pulled me back to the only sentence I had victoriously procured from Hamish. I'd been standing on a staircase, two steps above him and the hissing stills, and lip-read his rule of thumb for distillation:

Scotch whisky must be distilled twice. Do it three times and ye've made the Irish happy. Do it a fourth and all ye have left is vodka.

What I held in my hand certainly didn't taste like vodka. What it actually tasted like was so beyond my ken at this point that I found the last shred of the intact and functioning rational part of my brain directing my hand to surreptitiously empty the glass out onto the dirt floor behind another barrel. I heard the faint and uncertain whispers of the guys around me say words like *banana, pear, marzipan, ginger, a raisin-like smoke,* and maybe Graham chiming in with the word "purity." Had I known then that only three thousand bottles would be capturing this liquid, I would have smuggled that spirit out in my coat.

"My gracious, yer a lass wi' a stomach of steel, aye?" Graham said when glancing over at my liquid-less glass. "Well, then, you're in for a real treat now, I tell ye."

The real treat was "sampling" from private barrels. I was fairly sure back then (and positive right now) that, despite my lack of full connectivity to consciousness, *sampling* was a euphemism for *stealing*, but I was not the distillery manager.

Sure, I understood the importance and necessity of a distiller managing barrels, keeping a close eye on the spirit's development and progress to determine when to place the time stamp of "ready" on any cask. But I also put myself in the shoes of one of those barrel owners and thought about how I not only had shelled out a bucketful of money for a beautiful and unparalleled cask of whisky, but also had to swallow the bitter pill of the occasional sharing with the butcher, the baker, and the candlestick maker—aka the distiller, the angels, and the derpy students coming to study the art and craft of making such hedonistic liquor.

Two private barrels later—my heart hurt as I tipped those gorgeous golden liquids to the floor but felt a small measure of relief as, one of those times, I looked up to see the Tin Man giving me a conspiratorial wink of acceptance and encouragement.

He knew how much I could handle and would keep my secret safe.

Graham announced it was time for dinner—for those of us with room still in our bellies—and that tomorrow would be an exceptionally special day, for there was a chance we'd all get to see his beloved tractor. Then turning to me he added, "If you're lucky, ye might even get to sit on it."

Whisky Coproducts:
The Extra Bits and Bobs
Part 3 (The Heat Is On)

I love seeing the world creep toward the desire for planetary health. I get excited when industries put "going green" into practice. I get extra goosebumpy when it's an industry that I monetarily support. There's a smidgen of smugness I allow myself when pouring a dram from a distillery that I know is not only incorporating the *past* into each bottle but building a better *future* while they're at it.

The previous chapters on coproducts contained information about some of the whisky industry's clever answers to ridding itself of its merchandise's derivatives:

- Draff—the spent grains remaining in the mash tun after all the delectable sugars from starches have been removed, and a product often used as livestock feed.
- Pot ale—the high-protein liquid residue from fermented wort remaining in the still after the first distillation, often either used as a fertilizer or boiled down into a syrup (and then utilized as livestock feed).
- Spent lees—the remaining wash and coppery residue (from cleaning the still and other pieces of equipment),

which has no commercial value, but oftentimes must undergo treatment before disposal.

If you're still with me, then another coproduct that often goes by unnoticed (except to those in the industry) is heat. Yep, and there's more than your average thermometer-full. Some is generated from the need to heat the stills for distillation. Some is in the form of warm wastewater, left over from condensing the spirit vapors back into liquid form. And some breeds from the guy in the break room who's shouting at his coworkers for using up the last bit of milk for tea.

One way of utilizing the heat created in the distillation process is to recycle it back to the malting floors. Those barley grains need hot air to be properly dried and toasted before entering into the mash tuns for steeping. Recycling the heat generated from the hot stills is a viable, smart method for doing so. It's a little bit like robbing Peter to pay Paul, except Peter doesn't need his excesses. It's distillery socialism.

Some newer distilleries are fulfilling their needs for both heating and cooling by incorporating geothermal ground loops. A loop of pipe in the ground can not only dump excess heat created by the distillery, but it can access that heat energy and utilize it for the distillation process. Renewable energy makes people remarkably happy. Especially when they see their remarkably reduced energy bills.

For a little while, Glen Garioch pumped the heat from their still fires into greenhouses near the stillhouse to grow big, beautiful tomatoes. Old Pulteney gave back to the community in the form of a warm home to return to after a hard day's work in Wick; they chose to pump their surplus thermal heat into over 1,500 local houses. The North British Distillery kept young bodies and brains ablaze by gifting their overabundance of heat to local students attending Tynecastle High School across the road.

There have even been a few studies performed to determine whether salmon and trout can actually benefit from an uptick in temperature in their watery world. Stay tuned.

And stay informed. Of course, one must acknowledge not just Scotland's effortful adjustments to reduce their hefty footprints, but distilleries across the globe. From Norway to New Zealand—or Mexico to

Minnesota—manufacturers of spirits around the world are rebuilding, retrofitting, and rethinking the many things they can do to work within the realm of sustainability.

It's marvelous to know so much about the things we love, and even more lovely to know that through our affection, we're helping distilleries to make the world a marvelously lovely place.

How to Impress Your Boss
with Bovine Ailments

I woke early the next morning and looked out the window at the rain, which today had decided to adhere to our universal laws of physics. As it was gray, cool, and briny-aired, I dressed and felt like an insipid representative of a shelf-stable pickle.

Dinner the night before lay heavily in my stomach. Haggis, stuffed with chicken, wrapped in bacon. The variations were truly innovative. I sniffed the air to see if I could ferret out the scent of percolating coffee beans from the ever-present scent of cabbage and men. It was faint, but there, and it pulled me toward the kitchen, where I found Graham, as chipper and bright-eyed as a boy who'd snagged his first garden snake.

"Mornin'." He tipped his imaginary sea captain hat. "Heard ye all made your way again to Port Charlotte last night. Hadn't gotten your fill yesterday in the warehouse, aye?"

I smiled demurely. "I was there for moral support. It's a lovely walk. I just took in the air."

"I'm sure ye did, lass," he said with a wink. "Perhaps we should consider bottling our air instead of our spirits, aye?"

I rolled my eyes and reached for coffee at the same time he clapped his hands and called for attention.

"Rain slickers and Wellies today, crew. Head to the Bruichladdich van. Chop chop!"

I gulped hot coffee and then scooted to the mud room where all the rain gear was stored. Clearly, women's sizes were never given great consideration here, for yet again I was clad in a giant yellow slicker and a pair of rubber boots that Paul Bunyan might find roomy.

We drove (and occasionally had to get out and push) the van through the rain and mud to the new storage facilities Bruichladdich was nearly finished building. Currently, they were getting their organic barley from the mainland, but Graham said they were attempting to convince the Islay farmers to grow it for them. The farmers did grow the grain, but only for their animals, and planting organic grains would require a substantial boost of remuneration if they were going to be convinced to go down that path.

The only farmer they were presently buying grain from was a fellow by the name of James Brown. Yeah, the same chap who brought them their precious bottling hall water. The sticky wicket in their current supply chain would hopefully soon be rectified, as buying the grains from Farmer Brown was a good step in the direction of "buying local" apart from the fact that, until their proposed malting and kilning floors would be complete, they still had to ship the raw grain off the island to Inverness and then ship it back once it had been malted and dried—money, money, money just swirling down the drain.

Farmer Brown's farm—Octomore—was our van's next stop. There are easy words one can use to describe Octomore Farm: sprinkled with sheep, scattered with cows, lush with grain, but the same can be said to describe most Islay farms. It is much more interesting to describe Farmer Brown himself. The "constable" of this island, the local bagpiper, and a wizard at throwing the hammer.

A "hammer throw" features a 22lb metal ball attached to a wooden pole, which you whirl around your head and then toss toward the nearest planet—distance being the winning factor. It requires some strength to lift—pretty much the strength of a person who looks like Farmer Brown: taller than most ladders, as hefty as a full-grown man made from pewter, and as game as a five-year-old child sitting in front of cake. Imagine a flesh-colored Jolly Green Giant, but in overalls. That is James Brown of Islay.

Graham doled out sage advice in the van as we rolled up the farmer's driveway. "A surefire way to annoy a Scotsman is to ask for a hug."

As all of us were annoying Americans, the plan in the van was to rush the great goliath and embrace him with the true warmth of our homeland's typical bear hugs.

As is also rather typical of many Americans, we can be all gab and no game, and not one solitary soul leapt out of the van and into his arms. The men all shook hands, and when Farmer Brown finally saw me trying to peek around the Warlock, he moved with the speed of a raging bull, before throwing his arms around me and engulfing me like an enveloping softball glove.

Why? Who knows? But as I've often joked with friends that Wisconsinites' family trees show proof of the occasional breeding with farm animals, perhaps I reminded him of one of his recently deceased prize-winning sheep. The jury's still out.

Of course, the warm welcomes would not be over without a tankardful of bawdy jokes, as nothing says genteel and courtly like seeing a woman alone among men and testing her threshold for crudity.

I did just fine, thank you very much. All pinches and winks and raising of eyebrows. I was sadly used to it, if not somewhat immune. And by immune I do not mean resigned, as I still bristled like a porcupine with winter static issues whenever having to muscle my way into any interesting conversation about brown liquor. The world can move at an incredibly slow pace, but my feeling was that eventually I could break into those circles without a good chunk of the men within them acknowledging my presence only because they assumed I was there to take their order.

We were first given a tour of Farmer Brown's house and office. As a do-it-yourselfer (big surprise), James showed us the most important parts—all the nooks and crannies, drawers and cupboards, necessary for holding (or hiding) his liquor.

Glasses were passed around, as were bottles of things he adored. I did my best to excuse myself to the ladies' room after the first round, in order to keep the few wits I had and needed close at hand for the day.

We then moved outdoors. Tractors, trucks, and all farm accoutrements were proudly displayed and warmly admired. As I was the only true product of farm country within our merry band of lads and lasses, I was given a smidge more street cred for merely keeping pace with a conversation between Graham and Farmer Brown about calving and mastitis. Had I known I simply needed to utter the term "teat disease" in everyone's presence to gain respect, I would have thrown in the words *hardbag* and *udder sores* for good measure.

We traveled up to James's barley fields, to stand and admire the beauty of grain—a field trip (no pun intended) every elementary school child should be forced to go on, as they are mainly just small bodies filled with bread, cookies, and cake anyway. It's a beautiful, meditative experience—unless, of course, it's again raining sideways, in which case, it is much less a beautiful, meditative experience and more of a nettlesome, miserable one.

To make up for the rain, we walked to the highest point on the west coast, just south of Kilchoman and, despite the thwarting weather, had glorious views of both sides of the coast. Our eyes were treated to the sight of the islands of Mull and Jura, and even Ireland. Yes, it was worth the wet hike.

We made our way back to the house, where we shoveled down lunch before meeting back at the van for more field work—this time, *peat cutting*.

Peat cutting is so much fun.

I wrote that just to see if I could actually type out the words without stirring up a residual backache activated through some old neurological pain-pathway response.

Yep, it's still there. It still remembers. Despite my adoration for peat, peat cutting is not at all much fun. There is no fun in peat cutting whatsoever. And if anyone (namely a guy called Graham) ever tries to tell you as much, run from the giant shank blades and post-hole diggers he's trying to hand you. Run far and run fast. And then find a police officer to hunt that guy down so he can't "Bernie Madoff" anyone else's long-term investments in much-needed back and shoulder muscular support.

After we were properly educated and instructed on how to best handle the equipment used to slice through hairy chocolate pudding, Graham remained on the scene, encouraging us through the wretched weather not to be a bunch of pansies and give up.

"These bogs are thousands and thousands of years old, and ye never ken what relics ye might unearth!" Hereafter, Graham would sneak up behind each one of us and casually toss in a few miniature bottles of Bruichladdich's ten-year-old for us to draw up with the sludge.

(And now is where I whisper that peat cutting can be a teensy bit fun if one is lucky enough to fill one's pockets with enough treasures to make future global flights bearable.)

Whisky Coproducts:
The Extra Bits and Bobs
Part 4 (Biofuel)

This, I swear, is the last I'll write about the plethora of extras created during the whisky-making process. And as a bonus, it will allow us to appreciate the legion of clever clogs out there in the science world who have earned themselves a heartfelt toast of our admiration.

It seems our smart cars are growing smarter. As the auto industry continues to strive for improved safety standards, better gas mileage, and self-guided cars, the whisky industry has now tossed its hat into the ring and offered up an alternative to fuel. Instead of guzzling through gallons of gas, automobiles can now slake their thirst with the spent lees of spirits.

To be precise, the high sugar content in leftover draff and pot ale has been matched up with sugar-crazed bacterium. In exchange for its "all access pass to Candy Land," it will spin some gold in the form of beautiful butanol. According to studies from Napier University's Biofuel Research Centre (BfRC), this specific bacterium has been tested, and the results of its feast can be used as a direct replacement for vehicle fuel.

Tullibardine Distillery in Perthshire, Scotland, has offered up the spoils. Tons of it. Literally. And Celtic Renewables, a spin-off company born from Napier University in Edinburgh, has provided the test beds and scientists, but most importantly, the bacterium itself.

Yes, the spirit world is stretching out of liquids and into lab coats—but cutting-edge ideas or not, take heed. Industry leaders warn that making biofuel from whisky will not make siphoning gas any more palatable. And chances are, if you've been pulled over by police, you're not going to be able to pass off any alcoholic fumes emanating from the driver's side window by simply slurring, "Actually, officer, it's my car that's drunk."

In June 2017, the renewables company had their inaugural run of fueling a car with their new product, and in December of that same year, they secured planning permission to build a whisky residue biofuel plant to produce over a half-million liters of fuel each year. The most current news shows the refinery construction has been completed as of the fall of 2021. No doubt, many more great things are about to come from this marvelous sector. And indeed, Celtic Renewables has plans to build five more refineries worldwide within the next five years.

And now, enjoy your new knowledge that came from the peek behind the tour route and resulted in us pausing at the crossroads of industry and innovation. Wave to a cow, dig into that fish, study in that classroom, and go honk your horn—and do it all in the name of liquid gold and green technology. Not only do these colors complement one another; they also give a rosy glow to all our futures.

Graham's Great Exam

Our days were much of the same. Work in the mash house, still-house, and warehouse all capped off by rest in the pub house. In truth, it wasn't so much "work" as it was watch, try, listen, learn, sample, question, and do your utmost to remember every damn beautiful moment of it. There was no way to memorize the complexities of each piece of equipment, its quirks, and all the tricks one used to coax cooperation out of it. No method to sear dial settings, pipeline maps, or standard operational procedures into our brains—to make sense of them when they would no longer be in front of us. What we needed was a lifetime of study and application for that, but what we received was the realization that our tiny amount of time granted as apprentices was swiftly coming to an end.

I did my best to dodge the Warlock and stick close to the Tin Man. For it was so much more difficult to stomach stories about how much more accomplished than me the Warlock's wife was in the literary world, than to try to parse through and unpack the scientific language that came with the Tin Man's fascinating work within the Human Genome Project. I did not mind asking stupid questions of the Tin Man, and he did not mind answering them. Or more likely, rephrasing them so that they came out as worthy eighth-grade-level science class discussions and review sessions.

All too soon we were inching closer to gleeful Graham's "Distillery Exam"—an inevitable finality not so enthusiastically received by others. And by others, I mean four out of five of us.

Four out of five of us sat for the exam and understood that whatever the results, we would not immediately be offered jobs on the island, the country, or even within the industry. Maybe we could show our scores to some guy making moonshine in Kentucky and he'd be happy for the help, but otherwise, don't hold your breath.

One out of the five of us believed this was a career launcher.

Guess which one.

I think I even recall putting Jim McEwan's (the distillery's current Master Distiller) name at the top of my exam rather than my own. Graham could figure it out. He was about as sharp as one of those giant shank blades.

Hours later, or however long the blurry, brain-buzzing amount of time was, we handed in our exams and shared our last dinner together. Our last piece of haggis, stuffed with haggis, wrapped in haggis. It was delicious. And I wanted more of it. I loved those sweet ladies of the kitchen—The Fantastical Fenella and Reverend Mother Margaret of Meals and Miracles. They'd soothed my achy, sore muscles with hot, healing food, and they filled my heart and my head with the comforts of home. They would be missed and cherished.

We adjourned to the living room, where Graham came in with our test results. "Some of us," he said, glancing around the group, "did exceptionally well with memorization and science. Some of us," he said, meeting my eyes, "provided answers to a few techniques that science might not fully stand behind, although likely admires on behalf of effort and humor."

I swallowed. Please just let me have passed.

"You all *passed*," he announced.

Halle-bloody-loo-ya, I thought with a massive breath of relief.

"One of you," he continued, "had a perfect score."

Ugh, really? I had to hold back the scream of, "Oh good God no! He's already unbearable!"

Graham pointed to one of the other fellows in the Tin Man's trio. I nearly leapt for joy as much as he did.

The Warlock deflated.

"You did just fine too, son," Graham said, putting his hand up in reassurance toward the petulant man-child.

Just then, Farmer Brown came lunging across the living room threshold and shouted, "Are we all finished, then? Is it time to play? Who's up for a drink?"

When everyone answered with a rousing *hella yeah*, he bellowed out, "Off to the pub we go!"

And so, we made one last trek alongside the barley fields to the right and the frothy waters of Lochindaal, churning resolutely to our left, our spirits a mix of celebratory tones and bittersweet laments. We walked side by side and reviewed our time together.

At the pub, we bought each other drinks and toasted to our health and our families. On the pitch-black walk back home we sang songs, recalled our attempts to answer our exams, helped Islay's overly lubricated constable find his farm's driveway—and learned the Warlock's wife is a self-published writer of erotica.

I looked up at the sparkling pin-pricked quilt of sky and offered a profusion of well-wishes for the Warlock's wife—a woman who hopefully only knows of the deep and unending pride her blowhard of a husband has for her accomplishments.

And I took a moment to chastise and forgive myself. To boost my self-esteem for the undertaking and near completion of this great adventure, to frame the arc of sometimes untenable emotions into a story I could share once I returned home—if only in fragmented form. For who wants to hear of a quivering soul as the protagonist of such a story? Better to leave those less than shiny bits out but write them down to revisit on pages such as these.

We found our beds and rose the next morning for one final task. We were given a break on the costs at the gift shop and told to scan the shelves for treasures to recall the memories, one dramful at a time, back home.

I heard Sir Sackier in the back of my head, his punctuated British syllables warning me about airport duties and allowable amounts of liquor. I was unfamiliar with the exact statutes and, knowing my suitcase would already contain three tiny bottles found in the bottom of a six-foot peat bog and a prized bottle granted to each of us following our exams, I behaved conservatively and purchased just one extra bottle to bring home to Virginia.

The lads beside me were far less concerned about customs and bought copious bottles to pack into their extra suitcases, brought in anticipation of such an event. With warm and fond farewells, I wished them all luck, especially the Tin Man, and made promises to keep in touch as we continued on our paths through the world of whisky.

Fergus, one of the warm-hearted stillmen, had kindly offered to transport me back to the airport. The ride was filled with chatter about grandchildren, Islay life, and the things I'd learned whilst studying here.

Most importantly, I'd gleaned that I was not ready to return home. What a change from my initial trepidation those many weeks ago. We drove past a great number of the sites I'd stopped at and clambered over, the shops I'd visited, and the historical markers I'd studied. We floated over peat bogs and rumbled past barley fields. With each fresh memory came fresh ache. I realized I did not want to make the calamitous mistake of waiting for life to start—of getting ready to live. I couldn't envision a time when I would finally produce enough accomplishments, have enough knowledge, and have collected enough wisdom to say, "It's time. The real stuff starts now." What a terrible, ungrateful waste of today.

Fergus got out of the truck and helped to pull my bags. He grabbed me by the shoulders and planted a massive kiss on my forehead. "Come back, lass," he said, as he climbed back into his cab. I was left dumbstruck and heartsick, but also reassured and relieved.

Islay would still be here. As would all the memories and adventures. And somehow, I had the feeling that when I'd next return, it would be with far more skill, far more experience, and far more confidence than what my time on Islay had showered upon me. There was so much left to learn, and I had so much hunger to learn it.

PART FOUR

From Enthusiast to Whisky Woman

WHISKY GALORE

* BS

AS

* BEFORE SACKIER

When Opportunity Knocks

Finally. After what felt like a bazillion years (but was actually no more than six), I at last had an opportunity to make whisky again. Why so long, you might ask? Well, because a few things ate up all my time:

1. Raising two children whose father felt family life was much more palatable viewed from the other side of the world through FaceTime in between crucial meetings that might one day solve global problems and procure great fiscal compensation (with emphasis on the latter).
2. Publishing books at last, at last.
3. Growing the necessary backbone to divorce a man who frequently warned me how I'd be incapable of surviving without him. And I mean this quite literally. After he told me that, because of a recent spinal surgery, I'd never be able to find health insurance without him, I started eating calcium tablets by the fistful. (Backbone growth is a tricky little thing for most of us—injury or no.)

Not on the list, but definitely worth noting: there were no distilleries close enough to work at. Those a greater distance away would surely cause the school nurse to hate me when responding, "You betcha, I'll be right there to pick up my fevered, vomiting child. And by right there I mean two and a half hours, if the traffic works in my favor."

Funny, the parallels between a "so far out of reach" distillery and husband were ironically eyebrow raising, yet a steady yearning blossomed for only one of them.

Now, seeing the sausage made can blow the romance right off that glowing candle for some, but for me, when someone points at a stack of five hundred pounds worth of barley and says, "Shovel all that shit into that giant funnel," my ears interpret it as, (cue music from American Authors) *this is gonna be the best day of my li–i–ife.*

I think you get my point.

I really wanted to do this again.

Researching for a book that was, at last, about an actual distillery, and not just finding ways to hide and insert things about whisky into my middle-grade and young adult books, had me absolutely itching for a way to have my hands on a project from barley to bottle.

And I found it.

Finally. But that search brought more than the opportunity to fall in love again with the whole whisky-making process—it also brought me the opportunity to fall in love with the whisky maker himself. Total bonus.

ABOVE: The breathtaking bottles within the Claive Vidiz Diageo Whisky Collection, featuring 3,384 bottles of Scotch. *Credit: The Scotch Whisky Experience.* BELOW: The view from Loch Torridon Hotel. *Credit: Shelley Sackier.*

ABOVE: One of Scotland's countless burns. *Credit: Shelley Sackier.* LEFT: A visit to one of Islay's peat kilns.

ABOVE: The waterfall from Skye's Kilt Rock, comprising 180-ft-tall sea-cliffs made of colorful dolerite rock strata and mimicking a pleated kilt. *Credit: Shelley Sackier.* RIGHT: The "gifted" piper in the mist. *Credit: Shelley Sackier.*

ABOVE: Virginia's Highland Games; caber tossing. *Credit: Shelley Sackier.* BELOW: Virginia Highland Games; men of countless kilts and pipes. *Credit: Shelley Sackier.*

ABOVE: Burns Night; Chef Steven Wisniewski and sister "sous chef Shelley." *Credit: Judy Wisniewski*. BELOW: Scotland's myriad flavors of liquid gold. *Credit: Shelley Sackier.*

ABOVE: The quiet barley grains on an Islay distillery malting floor. *Credit: Shelley Sackier.* BELOW: Barrel building at Speyside Bourbon Cooperage in Atkins, Virginia. *Credit: Shelley Sackier.*

Barrel charring at the cooperage. *Credit: Speyside Bourbon Cooperage.*

ABOVE: A slightly thorny situation with a "heeland coo." *Credit: Shelley Sackier.* BELOW: Islay's Bunnahabhain Distillery. *Credit: Shelley Sackier.*

ABOVE: Seal? Or Selkie? *Credit: Shelley Sackier.* BELOW: Entrance to Islay's Bruichladdich Distillery. *Credit: Shelley Sackier.*

ABOVE: David Cuttino, proprietor of Reservoir Distillery. *Credit: Todd Wright Photography.*
BELOW: Sample bottles and grains; testing, tasting, and teaching. *Credit: Todd Wright Photography.*

Whiskey thieves always share what they steal. *Credit: Todd Wright Photography.*

Wallowing in the scent of time. *Credit: Todd Wright Photography.*

Discussing where flavor comes from. *Credit: Todd Wright Photography.*

ABOVE: Tackling the teaching of whiskey subjects sip by sip. *Credit: Nick Davis.* BELOW: Haggis the hound enjoys the beach but not bourbon. *Credit: Shelley Sackier.*

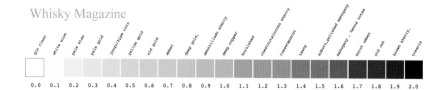

ABOVE: Whisky color spans the spectrum from gin clear to a deep treacle. *Credit: Whisky Magazine.* BELOW: The myriad scents and flavors of scotch. *Credit: The Scotch Whisky Research Institute.*

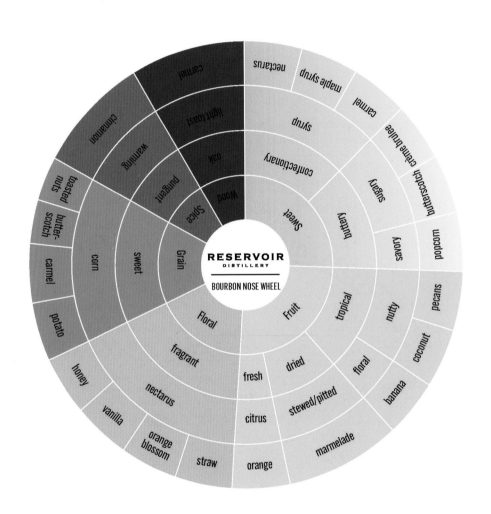

Reservoir's aroma and tasting wheel for bourbon. *Credit: Shelley Sackier.*

Belly Up to the Bar
(Part 1)

Learning the art of whisky nosing and tasting is a most pleasurable task made more agreeable by the fact that it must be done with great repetition. But for some, it can also be an undertaking filled with uncertainty. Many don't know where to begin in search of training and education. Too many give up, mistakenly believing you can only be born with the ability to smell and taste the complexities of whisky. Sadly, some see it as such a daunting endeavor, they throw in the towel before even using it.

Here is what I say to those folks. *Do you have a nose? Does it function fairly well—air passes in and out? Can you ferret out when it's time to change the cat litter?* If you have answered yes to all of these, then you, too, qualify as educable in this process—and lessons take less time than it would to make a sandwich.

This chapter is the first in a series of four that will help you elbow your way through the murky waters of your next "tasting" excursion—whether on your own, nestled before a fire and in your favorite well-cushioned chair, or in the company of men with no chins and cigar-smoking women, all who claim to be connoisseurs in the whisky world. You shall come through shining and unscathed.

Lesson #1—Color, Viscosity, and Clarity

So firstly, **Color:**

To the apathetic eye, there's not a lot of variation.

But that's like the execs telling the writers of *M*A*S*H* that the series run will be limited because the army isn't really a pool for humor.

The color of a whisky spans a spectrum from what's referred to as *gin clear* (a new-make spirit) to deep treacle.

A handy guide for identification from *Whisky Magazine* can be found on the fifteenth page of the image insert.

Color may identify both the type of cask used and the time spent in said cask, as the hue of a whisky is derived from wood contact: the longer the maturation, the more intense the color. Of course, some of this is dependent upon whether the casks were brand-new or originally housed bourbon, sherry, port, rum, Madeira, Sauternes, or even red wine.

Something I occasionally and regrettably come across is the discovery of a color additive—spirit caramel—used by some distilleries to enhance the outcome. It *is* legal to add to many whiskies, but not every country requires notification of its practice; so, if this bothers you, research the distillery. Often, they're quite proud to announce if they *do not* use E150A.

The simplest way to identify your dram's color is to hold your glass against a white background—such as a sheet of white paper—or your partner's face as they take in the latest credit card bill and discover how much you've been spending on whisky.

Now check the color chart. With hue identified, we move on.

Viscosity:

This is a measurement of thickness and may tell you a little bit about what's in your glass.

Swirl your whisky around to coat the sides, then stop and assess the legs—the bands of liquor falling from the rim back into the bowl of the glass. If they're as slow as a snail with a limp, you may have yourself an older whisky. Might even qualify for a pension.

And if it has long, thin gams like Cyd Charisse or Uma Thurman, your dram may be higher in alcohol. (Note: the conclusions from this observation are still highly debated, but one day science will sort out the truth. Until then, enjoy observing the mesmerizing drizzle.)

Clarity:

Some distilleries will chill-filter their whisky to eliminate any cloudiness that may occur naturally within the whisky-making process, but there is a common complaint that by discarding the oily compounds—the congeners that contribute to that hazy, floating particulate—it also negatively affects the whisky's flavor.

Whiskies with the non-chill-filtered style may go somewhat cloudy when water is added but will return to its clear state shortly—especially if you can raise the spirit closer to room temperature, where those compounds will redistribute themselves back into solution. (Flock or flocculation happens at colder temperatures—like when you add an ice cube.) Be patient. Many distillers believe they provide a richer, fuller flavor by keeping the whisky non-chill-filtered. I agree entirely.

So, there you have it. Lesson one and none the worse for wear. You've got a handy dandy color guide and a couple of interesting facts for your back pocket. Don't let this new knowledge go to waste! Next chapter there'll be a quiz. I'm kidding. Sort of.

Trusty Rusty Research

I need help.

Professional help.

It's a phrase I utter at least a dozen times a day it seems, and not every articulation is referring to the fact that shock therapy might be just the thing.

This time I was searching for answers to questions that did not reveal the meaning of life, or my purpose in the universe, or even advice on how to handle the creepy guy at the grocery store who is always watching me as I handle fruit.

No, this time I needed help with my new book. The "writing fiction" part is so much fun—but the "researching the fiction I just wrote and discovered wouldn't even be remotely believable" part is always a little hard to choke down.

Best to do them in tandem so I don't experience the *must rip out thirty pages* horrors I've suffered through in the past.

Being a stay-at-home parent left me truly little time to focus on my creativity.

Being a stay-at-home parent with little creativity time meant creativity would usually leak out of me in weird ways.

We can talk about all the questionable hair colors I went through, the ultimately unappealing recipes I created, or how I assigned one entire room in the house to unbridled imagination; four walls, a ceiling, and a floor held nothing but an invitation to draw upon them. Paint across their whitewashed walls, scribble with crayons, do your calculus homework—the sky's the limit. (I think everyone should try this.) But it was writing that took hold of me in such a way that it occasionally smothered the deafening calls to return to Scotland.

And as my primary focus in parenting was making sure I filled two children's brains with as much knowledge, resourcefulness, and comprehension pertaining to the world as I could muster, I soon figured out that just Googling interesting shit on the internet and sharing it at dinnertime was not capturing their attention.

I discovered that life lessons stuck to their little bodies in story form.

Need to teach your children about climate change? Throw in some self-invented mythology involving elemental fairies and have a few gnomes aid in their understanding of earth, water, air, and fire.

Need to instruct your wee ones about healthy diet and exercise? Give childhood obesity a protagonist who struggles with losing countless things in her life except weight. Make her plucky, relatable, and a heroine worth cheering for.

Make her fail.

Make failure a big part of your stories.

And then make getting up a bigger part.

Eventually, I also recognized that whisky, or distillation, or Scotland leaked into all my writing—it didn't matter what age group I wrote for, or what the point of the story truly was. The revelation clearly illuminated an unanswered call, and I was doing my best to send it smoke signals that I was still drawing breath, just far too many miles away.

Once finished with a rough draft deemed ready enough for critique, I sent the manuscript off to my agent and then went to work finding professionals and experts to either back up or correct the knowledge base from which I'd dipped when writing the story—this one truly about the subject of whisky. I mapped out all the Virginia distilleries at the time and narrowed my options of true whisky makers down to two that fit my profile needs. One I had visited before—as in before it had even been built and a few times along the way—and the second I was wholly unfamiliar with.

LinkedIn helped a little.

I decided to pursue the one most close and most familiar. So, I pleaded my case, called the joint, and set up an interview to make sure that my new manuscript wasn't going to entirely fit into the genre of *fantasy*.

Or an oval-shaped file under my agent's desk.

Ian Thomas, the director of operations at the Virginia Distillery Company, agreed to meet me on a foggy, misty morning when I could pick his brain. I planned to ask him a series of questions that could help improve the quality of the novel in ways that would display I possessed a level of comprehensiveness about the industry and wasn't just making up science like I have a terrible habit of doing.

Ask anyone. Or specifically ask my daughter, who at this point has a fancy piece of paper that declares her capable of regurgitating science in exchange for a paycheck. She believes my level of understanding the world relies too heavily on the answer, "The rest of it is just magic," whenever I can't quite grasp something with formulas representing modern-day hieroglyphics.

I tell her that her brand of science doesn't really count as science anyway, as she is a rocket engineer. And absolutely no one apart from another rocket engineer can understand their explanations of how the world works, as nearly their entire language is foreign to the rest of us. If we were looking at a Venn diagram of shared words between us, the only place where our two circles would intersect would be where coordinating conjunctions live—words like *and, but, for, nor, or, so,* and *yet.*

Everything else is alien. Which is fine for her and her teammates because that is the language for all the unearthly things those rockets are trying to get up close and personal with.

Ian, the distiller I was meeting with, was not into rocketry—thankfully. He was a biologist, and I understand about one page more of biology than I do aerospace. This added a few more words into our shared language, but for those that were incomprehensible to me, I took copious notes.

At first, I thought Ian, fairly new to his position, was worried about the time because, he was always checking his watch.

And then I thought for a second that maybe the fellow I was standing across from was fairly new to the concept of wristwatches, as when he looked down at it, he stared with intense focus for at least four to five seconds.

And then I realized that *I* was the actual idiot.

Ah. An Apple Watch.

Ian was getting about as many requests for attention as if he'd had a tiny toddler tugging at his pant leg—which, coincidentally, he'd have in a few short weeks, as he was indeed expecting his first child.

So perhaps coaxing a fledgling whisky distillery through its beginning years, full of growing pains, is exactly the kind of training a soon-to-be dad should be having.

If nothing more than to reinforce recognizing the blissful joy of losing consciousness for more than ten minutes in a row.

That, and maybe to discover what a bazillion new parents come to realize during the agonizing teething phase of their tiny tot: whisky can act as a damn fine benumbing agent . . .

For the parents, of course.

And this man was sitting on a gold mine.

The questions I needed answering were specifically related to the running and operating of a single malt distillery:

How much does each ingredient contribute to the overall end product flavor profile?

How much does the temperature and humidity in your warehouses impact the maturation process?

How many times have you tried to roll a full wooden cask of spirit into the back of your car to sneak home and feigned surprise when one of your coworkers discovered you struggling with the back hatch of the trunk?

Yup. All relevant.

We spent hours walking through the freshly built facility, and Ian patiently explained every piece of wholly familiar equipment and component involved in the operation: the gristmill, the mash tuns, the washbacks, and stills; the miles of plumbing, the resourceful recycling, the freshly plowed and planted barley fields, and the mile-long list of government officials he had to converse with daily to make this American malt find its way from barley to bottle—or grain to glass—or field to finally in my hot little hands.

Everything was crisp and clean. Not at all like the rundown, rickety-walled, ghost-filled distilleries of the motherland. But the equipment was the same—just shiny and brand-spanking new.

There was an element of it that I found disquieting—a hint that the industry was changing: some of the rooms were outfitted with computers and not people. It was modern, sleek, automated, and *expensive.*

Again, the same, but oh-so-different.

Ian gave me a taste of the new-make spirit—a thrill I'll never grow tired of. It's like seeing pictures of your unborn child, an exercise where you have an opportunity to nose and taste exactly what's just come off the still. A little like counting all fingers and toes, and maybe searching for an identifying marker that might give hints as to its as-yet-unrevealed character.

And like many of the heavenly scotches I've been privileged to taste in that raw state, it had the familiar traits of tropical notes: banana, citrus, and yeasty bread. My head spun with happiness. It felt like Scotland was rushing out to give me a God-we-missed-you-haven't-you-missed-us-too hug.

At one point, while talking in the warehouse that securely held the seven hundred wooden casks snugly embracing their aging spirit, Ian received the equivalent of another toddler tug that needed attention and stepped outside while I ecstatically and repeatedly filled my lungs with as much of the intoxicating, spirit-drenched air as they could hold. And then, profoundly lightheaded from hyperventilating, I suddenly worried that I had inhaled enough of the whisky-dense atmosphere to register as too intoxicated to drive home.

Maybe Ian's watch would keep him busy whilst I slept off the fumes and stretched out across a few ex-bourbon barrels.

We finished the day with Ian allowing me to further question him in hopes that he could provide answers for the stickiest parts of the book—things I was struggling with and that were critical to the book's authenticity and success: the biology, the chemistry, the plot.

"Okay," I said to Ian back in his office, "just in case this book goes bestseller and the only way you can fend off the sudden surge of paparazzi at the distillery is by locking yourself in the waste management warehouse and hiding behind a tank full of lye and caustic soda—is there anything else the world should know about Ian Thomas, young whisky maker hailing from Tennessee?"

"Ah," he said, glancing at his wrist again and staring at it intensely for about four seconds. "Well." He chuckled self-consciously. "I like casual strolls along the beach, I'm a good husband, I love my family and Virginia . . . and I'm working hard to make a world-class whisky."

I didn't doubt for one second all these things were true. Ian was a busy guy with a full life that was only going to get fuller in two shakes of a lamb's tail. A new dad. A new home. A new job. Yeah, he had his fingers in a lot of pots.

Copper ones to be precise.

And although I'm guessing for a minute or two, you might have been led to believe that *this* was the distiller I had fallen for—I assure you, he was not. And shame on all of you for thinking I'd somehow ruin a fresh new family! That is so not my style.

But teasing is. Which is probably why I fell for a guy who really knew the art of pulling pigtails. Especially mine.

Belly Up to the Bar
(Part 2)

I've heard one man say that nosing a whisky is like chasing a woman. The expectation is usually far more fun than the reality. Of course, this was a burly and bald-headed old master distiller who always had the pallor of unremitting constipation. I took what he said with a grain of salt, seeing as I'm not nearly as cantankerous and cannot draw upon his experience of hounding handmaidens.

Therefore, I'll tell you from my own practices, I find discovering the aromas in a dram to be equally as appealing as the actual taste. It's like unwrapping a present. The bows, paper, and colors beautifully add to the finished product.

The world of smell is available to most of us. But our recognition of it, our decision to incorporate that identification into our daily living, falls short of its true capacity. As with many of our other senses, we tend to insulate ourselves from their fullest experiences. And sometimes with good reason.

Who hasn't been to a concert where the music was deafening—to the point you simply wanted to leave and miss a potentially great performance?

On the flip side, can you catalogue the sounds around you right now and say you knew they each existed before you stopped to count them? The hum of the fridge? The birdsong outside? The click of your mouse?

Your spouse announcing they are leaving you because you won't leave the whisky blogs alone?

What about touch? Do you think about the steering wheel beneath your fingers? The rough calloused palm of the man whose hand you just shook? What's the texture of your daughter's hair?

We could go on with sight and taste, but let's skip to the smelling.

As suggested by anyone who is an imbiber of fine whiskies, find yourself a tulip-shaped glass. (Glencairns or copitas are perfect.) And because not everyone cleans their glassware with equal care, rinse the glass out in warm water, running your CLEAN fingers around the rim and inside, ensuring you're ridding the glass of any residual soap or contaminants that might affect the aromas and tastes. Lavender liquid detergent and whisky do not mix.

Pour a measure of the whisky into the glass, and if you're feeling frivolous, wasteful, and as portentous as Richard Paterson (master blender for Whyte & Mackay), then violently throw that dram out of the glass and onto the floor. It's flashy, gets the attention of everyone around you, suggests you're either out of your mind or a serious professional, and according to Paterson, rids the glass of impurities. Maybe he even chants a spell over the second batch to be certain.

Heads up, as there is a difference of opinion regarding the next step, and of course, repour if you did indeed toss that initial dram. Some say swirl the liquid in the glass, and others insist you keep it flat. Those that swirl believe the whisky needs to aerate: to help the alcohol leave the glass—and it's the alcohol that will carry the aroma compounds up to your nose, so this is important.

Those who maintain the method of keeping it flat feel that whisky, being somewhere around 40+ percent alcohol, needs no help evaporating from the glass and, by swirling, you're pushing all the aromas out of the glass at once, making it more difficult to identify the individual nuances.

Many professionals agree that the aroma compounds leave the liquid in layers based on their volatility, and each layer will reveal something different about the whisky. Typically, you'll have primary, secondary, and tertiary aromas to identify. Feel free to give each method a try and see what works best for you.

This next step is one of my favorites and has truly helped me distinguish scents existing in the glass that I might not get otherwise.

Dip a finger into the liquid and dab the whisky onto the back of your hand. Wave your hand around in the air to allow the alcohol to evaporate. Now smell. The aromas are much clearer, in many cases. If you detect leafy, grassy, or malty notes, the whisky may be on the younger side. Darker scents, like chocolate and spices, may signify something more mature.

One very important note; not everyone can smell every aroma compound, as there is a host of inputs that influence your recognition of said scent. How much of it have you been exposed to already (specific sensory fatigue); is it brand new to your neuroreceptors (and a neurological response hasn't been learned yet); what time of day is it (general fatigue)? If everyone around you is clearly smelling coconut and you aren't, it doesn't mean you're not trying hard enough.

Now again, we have some differing opinions on where to place your nose to obtain the best experience. Some distillers pass the glass beneath their noses quickly, others try inserting their entire face. I've run into a few folks who tilt the glass on its side and only sniff from one nostril, believing one side is dominant. I find three passes beneath your nose, in quick but separated succession, has been a good rule. The first deep sniff, your nose prickles with the recognition of *alcohol*. The second usually identifies the *sweet*, and the third, *fruit*. It's on the back of the third that I find the tertiary aromas: the smoke, peat, or brine. It can be entirely different for you, and most likely will be.

How aware are you of the scents in the room right now? Do you take the time to smell your food before you put it into your gob? Think about the scent of a crushed raspberry. Floor polish. Damp leaves. Oil-encrusted sardines. Sharp pine sap. The yeasty tang of crusty warm bread.

Do they snap front and center, easily recognizable? Could you identify them if your eyes were closed and the scent placed beneath you?

Memorization is key. As a human race, we tend to lean on multiple senses to quickly identify and process for maximum efficiency. But training your nose isn't about slick organization. This is an exercise meant for discovery, pleasure, and eventually, purpose.

Smell is related to memory and emotion. The whiff of a woman's perfume as you pass in the hallway immediately transports you through the fuzzy optics of time: your mother leaning over you in your childhood bed to kiss your forehead after she returns from dining out with your father. Security, safety, love. Have you ever driven past an industrial brewery and your mind is thrown back to your grandmother's kitchen, where you repeatedly peeked beneath the cotton cloth that covered the rising dough? Anticipation, warmth, glee. How about walking into a music store where the smell of cork grease is just present enough to remind you of when you fainted in orchestra class from trying to hold that oboe note for too long? Humiliation. Period.

There exists a patch of tissue about the size of a postage stamp located high in the nasal cavity that houses around four hundred olfactory receptors, but when counting the single or multiple aroma molecules it can bind with, new research suggests that our olfactory epithelium (that patch of tissue) can distinguish somewhere between a hundred million and a trillion unique odorants. Scent also triggers the limbic system, where our long-term emotional memories are stored. The challenge now is to identify those aroma components more specifically if you want to train your nose.

If you're keen to school your olfactory system, nosing kits are a must. You can purchase aroma kits for whisky, wine, and perfumes, where you'll receive a collection of small bottles containing the scents for memorization. Aromas that represent cut grass, roses, smoke, sherry, woodiness, citrus, nuts, and spices are some of the concentrations included. Some will be familiar immediately and identified easily. Others will need coaching, repeated and regular reminders. And a few may need to have new neuropathic roadways built for them. It all happens with persistence.

I love to incorporate the party game where I bring out my nosing kits and encourage dinner guests to test their memory and recognition for scent. It's a total hoot for everyone, and me especially, when I hand them a vial of something you definitely *don't* want to detect in the things you ingest. The fetid stench of decay is picture worthy, every time.

Sweet is a broad term, but you can train yourself to recognize particular forms of sweet with practice. Sweet like chocolate? Maybe honey? Like vanilla? Or flowers? What kind of flowers?

The same goes for many other aromas. It doesn't just have to be smoke. It could be smoke from tobacco, a campfire, tar-like, or earthy peat. If you say that something simply smells of "banana," you're definitely missing out because we all know that bananas have a spectrum of scent (and flavor) all dependent upon time. Is it a green banana, a ripe banana, an overripe banana, a rotten banana, or a caramelized banana?

Dive into the next layer and question what you smell. It's probably not going to be identical to the person next to you, and you should never judge your competency on another person's perceptions. Good lord, they may have just shoved a coating of Vicks VapoRub up their noses to prepare for the nosing session in hopes they'd "open up the passages."

Most people have no idea how much their noses contribute to the enjoyment of food and drink, although a massive number of people who have suffered through experiencing a coronavirus—and specifically COVID-19 with the symptom of anosmia (or smell blindness)—have gained a newfound appreciation. The nasal olfactory system should be applauded and held in high esteem for all that it provides. I'm not saying you should make a sketch of your appendage to tape on the fridge or insure it like the whisky world's beloved Richard Paterson for some astro-nomical just-in-case coverage, but don't turn up your nose at recognizing its contribution. Every whisky connoisseur *nose* it's important!

I leave you with this quote from Immanuel Kant:

All our knowledge begins with the senses, proceeds then to the under-standing, and ends with reason. There is nothing higher than reason.

And here's another good reason for training your nose.

Someday, someone is going to have to replace Richard Paterson.

Challenge Accepted

'll be back at 5:30. Sound good?" I asked my mom.

She looked over at Hung, the Vietnamese hairdresser she's been visiting for the last four years, the one who knew the special shade of fireball red she liked and needed, the shade that surely had the same ingredients as sriracha sauce. Personally, I thought the recipe needed a little toning down—maybe with some mayonnaise to soften it up.

Hung's whole face split into a wide grin. "Yeah, 5:30 is good. We take care of Judy. She's good here. We have wine."

I took a quick glance to gauge the sobriety level of the other clients. I was relieved to see that the only women whose chins touched their chests were the ones following their hairdressers' requests for ease of accuracy around the napes of their necks, so I backed out the door with a wave to my mom. She was already heading down the hallway to don her industrial-strength smock. She'd be fine. They had wine.

I got back in her reddish-brown Honda van—one with seventeen sliding doors and hatches, plus every variety of wheelchair, walker, and cane known to the physically unstable wedged into its fathomless back-seat area—and let my smartphone take charge of navigating. It was like driving a large, unwieldy brick down the streets of Richmond.

I had never felt sexier.

I had two places to visit. One for fun. And one for research. Okay, yes, technically—and it's a little hard to admit this to most people—I adore research, so it would be more appropriate to say *two* places for fun. In fact,

I once offered to do a spreadsheet about which humidifier a couple should purchase—with assurance that I'd do it with an independent drive to highlight truth, accountability, and integrity within the marketplace—and then wondered why they were looking at me so strangely until I realized that I eavesdropped on their conversation in a coffee shop. It's now that I start reeling in the admission that I'm a bit of a nerd.

But it's true. I love research.

Regardless, about a year earlier, I'd visited a new cidery, an unplanned stop I'd made when I'd found out that Chloe's flight home from Boston, for a quick fall weekend away from university lecture halls and laboratories, had been slightly delayed. The place had been in an old warehouse area—a funky sort of we-don't-give-a-fig-what-you-think-of-us, type atmosphere. I liked places like that. To me, it suggested they just needed a space to make a good product, and if it was good enough, people would step over the rubble and dodge the odd bullet.

And it was good stuff. The cider was surprising.

But they'd moved. Into a sweet little building with lots of great foot traffic, sufficient parking, and a large umbrella-bedecked patio that screamed, *Bring your strollers and four-footed friends.*

Suddenly, and sadly in my eyes, this place had lost the don't-give-a-fig charm I'd been drawn to, as I'm guessing "make it past the mortar and masonry for a thirst-quenching prize" really wasn't cutting it anymore. I popped in anyway, tried a few new things, and bought the same bottle I'd purchased last year.

Back in my car, I mapped out the other errand on my list—the important one, the research one, the anticipated one.

The distillery.

About a week earlier I had stayed overnight in Richmond for a writing conference. Even though my house was less than ninety minutes from the conference center, the last activity on the first night and the first class on the second morning convinced me to book a cheap hotel and spend the night.

In keeping with my antisocial personality trait requirements, I ditched the pro-social events on the first night and decided to go it alone—traversing the streets around my hotel and walking off a million hours of too much sitting and way too much interacting.

An event had been scheduled at the Poe House in town—a place Edgar Allan Poe had never lived in, but possibly walked around. I decided instead to visit one of the local pubs in honor of Poe's serious dedication to overindulging—a place, again, Edgar Allan Poe had never patronized, but possibly walked around.

I'd ordered dinner to go and sat at the bar, looking at the same predictable collection of scotches available in every watering hole, and grew annoyed at the endless selections of bourbons taking up valuable space. I'd wanted a scotch, as it was Whisky Friday for me—a special day of the week when finally I'd meet nose to nose with one of my Bens or Glens.

Scanning the shelves, I was intrigued to discover a whiskey from the other distillery I'd considered going to for help but had put off since I'd already spent so much time with Ian. I still had questions, but this distillery made bourbon. And I knew nothing about bourbon. I wasn't even sure they had similar production techniques to a single malt whisky. In my head, bourbon was like drinking liquefied brown sugar that hid a kick-ass scorching burn.

"I'll have a dram of the Reservoir rye, please." I nodded to the barkeep.

"A what?" he asked.

I rolled my eyes. "Shot. A *shot* of the rye." His tip had just rolled down to fifteen percent.

"And could I have it in a nosing glass by chance?"

"A what?"

Ten percent.

A tumbler slid in front of me, and I picked it up, holding it to the sallow, waxy light of the pub. The liquid moved thickly against the glass, coating the sides with its deep sherry and amber colored viscosity. I was suspicious and immediately wondered if they colored their liquor to get this sumptuous hue.

I passed it beneath my nose, and that appendage immediately sent up a warning to my brain that this was the wrong mash bill. *Grain alert! Grain alert!* This did not smell like barley. It smelled different. But not *bad* different—although everyone in my family knew that to me, different was dangerous. Different meant change. And change equals death. I avoided change at all costs and usually retreated to the safe, thin corridor I was comfortable skipping along every single day of my life.

Except, I had made a giant revision to that "no thanks to modifi-cation" motto two years earlier. With the blades of keenly sharpened pruning shears, I'd changed my world and removed the deadwood sti-fling my growth: a husband-type of deadwood, to be specific. Deciding to break through any cage of confinement can teach you a lot about yourself—namely, that reserves of strength will show up if you demand them to. It was time to be bold with a few other self-imposed constraints I was familiar with.

I took a tentative sip and let the spirit sit in the small hollow of my tongue. I breathed in air over it toward the back of my throat—an art that has taken me years to learn how to do without accidentally inhaling said spirit and coughing it all out in an unwelcome spray onto everything in front of me. That has lost me some serious street cred on occasion.

Swallowing the rye brought one clear and definitive thought to my head:

This does not suck.

And then it brought a second clear and definitive thought to my head:

Didn't I say this very same thing about the first scotch I'd tasted in Scotland?

Black pepper, vegetal notes, and Christmas spices filled every space in my head that aroma molecules could occupy, and a deep warmth fol-lowed the liquid down to my belly.

Yeah, this so does not suck.

I closed my eyes and held on to the scents, the warmth, the surprise. Good lord, did I like rye?

I asked the bartender for the bottle and studied the label. Maybe I should actually visit this place, this distillery named . . . Reservoir.

"These guys are local?" I asked.

"Yeah, I guess. But they're hella expensive, so you know."

I forced myself to keep the features on my face from arranging them-selves into yet another one that revealed incredulity about his synoptic connectivity.

"The two of them are not mutually exclusive," I mumbled into my glass. What I was sipping *tasted* expensive.

I finished the whisky, paid for my dinner, and grudgingly left a 20 percent tip and silently hoped the dullard would put it toward a few more hours of education. The world had an abundance of great bartenders, people who loved their work, their position, their potential for influence, but I'd still come across a slew of them who'd be far better as garden gnomes.

When I returned to my hotel room—a place that registered just slightly above sleeping in the back of my car—I cracked open my laptop and asked Google to get on with the business of revealing all of Reservoir's secrets. Or at least the people who were manufacturing their secrets.

Their website showed two fellas dressed in suits, one of them with a smile so roguish I half expected there to be a caption beneath the photo that said, *Come play with the devil. You know you want to.*

And sure enough, the next week, the three Fates must have rubbed their hands together in glee as they unfurled the ball of yarn I was chasing down a path I'd nearly ignored.

My mother was in the middle of battling a befuddling disease that had left her unable to drive, and I'd promised to take her for a haircut and color. Serendipitously, that hair salon was five minutes from the distillery. Time for further research.

After parking that saucy little sideloader on the street across from the distillery, I locked the door—pressing the key fob twice, as always reminded by my mother, "So you're sure the car is locked!" I rolled my eyes at the hefty announcement of my arrival via the high-volume horn. There's nothing like broadcasting your lack of taste in transportation by signaling your lack of consideration with clamor.

I looked across to the door—no more than twenty or twenty-five yards in front of me. A man was unloading a box from the back of his off-roading Jeep and glanced my way. Bingo. I'd made eye contact with the devil. And the devil apparently found time in his dastardly day to lift a few barbells. Or more likely barrels.

He made his way through the customer entrance of the distillery, and I followed about ten seconds later. Two bartenders nodded from behind a beautiful wooden bar, wiping dry the same type of Glencairn nosing glasses I believe every whisky begs to be poured into. They stood in front of a wall that looked like a live electrical grid barely holding back loose cables and the ever-present possibility of a spark. A chalkboard above it all said THE WORLD'S MOST DANGEROUS BAR.

I was certain the world's most dangerous bar owner was the guy at the other end of the sleek length of lumber, unpacking the box from the Jeep.

"Are you here for a tasting?" one of the bartenders asked.

"Umm . . ." I hesitated. I hadn't intended to do any tasting, as it was only around 4:00 and I still had a long drive—returning my mom to her house and then farther on to mine. "I was actually just coming in for some information. You guys make bourbon and rye, yes?"

"And a wheat whiskey," the barkeep said.

"Wheat?" I felt my brows rise. I'd never had that grain in a whiskey before, although I knew it to be in plenty of blends. But knowing that I had no taste for wheat beers and still shied away from blended whiskies, I figured I hadn't been missing anything.

"Well," I continued. "I'm doing some research for a book, and I was wondering if I might be able to get in contact with your distiller? Ask him or her a few questions?"

The rakish publican at the end of the bar piped up, "Oh? What do you write?"

"Mostly drivel. Some books for kids and young adults—"

"You write about whiskey for kids?"

I smiled and shook my head and wondered just how well I'd be received if I revealed that I've managed to tuck something whisky-related into all three of my middle-grade and young adult books. "I wish. No. This research is for an adult book—and that is not a euphemism for porn."

He laughed. Oooh, Lucifer had a killer smile, and I was reminded of the photograph where I first spotted him. "Are you by chance the owner? I Googled this place and—"

He pointed at me. "That's where I know you from. You were checking me out on LinkedIn, weren't you?"

I felt heat rush like two bright pink spots that settled onto my cheeks. "Like I said, I'm doing research and had a few questions."

"What kind of whiskey do you write about?"

I looked him straight in the eye. "The kind without an E."

He squinted at me.

"Scotch," I clarified. "I don't know anything about bourbon."

"Nothing?"

"Well, nothing apart from the fact that I find it way too sweet."

He returned my forthright gaze and reached for three Glencairns. "We're gonna fix that fallacy right now."

I watched the man pull three bottles from a shelf below the bar and thought about how this was a near replica experience of Balbirnie House with the Scottish barkeep who was determined to properly introduce me to single malt scotch. And then thought about my mom. I hoped her hairdresser discovered she needed extra time beneath the hood, or that after the color she'd need her nails painted and a few minutes in the heated massage chairs. Things were about to get interesting, with the upcoming throwing down of the gauntlet.

"I was just with a bunch of scotch guys in Sweden," the maybe-owner said.

Scotch guys? I thought. *Oh, for your sake I hope you did not call them that.* "Oh? Which ones?"

He shrugged while pouring the drams. "From Brewlayditch, I think."

I bit down hard on my cheeks and said, "Do you mean Bruichladdich?"

"What was that?"

"The distillery on Islay? Bruichladdich?" I pronounced it a little more slowly that time—brew-ick-lah-dee.

"Nah, I don't think so. Could be. No one could understand those guys." The proprietor quickly changed the subject and pointed up, at the network of electrical conductors on the wall behind him, to one latch that held a slew of ribboned medals. "San Francisco liked us."

The World Spirits Competition. The awards did not surprise me—if they were all for the rye I'd tasted the week before. He'd finished pouring. "That's wheat—start with that. That one is corn. And the last guy is rye. Everything is one hundred proof. Pure single grain. So you can mix and match and create your own mash bill once you know your taste buds and their liking."

"I know they won't like bourbon—no offense," I said, picking up each one and nosing the glasses.

A sly smile slid across his face, and his eyes sparked as they locked onto mine. "Challenge accepted."

Belly Up to the Bar
(Part 3)

When someone first discovers I'm a besotted fan of whisky, I see a slow reassessment of my character slide across their face. Their eyes widen, brows arch, and I can almost hear the reel of film footage whirring in their head.

But this is where most people get it wrong. I'm not a leather-clad extra at the bar in some Clint Eastwood film who slugs back a few before getting on her bike to peel out of the parking lot. *Single malt* and *slug* should never be uttered in the same sentence.

Learning how to taste whisky is an experience most folks want to savor. If your knees are knocking because you're about to enter stage left for the first time, or you're preparing to propose and are uncertain of the likely response, I suggest you choose a less expensive form of liquid courage. As so much of my work and writing life revolve around research, it never fails that when falling down the subject's rabbit hole to gain more insight and wipe away ignorance, I have this insufferable desire to do the same for other people. And apparently, I genuinely believe that I am doing so until I am reminded that my openings of, "Hey, did you know . . . ?" are often met with "I don't care." It appears most people are not dying to know how many different odor compounds there are in the world.

I have also heard from people I teach that I do not let them "get to the goddamn tasting part" quickly enough in my classes. This is crushing.

And true. But there's just so much to know and consider before your tongue meets that lovely elixir.

Just a few interesting tidbits to ponder before sipping:

1. What is flavor? It's an umbrella term that houses both taste and aroma, and as smell has far more descriptive language than taste, it repeatedly highlights how we struggle with a narrative for our experiences. Take for instance cheese. Think of the words you use to describe this food. Soft, ripe, runny, smelly, barnyard-like, nutty, fruity, grainy—these are pretty good when working across a broad spectrum, but what about comparing cheddar cheese to aged Gouda? Now what? One is cheesier than the other? Or what about the flavor of red snapper? It's not *fishy*. And stating it is of firm or flaky texture does not illustrate flavor. That is a different sensation entirely.

2. Flavor is more than a sensory experience as, remember, it turns on the light in our brain's limbic system and rummages around to immediately connect that taste and smell to an emotion and memory. Does what you taste transport you back in time? The complex flavors swirling within your glass can trigger the puckeringly sweet and heady marmalade your grandmother used to make, or the fourth-grade field trip you made to the pioneer museum with its widemouthed hearths still offering up the scent of applewood and toasted oak. Whenever I smell fish, I am flooded with the optimism of a marriage proposal. Why? Because after school I used to watch episodes of *Gilligan's Island* while eating Gorton's fish sticks and waited hopefully for the Professor to ask Mary Ann to be his wife and make perky, adorable, intelligent babies.

3. We have more control than once thought over whether we've birthed "picky eaters." We now have impressive data that shows babies will have an affinity for foods *if their mothers eat it while they are pregnant with said baby*. Hoping your tiny tyke will be asking for seconds on that

bitter bowlful of mustard greens? Start gestationally shoveling it in, Popeye.

I could go on but will spare those of you who are staring at your glass with a growing but uncomfortable longing.

The last thing I'll note before encouraging you to let tongue and taste-buds take over is that one should remember that whisky strength varies from bottle to bottle, and the correct alcoholic percentage for receiving the greatest flavors from the spirit is an ongoing debate. It's safe to say a good number of experts mark their answers at somewhere between 40 and 50 percent alcohol by volume (ABV). The majority of bottles residing on my shelves fall somewhere within that realm, unless they're labeled as *cask strength*, in which case they will possess the markings of 50–65+ percent ABV. No doubt, after downing a dram of something 130 proof, you may think twice about sitting too close to any open flames.

The industry standard for barrel filling is about 63.5 percent ABV in Scotland. (For American bourbon, it's 62.5 percent or 125 proof.) But during maturation, the spirit can lose strength to evaporation—as much as 2 percent per year (and a helluva lot more in some worldly locations). Just before bottling, the distillery usually chooses to add water to set the spirit where the distiller feels the flavors will shine. But this may not suit all tastebuds and may, in fact, anesthetize some. You, the consumer, can then play with the alcohol strength that suits you best, allowing you to identify all the whisky has to offer without suffering from chemesthesis, where the alcohol may interfere (via a burning/prickling sensation) with your ability to recognize flavor compounds.

So much for the lesson in percentages. Now let's get down to the business of categorization and consumption.

After making note of what strength your whisky is, play with it. Water helps to release aromas. Some whiskies swim better than others. Add a few drops at a time. Too much will break down the whisky's structure. If your tongue prickles when the liquid passes over it, feel free to add more.

Now take a sip, but don't immediately swallow. Swish the whisky around all the parts of your mouth: upper tongue, below your tongue, cheeks and roof of the mouth. Try chewing it a few times to help coat all surfaces.

As mentioned before, when I was first trained, I was instructed to take a sip and make a cup out of my tongue, allowing the spirit to rest there. Then I was told to open my mouth slightly and pull air over the surface of my tongue and the liquid, finally letting my breath flow back out my nose *and* mouth. Then I was told to stop choking and making an idiot out of myself. I had to practice a lot to get rid of the idiot part of the routine. At the end of the day, my clothes smelled like I'd spent the night in the pub but had no idea where my mouth was located. You might want to practice on your own—in private.

You should be asking yourself the same questions as in Part 2 when you're attempting to identify aromas. What is your tongue recognizing? After you swallow (which you can go ahead and do now), your nose will participate in helping with the task of identification.

The *delivery* of the whisky's flavors will happen at different times and in different places. There's your initial "entry," the springy and powerful meet and greet of something new and surprising in your mouth; the "middle palette," where the whisky has coated every surface and you embrace an explosion of flavor; and the "end" or "finish," but we'll talk more about that in Part 4. For now, notice the mouthfeel (Slippery? Thin?), the texture (Tannic and puckery? Thick and chewy?), and pay attention to the fact that both your nose and your tongue are working in concert to identify any aromatic compounds that then escalate flavor perception through two processes called orthonasal and retronasal olfaction. (This is simply the perception of odors and flavors via the pathway of your nose and mouth.) These terms might seem foreign at first, but with a little bit of pleasurable practice, they'll be as comfortable as old winter slippers.

And if you want to explore terminology a little further, there is a wealth of nosing/flavor wheels available online (and some I've made myself) for you to use as a guide in determining the compounds you may taste or smell. Of course, you can make your own flavor profiles for different whiskies and compare your observations with those of some industry experts, but remember: biologically, we're all different, and your interpretations are what should matter most to you.

Ultimately, the scents and tastes we experience are intricately interconnected to a vast array of our own bodies' unique systems, and our brain will weave the ingredients of scent, taste, sound, sight, texture, *and expectation* to create a full picture of "flavor." It goes without saying that we're too intelligent a species to answer the question, "How does it taste?" with something like, *I dunno. Pretty good, I guess.* Because answering that question is really, truly fun. It's all about the fun.

Except when it comes out of your nose. That would never happen in a Clint Eastwood film either.

Proper Whisky

I want to make proper whisky."

It was a wholly insulting thing to say, but Dave knew exactly what I meant and gave me the sweetest kiss on the forehead. "Then we will make that happen."

"I have peat," I added, giving him my best impish grin.

"I do not have a malting floor, honya." He paused to look out over the flush of blazing colors spread across the undulating mountains we were facing. We sat on my porch, a peat-soaked ten-year-old Ardbeg in our glasses, and slowly rocked the double glider in rhythm with drowsy summer crickets, refusing to let go of a season long over.

We'd been dating for a year, and for a year I'd been learning about the three grains Reservoir distilled, and how unique each one was to barley—the grain I was most familiar with. But more importantly, I'd been learning what it was like to be partnered with someone who viewed me as a person, not a project—a feeling I was most *un*familiar with.

"I do, however, know someone with a giant smoker," he said, now glancing up, clearly scanning the inside of his brain and not the peach-colored sky of an October sunset. He rubbed the underside of his chin, bristly as soft sandpaper.

"A *smoker*?"

"Yeah . . . Tanya—she's the Belmont Butcher—kick-ass in her field, probably one of the best in the state. You met her at the Autumn Olive Farm barbecue last month, remember? She catered the whole thing."

I nodded. "What would we do with a smoker?"

"Make it work like a malting floor. Maybe." He turned to look at me. "You start researching your big fat whisky science books, and I'll make a couple of calls. Between the two of us we'll figure this thing out." He flashed that million-dollar smile. "If my girl wants *proper* whisky, then we're gonna find a way to make it because"—he nosed his glass and held it up to meet mine—"Ardbeg. Hell, yes."

———

Dave's distillery is not like the one Ian works in. There is nothing there that was designed by a slick marketing team. Nothing shiny, sleek, stylish, or flashy to sway visitors on some distillery tour to empty their pockets in the gift shop and walk away with a bag full of facial scrub made from leftover grains, a set of wooden golf clubs made from old barrel staves, and a lavishly designed jam jar containing the special "source" water that Reservoir's whiskey is made from. In fact, all the swag they sell up front should basically just say, *Today only.* I'll explain in a minute.

And lest you believe that I am decrying the above, let me assure you that I would be first in line—and likely shove a few people out of the way to be so—to purchase that scrub, those clubs, and that jar. Because it all holds magic—including their spirit. And whisky magic is the answer to all my questions posed to the universe.

Now to defend Reservoir's business creativity, it's not that this distillery doesn't care about enticing its customers; it's that this distillery usually has all available hands on deck just trying to keep up with the spirit. It's really about the spirit.

In fact, most of the promotional paraphernalia they sell in their tasting room is a one-off and shows their playful ingenuity.

A chef made some insanely wicked hot sauce and we aged it in one of our old rye barrels for a year to see what would happen. We've got it till we run out.

A woman up in the mountains made maple syrup with our bourbon. We've got it till we run out.

A winery/brewery/cidery gave us two hundred gallons of some wine/beer/ cider they weren't happy with. We distilled it, aged it, and bottled it. Sorry, we've run out.

This is their theme, their mantra, their formula for focus on all things that aren't the bread-and-butter line of goods, the tried-and-true, tested-and-perfected three single-grain whiskies they built their business on.

Before cofounding Reservoir, Dave was an electrical engineer and then a bond trader on Wall Street with a brash Southern charm that still spreads as thickly as molasses. Smack dab in the middle of this intersection sprouted a trifecta of necessary revelations:

1. The value of money.
2. The value of doing things yourself.
3. The necessity of an enticing pitch.

A fair amount of the equipment in that distillery is, again, a one-off. Some of it is made by hand, some put together from reclaimed and restored hardware and machinery, and all maintained by a hope and a prayer.

The more time I spent in that distillery, the more I saw the parallels deepen between what I had fallen in love with overseas and what pulled on the same heartstrings here at home. Yes, copper pots make me all swoony—these were present and accounted for. True, the flavors and aromas of scotch were wholly unique and hypnotically connected me to people, places, and experiences, but I was at the beginning of a journey learning about the singular flavors present in *American* whiskies while attaching them to their own sets of sensory experiences here.

More than anything else, I recognized that, although I did not have the clan of men who molded so much of my most intricate thinking about whisky beside me, I had Dave, who played all their roles and then some. He was Farmer Brown with his unbound enthusiasm. He was Graham with his wicked and mischievous humor. He was the Tin Man with his strong intelligence and warm kindheartedness. And also, he was the Warlock, as Dave was nothing but buoyant with his excitement to share with others that I was a writer and *wasn't that amazing?*

And although Oz was far away, a still vivid and unforgettable utopia, I was in the middle of creating a pretty damn good Kansas—one that was taking on fresh color, newfound appreciation, and the ever-evolving definition of "home."

It's what I discovered slowly over the course of the first year I dated Dave, and what I discovered quickly during the first days we made whisky.

Belly Up to the Bar
(Part 4)

If you had to decide on anything you'd want to come to an end, you might volunteer such things as world hunger, or strip searches at the airport, possibly even the life of anyone who writes another vampire book.

Certainly, one thing no one looks forward to seeing is the bottom of an empty whisky glass.

Thankfully, this is not what is meant when referring to the word *finish* in the world of nosing and tasting. The "finish" alludes to those flavors and aromas that still linger on the palate after the alcohol has been swallowed. Personally, I think the whisky's job isn't over until it's established a small furnace in your stomach—a potbellied stove for some.

But as you note, or even record your observations on, the different whiskies you try, you'll find some finishes stick around longer than others—a little bit like the bloom of youth on Dick Clark.

A whisky's finish is often described with words like *long, dry, chewy, clean, fresh,* or *lingering,* but you can come up with your own terms that are meaningful to you. I'd hope you'd stay away from language like *yuck, horrid,* and *awful.* In these cases, switch your glass or change your whisky. I find the most satisfying thing to consider regarding the finish is answering the question *how long did the flavor last inside my head?* (Both oral and nasal cavities.) Some spirits have an initial punch of flavor but will fade rapidly, where others will linger and develop into something completely new and fascinating.

Now that you've had an opportunity to get acquainted with the enlightening and invaluable lessons of nosing and tasting, you can walk your guests and friends through the fun, coming off as the sagacious individual we all know you are.

Keep a notebook with your observations as they develop. Your growing assessments will be hugely helpful as you become a more learned and discerning connoisseur of whisky. And hold that guy close to hand. When you're shopping for and seeking a new whisky, that notebook will be your best bud.

So, to recap:

- Blow your nose, clean your glass, pour your dram, and note the color, viscosity, and clarity. (Part 1)
- Swirl or not. Dab a drop on the back of your hand. Sniff both hand and glass. Identify. (Part 2)
- Note the strength. Add H2O (or not). Take a sip. Breathe. Try not to choke. Locate your nosing/flavor wheel. (Part 3)
- Classify the finish. Select a notebook. Decorate with stickers. Consider yourself profoundly erudite. (Part 4)

School is out.

You may leave your teacher assessments on my desk, but remember I know your handwriting.

Now go forth and share.

Please . . . Let Me Explain

I glanced across the line of shelves filled with eye-catching boxes and broad-shouldered bottles, occasionally pulling one from the lineup to scrutinize with envious enthusiasm.

"I can't confidently say that I'm an expert at this time, as it's only been six months, but I figure another year and a half and most customers who walk through that shop door will find me to be a connoisseur of the craft—a malt maven, if you will."

I glanced up at the twenty-four-year-old soon-to-be scotch scholar and gave him an encouraging smile.

"I hadn't envisioned finding myself in this position years ago when in school in Finland—working as Mr. Worrall's apprentice, but"—he ran his hands through his buzz-cropped, fair-colored hair—"it seems the puzzle pieces just fell into place."

"I see," I murmured, pivoting from one tight space in the tiny London whisky shop to move past the long and lanky Finn toward another shelf filled with other amber liquids I'd yet to see or taste.

I picked up a bright canary-colored box. "Huh," I breathed out, twisting the carton in my hand to view all sides. A whisky made in New Zealand. I'd traveled to the country maybe a decade ago and had been disappointed to discover that the only distillation I came across was the furtive kind—with kerosene cans and rubber tubing. Nothing I could find on the shelves of duty free at the airport to take home. The box in my hand provided scant details.

"Where is this?" I twisted to glance up at the Lad McFinnland.

His eyebrows rose, and then quick understanding flooded his face. "Ah yes, New Zealand is a small chain of islands—two mainly—off the southeastern coast of Australia. Known for its mountains and glaciers generally."

I stood silent. Then I looked around for something that would cost less than one hundred pounds to throw at his head, as this was a *rare* malt whisky shop that carried nothing one wouldn't have to consider auctioning off a kidney to buy.

I sighed and rolled my eyes at Dave, sitting in the corner, wrapping up business with the shop owner. We had developed a few signals during this trip to subtly communicate.

I was tagging along on his travels across the UK, helping him navigate his unpretentious and ballsy bourbon around a country filled with its exclusive, gentry-filled single malt scotch drinkers.

The Virginian, whose teeth were cut on grits and grand plantations, was making use of my twenty-five years soaking up the Scottish, the Irish, and everything English.

"Your whisky tastes of Marmite and Ribena," one distributor had said.

I'd leaned over to translate. "Yeast paste and black currants."

"I'm getting a touch of candy floss."

"That would be cotton candy," I whispered.

"This one has scents of a water closet's urinal cake."

I looked at Dave. His furrowed eyebrows halted my words. "Yeah, I got that one."

I was also here, immersing myself in a side of the whisky world I was usually not swimming in—all for the sake of research. My newest novel in progress—a book about a suffering distillery on the verge of falling apart—had me seeking more than just the drinking of a dram. The more I know about the inside industry, the better the believability factor.

Traveling with Dave brought me needed experiences where I skimmed the deep abyss of his world—a world where he knew the players, had medaled in the art of a pitch, could assess his numbers, his audience, his competition. He knew what the person across from him likely cared about and wanted to hear, and more importantly, he knew what to leave out. Boy, that guy knows how to read a room.

And all this information was scribbled down, recorded for transcribing later, or inked onto the inside of my arm if I was out of paper. I'd use it all, if not for my book, then simply to add to my ever-growing database of the complexity of this liquid.

Alas, apart from my work with Dave, I once again found I'd entered the world of spirits where the main players erroneously assumed I had as much understanding and interest about the subject as I did about prostate cancer.

"We're talking about brown spirits, darling," one Englishman pointed out to me at a tasting event. "An utterly foul habit to the gentler sex."

"Mansplaining is something we find even fouler," I replied, looking up innocently.

"Surely not." He put a hand on my shoulder. "Perhaps we should get you a white wine?"

"A single malt, please."

"That's the spirit," he said with another wry, all-knowing pat. "I'll order you my favorite lest you find it distasteful."

This industry has been slow to change. Like the pivoting of a large ship, the whisky world protects its stability. Women can make things tipsy—both literally and figuratively. And parts of the world I travel to are reticent to allow the hands of time to tick as quickly as it wishes to. But there is a growing number of "that gentler sex" that persevere, and as I believe it's an arena that many still find too intimidating to enter, I place great value on the women who are effortfully and boldly clearing the path forward.

I crave standing in the intersection of the two things I love most: writing and whisky. My aim for the last two decades has been to make it into a panoptic crossroads, adding food and nature, folklore and peat smoke. To me, this ingredient list illustrates how Scotland can present itself purely in liquid form.

Despite the heavy hand of doubt I'm often greeted with on this male-dominated turf, I'd be remiss if I neglected to point out the bright moments where I'm caught by surprise and filled with delight.

"So," a tall Welsh actor beside me starts, "have you been dragged here by a companion you're unfortunately in debt to, or are you as besotted with this juice like the rest of us poor SOBs at this whisky tasting?"

I turned and glanced up. I wanted to hug him. "Definitely not dragged. There's nowhere else I'd rather be."

"Ah." He nodded grimly. "Then I feel doubly sorry for you, as I'm sure, like us, you're continually searching for and finding the next Holy Grail, only to discover, after a sip from that chalice, that it's usually just a few too many precious pennies out of our budgets."

I laughed and then sniffed the pricey elixir in my hand. Finally, a true compatriot.

He continued. "So, what have you been dying to try that seems a little out of reach?"

I thought back to yesterday, in the rare malt shop. "Oh," I breathed out dreamily. "A new single malt from New Zealand."

His eyes lit with interest. "Really? Where's that?"

I couldn't help myself, and I snorted with laughter as the words tumbled out. "Ah yes, New Zealand is a small chain of islands—two mainly—off the southeastern coast of Australia. Known for its mountains and glaciers generally."

Boozy Broads and
Whisky Women

W hat does it take to gain notoriety? If you're a wannabe celebrity, you've got to make a statement that attracts some attention. Find a butcher and have someone cleave you a meat dress. Post something shocking on eBay: sell the ghost in your basement, or the peace of mind you just received from hosting a middle school fundraiser that auctioned off only confectionary and baked goods made with the main ingredient *kale*. Or stockpile as much tea as you can and toss it into the Boston Harbor as a commemorative gesture. Be brave. Be bold. And get it on video.

But what if you're not a person, but a thing—a widget, an object, or even a way of life? You want to be desirable, you seek to build brand loyalty, you strive to gain a lifetime of devotion.

Best bet? Put that gadget in the hand of the woman wearing the meat dress.

There you go, now everybody wants one.

In this case, we're talking about image. On both a small and large scale.

This has happened to me too many times: I'd sit down on a barstool and an attentive barkeep would hand me the drinks menu conveniently opened to every flavor of cosmopolitan available to the human tongue. I'd smile politely and flip to the back page, where the list of single malts usually lived. I'd order something with the intention of removing all dental plaque, and the barman would then turn to my husband to correct my endearing confusion. Apparently, I had lost my marbles, the ability to hear, and the gift of language.

Usually, Sir Sackier said something along the lines of, "Just get her the damn scotch, and now you'd better make it a double."

Responses like that always perked me up.

Thankfully, that scenario is diminishing—likely because of a growing spate of tenacious women who have no problem lassoing the bartender with their purse straps, tying him up with the seltzer hose, and leaping over the bar to pour themselves a glass of something they really want.

Whisky has had a rough time in the past when trying to appeal to women, evoking a reputation based on those who regularly use the back end of their stilettos as both a weapon and toothpick. Is it the drink that gives them a hard edge? Can soft-spoken women—maybe those who have been raised in the stacks of great libraries or reared by Care Bears—find whisky enticing?

I think so.

Maybe not in vast quantities, but there is a growing body of females who are not only trekking across the whisky trail—and not trailing behind their husbands—but blazing a few new trails for the cool kids to follow.

Once whisky (and soda) became a standard for Sherlock Holmes, and Charles Dickens stockpiled case after case of Pure Highland Malt (Cockburns of Leith) in his basement, the rest of the world fell in line.

Winston Churchill, Dylan Thomas, and Humphrey Bogart were all somewhat reliant on scotch. Mark Twain waxed lyrical over the drink, and the Rat Pack, while on stage singing, likely sucked up more of the juice than they did air.

Sure, Lady Gaga has stated that when songwriting, the typical accompaniment to her melodious muse is a vat of scotch and some Mary Jane, and other hipster girls, like Kate Moss and KT Tunstall, have pitched in to the celebrity profile by slugging back, but for some women, they aren't seeking the bad-girl glory with their choice of liquor. They're wanting something more along the lines of *smart and classy* instead of *tart and sassy*. Not that there is anything wrong with the latter. It's a matter of which hat you feel like donning that day.

Perhaps a combination of both is what the whisky world is after when marketing to women. Liqueur companies have tapped into their sweet tooth, mixologists have concocted cocktails, and Jack Daniels created a campaign encouraging women to ditch the eggnog and spike the cookies for the holidays. (Because who doesn't love to see little kids try to decorate the Christmas tree, boozy after eating/drinking a dozen Santa Claus–shaped sugar cookies?) Diageo—which owns Johnnie Walker—threw their bonnet into the ring and, in March of 2018, began selling a limited-edition run of a quarter of a million bottles with "Jane Walker" striding across their label, complete in top hat and tails. Sadly, that marketing idea left numerous women feeling patronized, as it piggybacked a few political and social movements.

And then there are those plucky pioneers I mentioned earlier, the ones who are influential not simply because of what they drink, but because of what they *make* to drink.

I touch upon some of them in more detail within this book—those who long ago were manning the stills whilst their husbands farmed the fields—but their contemporaries today deserve a tip of that proverbial top hat, too. Rachel Barrie, with over a quarter century of time within the industry, is continuing to draw headlines as a respected whisky blender, originally at Morrison Bowmore and now at Brown-Forman. Jill Jones was the executive vice president of Brown-Forman—a global spirit company—working with them for over eighteen years. Gillian Macdonald was the distiller at Penderyn—the spirit of the Welsh Whisky Company—and is now with Glenmorangie as head of analytics and whisky creation. Angie Morrison broke new ground as the first female whisky sommelier while working at Cape Town's famous Bascule Bar. Angela D'Orazio, who probably has the coolest job title of master blender and chief nose officer, works for Mackmyra Svensk Whisky. Marianne Eaves, previous master distiller of Castle & Key, is the first female master distiller in Kentucky since Prohibition, while Julia Ritz Toffoli is the founder of one of the most successful international whiskey clubs, Women Who Whiskey.

Want me to go on? Probably not, as I think you see my point. But what does this say about the industry? I'd say good news for shareholders, less typecasting for women, and a few Christmas photos you might want to keep out of the hands of child protective services.

Yes, the future will be fun, but it will also be arduous, as there is a great deal of work ahead of us when lifting the lids off the pots labeled "inclusion" and "representation." A peek inside those vessels reveals a true deficit—one where many people deserve and would benefit from attention, support, and recognition. Whether speaking about minorities, women, or the countless colors of diversity our planet holds, surely the industry has room for as many as wish to participate. And it's not enough to wait to be "picked," as it is up to each of us to choose our path and march down it because we wish to go in that direction. We cannot wait for an invitation. Show up at the party, or better yet, throw it yourself.

The Malting, the Making, the Whisky, the Waiting

P eat?"

    "In the back."

"Barley?"

"In the back."

"Hound?"

"In the driver's seat."

"Hound goes in the back with the peat and the barley, honya. Unless you've shown him how to drive three on the tree?" Dave said with a smirk.

I smiled, shook my head, and convinced Haggis to move into the thin crack of storage space behind the two front seats in the cab of Dave's old pickup truck. I'd rather have my dog be slightly squished behind us than tossed about in the bed of the truck as we drove to Tanya's butcher shop, where we were about to start peat-smoking our grains. I preferred Haggis in an unbruised state. The peat and barley would be fine.

The day had come at last, and finally, we had all the ingredients necessary to work this experiment. It was going to be a small run, the first time around—but could we make a peaty, smoky, maybe even briny single malt whisky with Dave's equipment? Would it work like the machinery I'd learned on in Scotland? Would Dave finally throttle me after I'd uttered the phrase, "That's not how we did it in Scotland," for the thirtieth time? The fiftieth? I'd have to see just how long his thread of saintly patience held.

The small run would fill maybe five quarter casks. I wanted to label the finished spirit *The Barley Bottles*, but I knew leaping ahead three years into the future might bring about bad luck and that perhaps I was tempting fate by putting the cart in front of the horse.

There were no washbacks, or mash tuns, no low wines and spirit stills, and no spirit safe to make me feel at home with the equipment. What I was introduced to was a cooker, a chiller, the open fermentation tanks, a stripper still, a rectification still, and a trusty rusty hydrometer.

Thank God for the hydrometer. It was the one thing I recognized as friendly and familiar.

I take it back. The air was perfumed with the heady organic compounds that had long ago glued their scents onto my cells and suctioned themselves into my heart. The familiar aromas of sweet, crushed cereal, of tangy yeast, and of fermenting wort, tangled with the bright pungency of metallic copper, of tropical distillate notes, and of oak in all its various stages of maturation as it breathes an aging spirit in and out of its pores. I was a pig in muck.

And although some of the machinery was unfamiliar to me, they all worked in similar ways, and all of it accomplished what needed to be done.

The first time we ran the stills, it was a test of ingenuity, patience, research, and humor. Not everything worked perfectly, and some things worked in ways that left us with hours and hours of cleaning up all that could not even come close to working perfectly. It was science in action, and a little less magic than I had imagined.

But the magic came, as it always does. And as the new-make spirit trickled off the still, the estery aromas that filled the air around the parrot spout of the copper pot made me dance with glee—the pineapple, banana, pear, and soap. The bite of those clean flavors signified the spirit's proof and also provided "proof" that we may have succeeded—both a welcome greeting of data. And once all the spirit was snugly tucked into each barrel we'd chosen, those casks were nestled in for sleep—at least a three-year nap, but a nap that would feel like three lifetimes for my impatient tastebuds.

The casks received the occasional gentle nudge over those next few years, when we'd peek to see where its contents were on the scales of oak curve and maturation. Five-gallon ex-bourbon casks provide more wood-to-solvent ratio, and along with the vast temperature and humidity fluctuations here in Virginia, where the whisky is aging, and an extraordinarily clean distillate, one sees results much more rapidly than what is standard elsewhere.

And as much as I have pleaded with Mother Nature and science to make haste, I am fully aware that I have control over neither. There is only so much a distiller can do except practice patience once the spirit is resting on wood. In fact, I'm reminded of the well-known sentiment among distillers, excitedly acknowledging that the cask has blessed you with a plethora of mixed flavors during the first several weeks of aging, and then you spend the next several years praying the cask will now take back a few stinkers no one wanted to begin with. It is the complexity of wood science—a subject I am sure will be the focus of many years in my future.

Now in case you are wondering, the Barley Bottle results were truly lovely, although not award-winning. And as Rome was not built in a day, neither are the skills of an apprentice. But perhaps like Rome's appetite to acquire more land, I shared that same appetite with the desire to acquire more skills. As I sat looking at those five barrels, I realized I would have ample time to grow fat and conquer.

Cardhu and Helen Cumming:
Cunning Doesn't Even Come Close

Helen of Troy; daughter of Zeus, hatched from an egg, coveted by both Greeks and Trojans.

Helen Churchill Candee; Titanic survivor, campaigned to women about independence from men.

Helen Thomas; ballsy White House journalist who thrived on asking questions that made presidents squirm.

Helen Cumming; wife, baker, sly whisky maker. Cardhu Distillery takes a bow in her honor.

Is it the name? I doubt it. For many it evokes the image of an elderly auntie at a family reunion, the one with lipstick on her teeth and a Miracle-Ear the Smithsonian has dibs on.

Yet it must be said, the exceptions to the rule are truly rule-breakers. Girls with guts and revelers of a rush.

Helen Cumming, a pioneer in distaff distillation, clearly took part in elevating her name by taking the lead in an industry that was not only absent of female recognition, but illegal to boot. Bootlegging wasn't a traditional career choice for women in the early 1800s, though Helen took a great deal of pride in it.

Married to John Cumming of Cardow Farm, it was clear Helen realized her husband's skills were deemed necessary in the fields, which meant *she* oversaw the stills. Working illicitly for more than a dozen years,

Helen churned out the spirit in the farmhouse and set up a drive-thru window for the convenience of her customers. And given the opportunity, her patrons would likely have thrown a parade in her honor for the protection she offered against the wily excisemen.

Welcoming any taxman into her home, she found tremendous success in serving tea and scones, waving away any curiosity regarding that yeasty-like smell as the consequence of all the hefty baking a good farmer's wife is required to do.

In the meantime, while the regulator took a respite from the unforgiving demands of his profession, Helen made sure the rest of his day would be less *taxing* by slipping out of sight to raise the flagpole's red banner of warning to any clientele heading her way, and to other distillers in view of the farm. Warm and welcoming, facile and furtive, Helen Cumming probably had more likes on her Facebook page than Cristiano Ronaldo and Rihanna combined.

It takes dedication to create a fine spirit, and luckily for whisky lovers, she passed on her devotion to her daughter-in-law Elizabeth.

Young Lizzie handled the reins of the finally-legal distillery with aplomb. Not only did she continue to create Cardhu's robust (at the time) Speyside standard, but she soon rebuilt the facility, furthering its future potential.

To top it off, Ms. Cummings pulled off the business feat that many an industry expert would give their left lung to enjoy; authority without responsibility. She sold it on to John Walker & Sons—distinguished regulars who knew a gem when they sipped it—with the caveat that her family still retained control of the operation. A Wall Street frontiersman (or frontierswoman) in the making.

The whisky went on to new owners and operators, and its flavor camp may have jumped from classical to verdant and vernal, but its history packs a punch, even if its character treads lightly.

Cardhu was the crown the "Queens of the Whisky Trade" wore with pride and with purpose. But these ingenious women were not history's first women distillers. There are scores of them, no doubt. But their critical contributions were not catalogued in the same way their opposite-gender counterparts' were, and the lack of canonization misleads many into believing women played a small or irrelevant role in the history of distillation. Although there are few published books available on the topic—*Whiskey Women: The Untold Story of How Women Saved Bourbon, Scotch, and Irish Whiskey* by Fred Minnick being the most well-known—the tales do exist. Likely in the form of journal entries, farm account books, and ancient family scrapbooks. They need to be unearthed. They need to be celebrated. They are the fire and fodder for new generations. And although toasting to their good health will be ineffective, raising a glass in honor of their efforts and accomplishments is a salute long overdue—with perhaps an additional toast to a new generation that will continue and grow their legacy.

The Lass Gets a Title

I think it's time we put you on the payroll."

I glanced over at Dave to see him take a sip of one of the two whiskies we were drinking that night on his front stoop. It was Whisky Friday—the once-a-week ritual we now shared, where we'd pull two bottles of scotch off my shelves to practice nosing and tasting, but mostly revel in the surprising differences among the vast spectrum of flavors across Scotland.

It usually followed with some bit of knowledge, trivia, or folklore I'd picked up along the way about those two particular bottles.

"What would be my job description?" I asked as I took a sizable swallow of Caol Ila—an eighteen-year-old beauty from the island of Islay—and focused on the path of the peated, honeyed liquid.

It's not like we hadn't discussed the topic a few times before, but Dave seemed more focused on it tonight. During the past two years, I'd worked the stillroom floor, the tasting room, as a brand ambassador in festivals and private whiskey events, and as part of a team to put on a grand Burns Supper in a luxury country house hotel. I freelanced blog posts and any editorial work the distillery needed, and I taught a class for them called Women & Whiskey.

"I'm not sure," Dave mused. "We'll have to think on that. But I've spoken to the accountants, a few investors, but most important to the rest of the team. It's agreed."

There were mutinous emotions roiling about my insides, refusing calm containment. Part of me wanted to leap with unadulterated euphoria—just jump off the stoop and do some awful and clearly unrehearsed version of an end zone dance, although I'd hold back on spiking my Glencairn glass. It was the culmination of a secret dream I had harbored all those years ago as I knuckled down that test at the end of my apprenticeship. And another part of me was gripped with fear—what if I wasn't happy with the work I'd be asked to do? What if I was a disappointment with the results of that work? What if . . . what if Dave and I broke up?

I refocused on the second dram we'd chosen and buried my nose into the heady scents of fresh cut grass and autumn fruits from a young Wolfburn single malt. I glanced at the mystical sea wolf they used as their logo—a creature that could walk on water and bring good luck if spotted. Then I spent a few moments pondering the old Cherokee teaching about the two wolves within us all: the one that is evil, holding anger, greed, sorrow, and regret; and the one that is good, exuding humility, empathy, peace, and hope. The fight between the two is horrific at times, but the one that survives is the one you feed.

"I will not let you down," I told him, looking him in the eye.

He gave me that devilish, knee-weakening side smirk that has become his trademark. "Don't forget, honya, I spent years workin' Wall Street. I know a good bet when I see one."

A short time later, I was granted my official title and a full box of business cards.

Shelley Sackier
Director of Distillery Education

I'm guessing you may be wondering just what a distillery educator does. This answer depends upon the calendar, and sometimes even my ability to persuade someone (ahem, Dave) that this is what *this* distillery educator does. When I am not teaching a variety of master classes, training employees, and developing podcasts, blogs, and newsletters for the education and enjoyment of Reservoir's followers, I'm often writing articles for industry publishers, scouring through grain research and scientific trials, and parsing through dissertations about wood composition, attempting to translate the information into usable data for our team. I've created spreadsheets that catalogue and track all the data collected from myriad ongoing cask experiments we're conducting, including a calendric oak curve based on our barreled inventory, a vertical study on aging barrels at different heights within the warehouse, and analyzing whether aging our oak staves before coopering them into casks will impact the spirit favorably.

I spent months developing complex aroma and flavor wheels for all our whiskies, years designing and implementing industry partnerships for barrel-finishing projects, and way, way too long creating a standard operating manual for all the machinery within the distillery. (Technical manuals are uber challenging for me as none of the machinery is allowed to have dialogue, nor emotions.)

During the pandemic, our distillery refashioned a large portion of our new warehouse and transformed it into a hand sanitizer manufacturing plant. We may have been making hundreds of gallons of whiskey each week, but now we were also making *thousands* of gallons of Handshine™, as well.

My job then included filling out unending applications to state and federal organizations, seeking grants, loans, or any elusive pot of gold. I was negotiating with the FDA to create labeling for our new "drug." I read through reams of ridiculously scripted instructions for how to trademark items. As restaurants and bars shuttered, we shifted to ecommerce, and I negotiated contracts with shipping carriers and direct-to-consumer internet selling platforms. My days were filled with phone calls and emails with accountants, bookkeepers, bankers, loan officers, government workers, and oh . . . so . . . many . . . call center agents.

I made friends with hundreds of people whose days were filled with angry customers, consumers, and applicants, simply by first offering the phrase *I know you must be totally overwhelmed, so thank you for taking my call, and I fully understand if you can't answer this, but we're just gonna give it a shot, okay?*

It seemed to set the tone of expectation, put them at ease, but mostly, give them the firm sense that I wasn't going to shout at them for letting our business die.

Along the way and still to this day, I've also been pushed to wear more than one uncomfortably fitting hat that was typically thrown at me without any warning. And they all came from Dave.

Create us a Wikipedia page.

"I don't know how to do that."

Figure it out.

Or . . .

I need you to source used barrels for me—nationally or internationally, get pricing, sizing, shipping costs, and prior contents, but don't give away any of our details.

"Wait—I don't know how to do that."

You'll figure it out.

Or . . .

I've told a journalist you're a rye grain expert. You're doing an interview with him first thing tomorrow morning.

"Wait—what?! I'm not a rye grain expert!"

You will be by tomorrow morning, honya.

My levels of stress have skyrocketed on umpteen occasions, and they have been relieved nearly as many times simply by going through the arduous but not impossible act of problem solving. Occasionally, my boss has helped alleviate those pressures with his indefatigable Scottish humor by reminding me that we're not making defibrillators and could I maybe head out to find him a pail of striped paint for the tasting room.

My grandmother once filled me in on the adage, "If you're going to eat an elephant, you've got to take it one bite at a time."

And she also used to say, "The harder you work for something, the dearer it becomes to you."

I cherish both statements, and have held them close to my heart, as they have seen me through the most challenging ordeals. I've posted them on colored sticky notes above my computer, right next to my other most critical lifeboat quote:

I don't know about you, but I've thought about running away more as an adult than I ever did as a child.

Dave has a motto we've all been told to tattoo on our foreheads backward so that it's the first thing we see in the morning when we look at ourselves in the mirror:

Adapt, Migrate, or Die.

There are times when each one has signaled it is the best option, but I make sure to call a friend to talk out my plan before truly acting on it.

In times when I have moments to reflect on the mercurial trajectory of my path, it's easy to see how much I wanted certainty—a sure-footedness that would guarantee a safe and elegant trail from the present moment to the last draw of breath. I was given volatility instead, the Universe stating my request was a gift no one would be granted. The choice then was to develop the one skill that would see me through the turbulent times—the ability to shed light on what was a problem to be solved and what was simply a situation that must be endured.

Shackled with the chains of others' expectations left me living an inauthentic life, left me squinting toward a horizon that did not necessarily belong to me, and through the optics of a distorted, cataracted view.

I wanted to move forward, to no longer ignore any magnetic pull because it did not fit within someone else's scope of a defined future. I wanted to move in a direction where I could one day glance back and gasp with the thrill of that path—*my* path, my footsteps, my stumbles, my milestones.

Working with Dave, with my new distillery family, with so many warm and welcoming people within the industry has proven not just the possibility of that, but the probability of that. The questions I now ask myself are no longer, "How do I do this right?" but rather, "What's the next right thing to do?" The difference between finding an answer from the indifferent void and finding an answer from within illuminated the value of calibrating my own compass.

Ultimately, this job, this work, this great love of mine has repeatedly pushed me to stretch myself to a point usually just beyond the feeling of delicious discomfort. It's *real* discomfort. But the delicious part does come. It's effortful, knee-bruising, and sometimes a bit soul-crushing. But it comes. And although the flavor may at times be bittersweet, I remember my first sip of whisky as well, and what a long road I'd traveled to finally call that liquid bliss.

When the Spirit Moves You

Long ago, I fell in love with Scotland (Islay in particular) so hard I found myself scribbling the name on every dusty truck hatch and barn window. I secretly christened certain parts of the mountaintop where I'd lived for so long with names from that tiny island. I pleaded with my family to let me call one of the animals Islay—except that they all possessed names already. And no one was that keen to retrain.

I was sent to this sacred land to finally learn the art of spirit making. To stand at the sides of master distillers as they tinkered with knobs and stirred the vast cauldrons, sniffed at their potions, and tasted elixirs. It was the Hogwarts of scotch. An opportunity unlike anything I could have ever imagined.

I returned to a life where I dispersed that learning in, around, and onto nearly everything I touched. It was in every novel, on every menu, and predominantly present in my conversations. It hung in the air like the angel's share, making life heady and rich, and sometimes just bearable.

I've seen myself move along an endless graduated table of growth and evolution. I've revisited every entry in all my videos, all my journals, all my blog posts and essays, to see this slow progression of accomplishment. Every day I learn, every experience slakes a thirst for more, every opportunity provides greater context and insight down toward the unplumbed depths of the foundational knowledge I crave.

But throughout these many years I've also gained a greater understanding that no matter how many opportunities, or how much context and insight I might possess, this world is still one where women must go the extra mile to get the standard mileage.

Even writing this book I have experienced progress-halting advice from those who are the gatekeepers of the publishing world:

You need more visibility. You need more followers. You need to be seen by others as an expert.

But what makes a person an expert? Is it the individual who finally allows you to gain experience? Is it the experience itself? Or is it more like what Nobel laureate physicist Niels Bohr stated when he said: *An expert is a man* (ahem, or woman) *who has made all the mistakes that can be made in a very narrow field.*

I vote for door number three. I vote for not waiting to get picked. I vote for identifying that narrow field and then stumbling through it despite its being riddled with potholes and cow-pie patties. Yes, chances are you will come out the other end somewhat bruised and oddly perfumed, but you will also come out more experienced and with a marvelous story to tell. And I feel like that chance at observation, at participation, at accumulating skills and knowledge and know-how are worth it. Not only to you, but to furthering the understanding (and enjoyment) for the person who comes next. A housewarming—or *field*warming gift, one might say.

I wish it weren't so difficult to offer that gift.

But I will do what I must do.

I will work my way in and around what, to some, still rings true with the comfort of an all-boys club. And although I've fondly referred to the collection of my bottles as All My Boys—highlighting the many names beginning with Glen, Ben, Craig, or Mac, that labeling also gives a nod to the many men who have both helped and hindered my route. Without all of them, and the daunting and provocative lessons they provided, my life might have been vastly different. In truth, I have learned enough about my own stubborn ways to see that I have, in part, reinforced that very mindset—that fraternal guild. I have often waited for permission. I have scanned male faces to see if it is finally my turn. I have held back in fear of failure.

At this point, I've fallen down enough times to finally realize that my success does not rely only upon battling patriarchy, sexism, and gender discrimination; nor does it rest solely on my ability to pick myself up following rejection or setbacks. It is also vitally important to possess a willingness to pick myself up and then *move forward* toward that Holy Grail of accomplishment and inclusion. To grasp more, taste more, and throw two open arms toward chance and occasion.

I feel very much like I've lived the life of a casked whisky: created by loving hands, determined as sharp and fiery in the beginning, labeled, ignored, remembered, assessed, examined, tested, monitored, and controlled. But I've also been admired, coaxed, anticipated, and adored. It is a life cycle I've chosen because of my ambitions.

I want not only to be a member of Women *Who* Whiskey, but also a woman *in* whisky. Who wouldn't wish to be part of an organization where your curiosity and thirst are both quenched? But I want more. I want to be a woman who is welcomed to learn and then pass on that education, a woman who provides the new data, conducts the new research, and creates the new products. For nearly thirty years I've worked toward my goals, and those goals are as crystal clear to me as the sparkling new distillate that pours from those copper stills.

Over and over, since I've been working in this new world, with these new people, and in this new position, I have found myself ripening—flourishing—in *response* to somebody rather than *despite* them. It is a curious, but delicious, discovery, an internal iteration I soon came to see as an experience I would need to pay forward.

One day I may have collected enough mistakes to be considered an expert. In the interim, I'm determined to work on that turf—harvesting the "grains" of knowledge in that very narrow field.

PART FIVE

Extras to Sip On

FAMOUS SINGLE MALTS: "LAPHROG"

LE WHISKY

ROB.

If you're like me and simply can't get enough of all things whisky, then this section is sure to present a new arsenal of delights. From book recommendations to recipes and libations, enjoy these dram-worthy extras, on me!

A Nip, a Novel,
and Knowledge

I t's not often one gets the opportunity to read about their passion *and* experience it at the same time, but luckily for any whisky drinker, you can learn and imbibe from the comfort of your La-Z-Boy. Read, sip, ponder, and welcome the "aha" moment as it wheedles its way through your web of firing synapses.

We have the advantage over someone who may have the hobby of skydiving, where turning pages with all that wind is a little challenging, or pole dancing, where the audience can easily lose the mood when you shut off the music and turn on the lights to glance at the manual, or even hunting, where animals on the other side of the barrel are going to be much less patient while you thumb through the last chapter, searching for the exact mark on their bodies to place in front of the crosshairs.

From that perspective, we've got no worries. And speaking of angst, you should have none when it comes to running out of material to keep your mind engaged and your learning on track. There is a surfeit of individuals churning out page after page of spirit-related information today, saturating the market with their knowledge of the industry, their review of products and availability, and in a mind-blowing flurry of ever-increasing occasions, their personal experience.

As is true for many pastime pursuits, others enjoying the same activities want to share their thoughts with the hope that you will have a richer adventure, an expanded awareness, and a sumptuous memory to tuck away for future delight. It's simply human beings acting benevolently.

With that in mind, here is a not staggering, but also not scant, list of my favorite wintertime (or anytime) whisky reading that has kept me snug in my favorite chair, learning a little, enjoying a lot, and loving it all.

The World Atlas of Whisky by Dave Broom

Dave Broom crisscrosses the whisky world—explaining the similarities and differences between most whisky-producing countries' elixirs. A top-notch book, a must-have in my opinion, and one that will have you grateful for the short, sweet, and synoptic method of writing.

The World's Best Whiskies by Dominic Roskrow

For me, a winner in that it touches upon not only the spirits themselves, but the places and the people behind them.

Peat Smoke and Spirit by Andrew Jefford

This book is more dog-eared than my hound. It is a must-have for anyone with an insane love for Islay and all she has to offer the whisky world.

Malt Whisky Yearbook 2021

The latest updates on distilleries (worldwide), viewpoints from knowledgeable experts, tasting notes, cocktails and recipes, interviews, a look back at trends and newsmakers, and hundreds of pictures to whet the appetite. Truly, a yearly event worth waiting for.

Malt Whisky Companion by Michael Jackson

One of the most authoritative voices the spirit (and beer) world has enjoyed. And a book (this one strictly about *malt* whiskies) you'll find on most whisky aficionados' shelves.

Wort, Worms & Washbacks by John McDougall and Gavin D. Smith

A peek behind the curtain—something many of us wish we had more of—in a delightful memoir filled with personal tales of John McDougall's time working in the industry, beginning in 1963 through the publishing date of March 2001.

Beam, Straight Up by Fred Noe

Part memoir, part method, part mission, *Beam, Straight Up* is a look at Noe's bourbon world from the Beam command post. Carrying the mantle of responsibility, Frederick Booker Noe III pens his experiences growing up within the seven generations of whiskey-makers. Mr. Noe imparts wisdom to those wishing for business insight, but also addresses the shaping of the bourbon industry and his family's influences within it.

The Whisky Distilleries of the United Kingdom by Alfred Barnard

It's 1887 in Barnard's time, but whatever year it happens to be when this book finds its way into your hands will prove that it's still a relevant and cherished classic.

Whiskey Women: The Untold Story of How Women Saved Bourbon, Scotch, and Irish Whiskey by Fred Minnick

Title says it all, doesn't it? *Whiskey Women* illustrates the everyday, ordinary women who distilled alcohol for home, medicinal, and family use as well as the trailblazers who helped shape, albeit rather silently and with little acknowledgment, the industry on a more global scale. Whether a farmer's wife, a woman heading the temperance movement, a Prohibition barmaid, or a modern-day master distiller, clearly there are women who have left their fingerprints on the industry and have contributed to the history of the spirit.

And speaking of women, have a glance upward once more and identify what's missing. If you said the perfect whisky paired to your Zodiac sign, then you'd be right, but off the mark for the larger point. If you said *women authors*, then well spotted. And good Lord, *where are all the women authors?!*

It should not be that difficult to find books written *about* whisky written *by* women. And yet I struggle to locate them. Below are six that deserve a place on our bookshelves, and in some cases, a place in our hearts.

The Bourbon Bartender: 50 Cocktails to Celebrate the American Spirit by Jane Danger and Alla Lapushchik

Two whiskey experts provide recipes, history, and even a few profiles of the best bourbon bars. A gorgeous book. A must-have resource.

But Always Fine Bourbon: Pappy Van Winkle and the Story of Old Fitzgerald by Sally Van Winkle Campbell

The story of the Stitzel-Weller Distillery and its infamous Van Winkle family. And although it may ultimately be the tale of the legend himself, it is told by his granddaughter and will have you profoundly immersed in their world and their welfare.

The Birth of Bourbon: A Photographic Tour of Early Distilleries by Carol Peachee

An armchair traveler, are you? *And* a history buff to boot? This marvelously rich and color-saturated collection of photographs will capture your imagination and fill you with wonder, providing you with an unparalleled glimpse of the resplendent and haunting pictures of distilleries from the past.

WitchCraft Cocktails: 70 Seasonal Drinks Infused with Magic & Ritual by Julia Halina Hadas

As a writer of fantasy and historical fiction, I am always filled with curiosity and great anticipation the moment I come upon a grimoire. And a spell book filled with drinkable potions? Hella yes. The fact that Ms. Hadas is a bartender and past employee of a distillery makes me somewhat giddy to actually locate the giant cauldron we have for making Brunswick stew and put it to good use. Oh, so much fun to be had!

Whiskey Distilled: A Populist Guide to the Water of Life by Heather Greene

As New York City's first female whiskey sommelier, Heather Greene has written an annotated guide for the novice whiskey drinker, helping to lead them through the vast aspects of whiskey's many subjects, including the fundamentals of nosing and tasting, general explanations of whiskey terms and types, cocktail/food pairing, and a great deal of comparisons to wine for readers more adept with that subject and its terminology.

Whisky: A Very Peculiar History by Fenella Macdonald

I have saved my absolute favorite for last! Full of truthful tales and bewitching mythology, and whimsical in a wholly magical way, this book has been my companion for years. Written in tiny bite-sized chunks with charming illustrations, this small book is the perfect accompaniment to your fireside dram. With each seductive sip you learn more and thirst for more. (I so wish I had written this book.)

So, there we have it. A not-so-tiny list for your library. Leave it around the house and casually bring it up a few weeks before the holidays or your birthday. The pursuit of knowledge is a worthy task. Surely your family and friends will want to help further advance your education, right?

The Distiller's Handbook:
The Mirth of Mixology

People are crazy.

And inventive.

And did I mention crazy?

Traditionally, the drinks industry, namely the ever-expanding hip crowd of mixologists, follows close on the tails of bored—sorry, *ingenious*—chefs who are always inventing new ways to get food down our gullets and hopefully a three-page story in a gourmet magazine as a side bonus. I'm beginning to find chicken-flavored doughnuts infused with a pocket of vodka-spiked BBQ sauce laying on a bed of gently trampled reindeer moss a little cliché. You too? I'm not surprised.

Personally, most of my meals are consumed crouched over the raised beds of my vegetable patch and berry bushes. I don't even hose anything off anymore before I eat it. If there's dirt on it, I tell myself it's Earth pepper. Speckled with microscopic bugs? Extra protein. Find out I've just bitten into a squirty cluster of copper-colored squash bug eggs? A twofold bonus:

1. I've gotten to them before they've hatched and eaten all my zucchini, and
2. I may have discovered the newest form of caviar. Bully for me.

I love food. I will try most everything. And I find I like a lot of it. Because of this obsession, I easily discover myself surrounded by paper walls of stacked magazines and cookbooks or staring at too many open tabs on my browser, each waiting patiently for my eyes to return to them.

I like learning about food and beverage industry trends and oftentimes I give them a whirl in my own kitchen. There were four entire seasons where no one ate anything solid because it was *the year of foam food*. I don't think a body should hold that much nitrous oxide. I'm still experiencing the side effects.

Following along with the cocktail crowd can be a full-time job for many. Lately, the brews are smoldering. You can order something on the drinks menu that sounds appealing and find it presented to you in a goblet worthy of a *Harry Potter* scene, white tendrils of smoke floating up and rolling over the brim due to a quick discharge of liquid nitrogen. People are smoking everything, from their ice chips to Shirley Temples—cherries included.

One bar will even serve you water steeped in tobacco. Um . . . pass.

Since I tend to take my liquor straight, the pioneering procedures in the cocktail world had not been catching my eye; that is, until I started coming across books and articles that appealed to me from the angle of *infusion techniques* and after our distillery hired Michael Hanbury, our new resident publican and infusion master extraordinaire.

It's easy enough for any of us to now locate a gazillion recipes to create straightforward infusions—or even the unfathomable and complicated ones, where it helps to have access to your local university lab. Sometimes I'd swear I was entering an apothecary shop at work when I see endless old jugs, barrels, and mason jars filled with Mike's latest recipes.

But I like the word *infusion*. It's a little hip without being pretentious. It suggests you might know what you're doing and will raise a few eyebrows without turning any stomachs. Funky blends like Cucumber Gin, Raspberry Cognac, Sour Cherry Whiskey, and Horseradish Vodka are just a few that I've dog-eared and set aside, but maybe you're more the sort who'd gravitate toward Habanero & Mango Tequila,

Lavender Liqueur, or even Smoked Bacon Bourbon—or what I like to call breakfast.

A little while back, as I was up to my earballs in final research for a young adult novel I wrote about magic and *flora homeopathica*, I had to research and travel to any herbalists and apothecaries I could rustle up an address for. Lucky for me, the area where I live is just bursting with hedge-witch craftiness, and everyone and their dogs were now whipping up home concoctions of shrubs, tinctures, and bitters—for both medicine and amusement.

Nettle orange bitters, elderberry lavender shrub, rosehip hibiscus, and lemon cardamom tinctures—a million ideas, a million ways to play, countless satisfying results.

My first run was an effortless achievement. I made cocktail-ready mixers: Blueberry Bourbon and Sour Apple Blueberry Rum. I usually have such an overwhelming surplus of blueberries in the garden that by mid-July I begin to look a little like Violet Beauregarde from Willy Wonka's Chocolate Factory. By that point, I'm thinking of chucking anything else into the freezer from the outdoors that turns blue; we'll thaw it all out come November's pancake season.

I've also decided that everyone is getting hard liquor for Christmas—even all the kids on my list. By the time they turn twenty-one, the flavors should have matured to perfection.

Once I've made my way through all the alcoholic infusion recipes that tickle my fancy, I'm going to need a new culinary project.

Maybe I'll buy my own food truck and sell freshly grilled roadkill kebabs.

I might try to create a scratch and sniff app.

It very well might be the year of eating only foraged food.

I'm always looking for ideas.

The rest of the family is super excited, too. Because *inventive* is my middle name . . . right after *crazy*.

———

(For your pleasure, below are two recipes that are not *crazy* but might be for *curing* all your teeny tiny soul cravings.)

NORTH WOODS PINE NEEDLE TEA

I remember the first time I heard the phrase, "We're makin' pine needle tea." But I've long lost count since then. Having been raised in Wisconsin, where winters are serious about bringing down the national average for temperature and hoisting it for snow, hearing the medicinal-benefit-of-tea talk wasn't a rare occurrence. In fact, it was customary to walk into most anyone's home and realize that, within the chunk of time it took you to pull off your snow boots, mittens, scarves, hats, parka, and the two extra pairs of pants you wore on top of your true chosen outfit for the day, you were being sized up for sickness on the North Woods Symptom Scale.

1. Nose running? Chances are it's the icy air effect.
2. Cheeks red? A quick hug and a brush of skin while doing so would instantly reveal whether you sported ruby spots from frigid temps or fever.
3. Eyes glazed? Were you by chance in an impromptu snowball fight just before reaching the door and got walloped with flawless aim to the back of the head? Perfectly reasonable.
4. Coughing? Interminable smoke from the belching wood stove can take anyone a minute or two to get used to after being outside in air so dry it crackles.
5. Lethargic? Regardless of how many air-activated, ten-hour hand and foot warmers you strategically insert into your clothing, if your blood is running through your veins without a quart of antifreeze in it, you will be sluggish until you thaw.

If North Woods logic failed to explain away your symptoms, you'd likely next hear those beautiful words (in quotes above) uttered in any variety of flat, vowel-stretching, Lutheran-influenced accents that make up the region's settlers. Your response?

"Pour me a cup, please!"

This nifty nightcap has been long touted for its medicinal benefits by nursemaids, mothers, and frozen-to-the-bone trappers and hunters.

Sadly, funding by government health organizations for in-depth research remains tragically low, forcing thousands to use their own discretionary funds to purchase ingredients and collect personal data on its efficacy.

A typical North Woods Tea concoction contains the following ingredients:

- a spirit (whisk(e)y, brandy, rum, etc.)
- pine needles (pine, spruce, or Douglas fir needles—young tips are best, but please note: some needles are toxic, like ponderosa pines and Norfolk Island pine, so make sure to be certain of your evergreen ingredient or you'll need something a lot stronger and more expensive than tea to feel well again!)
- a sweetener (sugar, dark maple sugar, or honey)
- a warm base (usually boiling water or pre-steeped tea)
- spices or flavorings (cinnamon, cloves, lemon, or orange peel)

There are copious variations limited only by one's imagination, so dabble away, but typically we would muddle one cup of pre-simmered pine needles in a glass. (Don't boil the needles, as doing this will break down their vitamin C and release bitter terpenes into the infusion—just simmer ½ cup of needles for 10–20 minutes in three cups of water.) Then transfer and infuse them in a closed jar with 4–6 ounces of whisky (enough to cover the needles) for 5 to 10 days. Strain the infusion, then warm in a pot:

- 2 ounces of pine-infused whisky
- ¾ ounce dark maple sugar/syrup
- 4 ounces brewed Darjeeling or Orange Pekoe tea
- An orange or lemon slice
- 1 cinnamon stick

Once just below a simmer, hold warm for a few minutes to allow the flavors to meld. Pour into a mug and enjoy this antioxidant, vitamin A and C–packed immune booster.

As an accompaniment to this fine potion, might I suggest the perfect reading material? *How to Eat Your Christmas Tree* by Julia Geogallis. So many ideas . . .

Stay warm, stay healthy, stay in bed until spring, maybe!

———

SINGLE MALTED MILK CHOCOLATE BALLS

I think we all know the phrase, "No man shall live on bread alone."

It was probably written by someone who's never tasted a perfect croissant. Furthermore, I believe there may be a whole slew of teenage boys out there who would fervently disagree.

But what if you had to choose just one thing? One thing to carry you through from one day to the next. Ad infinitum. What would it be?

Cheese?

Filet mignon?

Champagne?

I couldn't do it. I could not choose *one*.

But I could choose TWO.

Chocolate and whisky. Absolute musts for a fine and fulfilling life.

As I'm penning this chapter, we're in the thick of the blustery winter holidays, and I've been buried beneath heaps of flour, butter, and sugar in between making sure the sheep in the barn aren't *sheepcicles* come morning. Therefore, I decided to put my less-than-stellar skills to the test in the kitchen to prove three things.

1. Whisky and chocolate belong together.
2. Most everyone—especially when forced to—will eventually agree with you.
3. Most sheep cannot be convinced that whisky and chocolate belong together.

That said, the results of my efforts are being shared with (read thrust into the hands of) everyone I love, given as holiday gifts, because nothing says, *Happy Saturnalia!* like an overdose of things meant to be consumed in moderation.

And just so I'm not caught on a technicality for the "surviving on one thing alone" challenge, I shall marry my two must-haves together. (Okay, the other technicality might be that there are a few more than just two ingredients, but once all together, it's really JUST ONE THING.)

Single Malted Milk Chocolate Balls

Ingredients for balls:
> 1 cup high-quality chocolate (milk or dark is fine)
> 3 scant tablespoons malted milk powder
> 4 tablespoons single malt whisky
> 3 oz. of chocolate wafer cookies
> Rolling powder:
> 2 teaspoons malted milk powder
> 2 teaspoons ground chocolate or Dutch processed cocoa powder
> 2 teaspoons espresso powder

Cooking:
To prepare the balls, melt chocolate over a double boiler or heat gently until just melted in a microwave. Add the malted milk powder and stir to combine. Pour whisky over the mixture one tablespoon at a time, stirring to incorporate after each addition. Using a mortar and pestle, crush the wafer cookies into powdery crumbs and stir into the chocolate mixture.

In a small bowl, combine the last three ingredients and set beside your chocolate mixture with a cookie sheet lined with a strip of wax paper.

With clean hands, roll truffle-sized dollops of the chocolate mixture between your palms and then place in the powder bowl, rolling with a spoon to coat the sphere evenly. Remove and place on the cookie sheet.

Once you've finished rolling out all the dough, place the balls in the freezer for thirty minutes to harden, then pop into a pretty wax paper–lined tin and gift away to your favorite adults (but no bovidae).

As a toasty bonus, serve with a warming dram.

Singing the Praises of Whisky: Drinking Songs

There are plenty of drinking songs one learns (or hears strains of) while growing up—the pub singalong, the frat-boy lawn parties, the guy in the back of a squad car filmed singing the entire five minutes and twenty-five seconds of Queen's "Bohemian Rhapsody," word for word, and beautifully, if somewhat inarticulately, broadcast for the world to admire on YouTube.

If one is to stick with the most agreed-upon definition of a drinking song, it is universally accepted that it is a song sung while drinking (drum-roll here) . . . alcohol. Oftentimes catalogued as folk music, drinking songs are communal in nature (unless enjoying that solo paddy wagon ride to the station), typically somewhat catchy for newcomers or those thick of tongue, express shared beliefs, and are merrily passed down because they are fun.

It's likely every country and culture have their own versions, and of course whilst in Scotland, I learned the lyrics to quite a few, despite knowing a fair handful from my own homeland. But wherever one may be, and with whomever one is drinking, a drinking song can magically erase borders. They unite us in a harmonious voice, a choir of musical expression giving rise to joy, all fueled and fostered by liquor.

I provide for you a list—in genres that are both typical and surprising. I culled through hundreds of songs (slogged in some cases), filtering and compiling a list of tunes I felt worthy of bringing to your attention. Some have videos—easily accessible, some are simply unfilmed audio one must hunt down—but all may be worthy of a dram for companionship.

    "Whisky in the Jar" (Three vastly different versions.)
        —The Pogues
        —The Dubliners
        —Thin Lizzy
    "Alabama Song (Whiskey Bar)"—The Doors (A fine mix of German opera and circus, but you decide for yourself.)
    "One Bourbon, One Scotch, One Beer"—John Lee Hooker, 1966 (Blues from the Deep South. This one needs something smoky.)
    "Whiskey River"—Willie Nelson, live 1974 (You're gonna need to dance in the kitchen with this guy.)
    "John Barleycorn (Must Die)"—Traffic, 1968 (Good for those reminding themselves of the year they lived in a traveling van.)
    "Whiskey Lullaby"—Brad Paisley (Warning: this one is for those wishing to cry in their beer with a whisky chaser.)
    "Take Your Whiskey Home"—Van Halen (I wish the whole song were just like the first forty-five seconds.)
    "Whiskey and You"—Tim McGraw or Chris Stapleton (Stapleton is the composer of the song, and according to many, the better choice to sing it. Again, decide for yourself. No. Choose Stapleton. There, I made it easy.)
    "Wasted Whiskey"—Rodney Atkins (Words to live by.)
    "Whiskey or God"—Dale Watson (Old-school country.)
    "Tennessee Whiskey"—George Jones (Even older. Historic. Antique. Cobwebbed and archived.)
    "Streams of Whiskey"—The Pogues (Love these guys.)
    "Well Whiskey"—Bright Eyes (American indie rock.)
    "Rye Whiskey"—Punch Brothers (Progressive bluegrass. Oh, yeah.)

"Sue Jack Daniels"—Reverend Horton Heat (Texas-based psychobilly trio. I swear I didn't make that tagline up. That's how they describe themselves.)

"The Whisky Song"—John Paterson (Scottish drinking music video; a lovely audio version is available on SoundCloud. A fine fiddle.)

"Farewell to Whisky"—(I have been told it's a song taught in Scottish secondary schools, and apparently its title raises not even a few eyebrows when parents discover it on the program at the school singalong.)

"Whiskey, Whiskey, Whiskey"—John Mayer at the Hotel Cafe, L.A.

"The Scotsman"—Bryan Bowers (I saved the best for last.)

Here's to All That Gives You Pleasure: Toasts and Tributes

Sláinte!

If, like me, you are a scotch whisky drinker, we all know it, at times have said it, or at least have heard it. Chances are you've tried uttering that word with as much mustered panache as Rick displayed when toasting Ilse with his, "Here's looking at you, kid!" *Casablanca* quote.

But the art of toasting is slowly slipping away.

And with the huge influx of innovative and enthusiastic spirit makers across the world—not to mention the great vintners, bartenders, brewers, mixologists, and, most important, the consumers—we need to reach back into history and take back the toast.

I'm not talking about the forty-minute lament given at state dinners or ambassadorial functions, and certainly not the half-dozen words flung out in an inebriated slur, honoring a newly wedded couple with, "Here's to the gride and broom!" Instead, I'm hoping you might find that same sliver of urgency that tugs at *my* sentimental heartstrings—the one that insists we're losing the plot when it comes to raising a glass.

We've filled our lives with a profusion of moments of recognition and celebrations—from baby's first steps to finally pulling the plug on Facebook. Countless gurus, psychologists, self-help guides, and insides of bottle caps encourage us to *seize the day, cherish this accomplishment,* and *make every moment count.* And because of that and the strength of mass-marketing to those sentiments, we try our level best to fulfill those suggestions. We find reasons to pop open a bottle and mark occasions to note one's age, to acknowledge a death, to support our team, and to welcome friends back. Occasionally, we make an about-face and reverse the form, throwing out plagues on our enemies and wishing ill luck at every turn.

But most of those are reserved for diplomatic dinners, where prickly critiques are well-disguised and nestled within perfectly wordsmithed acknowledgements. Likely, nearly all of us find ourselves at less formal affairs, or at least among folks who understand that if we make a gaffe in conversation or protocol, there's little worry we've breached a treaty and war will ensue.

As most of us these days are usually in the thick of preparing for some family event or holiday season, there are ample opportunities to research and practice a toast of first-rate quality and class—if not for that event right around the corner, then for the one that soon follows.

And to help you on our quest, I offer you a few of my favorites, a fraction of available verses ready-made in case your mind is blank, and your tongue grows tied at moments of needed inspiration.

> **Birthdays:** May you live to be a hundred years with one extra year to repent! ~ Irish
>
> **Christmas:** Here's to the holly with its bright, red berry. Here's to Christmas, let's make it merry. ~ anonymous
>
> **Death:** Though life is now pleasant and sweet to the sense, we'll be damnably moldy a hundred years hence. ~ Old pirate toast
>
> **Friendship:** Never drink anything without first smelling it, never sign anything without first reading it. Never dive into pools of depth unknown, and rarely drink—if you are alone. ~ 17th century philosophy
>
> **Grace:** Lord keep our pots distilling weel. Lord send the excise man to the de'il. Lord bless our couthy meal. Amen. ~ Scottish

<u>Health and Prosperity</u>: May you live as long as you like and love as long as you live. ~ Robert A. Heinlein

<u>Humor</u>: In Vino Veritas! Which means a man's a very ass in liquor. The thief that slowly steals our brains makes nothing but the temper quicker. ~ Scottish

<u>Husbands</u>: Here's to the man who loves his wife and loves his wife alone. For many a man loves another man's wife when he ought to be loving his own. ~ anonymous

<u>Love</u>: Brew me a cup for a winter's night. For the wind howls loud and the furies fight; Spice it with love and stir it with care, and I'll toast your bright eyes, my sweetheart fair. ~ Minna Thomas Antrim

<u>Luck</u>: As you slide down the banister of life, may the splinters never face the wrong way. ~ Irish blessing

<u>Misbehavior</u>: May the pleasure of the evening bear the reflections of the morning. ~ Scottish

<u>New Year's</u>: As we start the New Year, let's get down on our knees to thank God we're on our feet. ~ Irish

<u>Weddings</u>: Look down you gods, and on this couple drop a blessed crown. ~ Shakespeare

<u>Women</u>: Here's to the lasses we've loved, my lad, here's to the lips we've pressed; for of kisses and lasses, like liquor in glasses, the last is always the best. ~ anonymous

I leave you with one last sentiment—a quote, to be exact, from Winston Churchill, who said, "Success is not final, failure is not fatal; it is the courage to continue that counts." Therefore, I raise a glass to us both—one to my young self for pursuing this far, and one to you for reading this far. May we all continue with courage!

Where to Find Your First
(Or Next) Whisky

O kay, I can hear you. You've just finished the book, and although you're not quite keen enough to hunt down the nearest distillery and apply for a job (but might be persuaded if the distiller makes you go weak in the knees), there's a fair to middling chance that right now you are keen enough to hunt for your first bottle of whisky. But the resounding word in your head is basically, ACK! And that guy can get in the way.

So, here is my solution. Firstly, if you are lucky enough to live in a location where your village has a whisk(e)y bar . . . go there and pull up a stool. Go there with four friends. Three who will buy different drams than you, so you can pass and share, and one who will play the part of the Uber driver if that service does not exist in your neck of the woods.

This is the least expensive way to try many different whiskies and to get a feel for what you like and what you do not. If the bar list does not have tasting notes on it, make friends with the barkeep and ask for his/her opinion if they have one. If they're good at their profession, they should have ample words to share.

Jot down the names of the whiskies you gravitated toward, and then, in a day or two, after you sober up, head to your local liquor store, or online (again, if you're lucky enough to live in a state that offers Direct-to-Consumer shipping of spirits) and see what you can afford. It will be a good indicator that the price of the dram reflects the expense of the bottle.

Now, if you do not have a whisky bar within a reasonable walk or drive, then we move on to solution #2. Ask your friends if they keep any whiskies at home, and if they answer in the affirmative, then ask them to invite you over so you can mooch a sip or two. Tell them it's for research. It's for science. It's for charity—doesn't matter. Just cast a wide net and see who burbles up to the surface.

My solution #3 is called "A List of Recommendations for First-Time Scotch Drinkers or People New to Brown Spirits."

Currently there are around 130 active distilleries spread across Scotland, typically assigned to one of five whisky-producing regions: Lowland, Speyside, Highland, Campbeltown, and Islay. These are the "official" regions that the Scotch Whisky Association indicates as classifications.

To give some context to that, there are around two thousand distilleries in America today. As this book mostly revolves around my Scottish whisky experiences, I will stick to suggestions that are available from Scotland and not venture into making recommendations from the world of bourbon. But of course, if you're desperate for a taste of stateside liquid luxury . . . ahem, Reservoir Distillery, located in Richmond, Virginia, has got you covered.

But back to the topic at hand: now when we talk about terroir, we're led to believe that regions have flavors. There's some dispute about this. Some research argues that it's not so much the patch of earth that brings the spirit its flavor, rather the people making it. Although we cannot disregard any influence brought in by their background, culture, and traditions, it is oftentimes a distiller's choice of ingredients, decisions on machinery shapes and sizes, operational procedures, and ever important and overlooked factors such as the ambient temperature around the fermentation tanks that weigh heavier on the scale. I'm not suggesting that terroir doesn't have an influence—it surely does! But human factors are remarkably seminal when discovering where flavor stemmed from. I would also be remiss in not pointing out that a whisky's flavor is significantly affected by barrel choice, as within America, the brand-new oak barrels contribute anywhere between 50 and 80 percent of the flavor profile. (Scotland more typically uses ex-cooperage, where the casks have much less flavor to impart, because they've been used anywhere between one and four times previously.)

Nonetheless, in 1988, the United Distillers & Vintners (soon thereafter owned by Diageo) launched the "Classic Malts of Scotland" range with six whiskies representing different malt-producing regions of Scotland and, according to a slick London marketing team, were blue-ribboned winners representing the best Scotch whisky around. This marketing push was typically displayed in bars and liquor stores.

The original six included in the display were:

- Glenkinchie 12 (Lowland)
- Cragganmore 12 (Speyside)
- Dalwhinnie 15 (Highland)
- Oban 14 (West Highland)
- Talisker 10 (Islands)
- Lagavulin 16 (Islay)

Two notes regarding the list. Firstly, although I agree that nearly every one of these fellas deserves their spot here, my personal suggestion is to also include (if not replace Cragganmore with) Aberlour under the umbrella of Speyside, and I'd also swap out the Oban 14 for Old Pulteney 12 (Northern Highland). To me, and to a tremendous number of other people I have presented this whisky to, it shines as an overwhelming beacon of all the most palatable and prized flavors a scotch could hope to capture in a bottle.

My second note is to exclaim wide-eyed with horror over the fact that Campbeltown is not represented, but this is easily explained by the fact that, at the time, United Distillers and Vintners (and then Diageo) did not own anything on that tiny but important spit of land. Therefore, I have added a seventh whisky recommendation: Springbank 12 (Campbeltown).

Now, although Diageo wants us all to believe that flavor is regional, we know it's not; there are plenty of distilleries in the Lowlands and in Speyside choosing to make peaty whiskies when they wish to.

Instead, I'll refer you to whisky writer extraordinaire Dave Broom's method of identifying whiskies into five "Flavor Camps"; and as someone who hesitates on sharing tasting notes (you taste what you taste, and like what you like), I especially appreciate this style of classifying realms or groups of flavors:

- Fragrant and floral (like fresh-cut flowers, grass, light fruits like apple, pear, and melon)
- Malty and dry (understood as drier on the nose, crisp, cookie-like, sometimes dusty or like flour, cereal, and nuts)
- Fruity and spicy (ripe orchard fruit—think peach, apricot, or mango. Also, creamy notes like vanilla, coconut, and custard and spices like cinnamon or nutmeg)
- Rich and round (fruit here too, but dried: raisins, figs, dates—sometimes sweet, sometimes meaty, mostly deep)
- Smokey and peaty (sooty, lapsang souchong, tar, kippers, smoked bacon, burning heather, woodsmoke; also, oily)

Some of the above suggestions will fit neatly into one flavor camp, but others may bounce around a bit or cross borders with multiple groups. The point is not to make you over-obsess with labeling everything, rather to give you a wide spectrum of all the interesting aroma/flavor profiles that may pique your interest. This is not a list of all my favorite whiskies, although each of these listed is near and dear to my heart. Unfortunately, many of my favorite whiskies are ones no longer available, and to list them here would send you on a disheartening chase that will only end with hate mail directed to my inbox. We shall avoid that at all costs.

Instead, I simply ask that you remember these are recommendations I have made repeatedly to friends, family, and students—but know that not everything I suggest may appeal to you. My hope is that I have enticed and intrigued you sufficiently to give something new a try or encouraged you to experiment and explore further. Because I love whisky. And I love people who love whisky. And chances are, you're going to end up being a person I love.

Acknowledgments

One of the most exciting pages in any book I'm reading is typically the acknowledgment page, for it highlights the enormous amount of teamwork and the true collaborative spirit required to nudge (and for some of us *shove*) a book beyond the stages of concept and development through to publishing success. Therefore, even if you skip past these paragraphs of printed gratitude, if you enjoyed this tale and its contents, just send a little thanks skyward for all the many individuals who helped to make it so.

No doubt, the first mention of indebtedness must shine a light on Jennifer Unter, my agent. The effort she puts into finding my books a home—or sending them back to the drawing board—is immeasurable. Whether with tea in hand or whisky held high, I toast to your good health and fortune every day.

I'd also like to send a massive hug to one of the most talented women I've come across yet. Rachel Knowles's editorial work during the early days of development was truly one of the best ways to spend a Sunday afternoon for seven straight months. If I could keep you in my pocket always, I would. And there is no doubt your mother is a thousand times thrilled—still seeing your immeasurable talents.

I owe a debt of gratitude to my editor, Jessica Case, who took a chance on this book and gave it some shelf space in the already highly coveted berths that she so masterfully tends to within Pegasus. And to the rest of my Pegasus family—Jenny Rossberg and Meghan Jusczak, whose efforts in announcing this book's arrival continue to thrill me to no end, Drew Wheeler for his copyediting, Stephanie Marshall Ward for her patience while proofreading, Victoria Wenzel for her careful attention reviewing all edits, and Maria Fernandez for interior design—I owe you so many thanks and a couple of stiff drinks. And lastly, massive compliments go to both Derek Thornton and Timothy Park for putting their talented fingerprints all over the cover.

To my Reservoir family: Leslie Griles, to have you laboring on behalf of this book is a pure honor. Nick Vaughan and Mary Allison, I thank you for being so *so* much of the reason we are celebrated and embraced, as your daily toils and talents are truly medal-worthy in and of themselves. Michael Hanbury, I think I have no words apart from "please don't ever leave." You are a walking Netflix comedy special, and the joy you bring to all of us is incalculable. Kevin Hatton, Dylan McMahon, Matthew Tucker, and Chris Mitchell, we grow because of your presence and are so much better off because of it.

I'd like to express my appreciation to the countless individuals who I phoned, emailed, visited, or hunted down to collect information, to corroborate my research, to seek explanations for complex science far out of my wheelhouse of understanding, and to read through sections of this book to provide accuracy and interest: Patrick Heist, Adriana Bailey, Dave Scheurich, Ian Thomas, Gary Spedding, Barbara Cole, Chip Frazier, and Jacob Lahne are the tip of the iceberg but undoubtedly noteworthy.

I must pass on my thanks to Phil Duffy and Harry Georgiou for making their invaluable introductions. Rhea Baldino, your words and your instruction still resonate every day with as great an impact as they first had. William Plail, I still hear your bagpipes and still feel their resonance. Todd Wright, your art and talents are breathtaking. Ralph Beaudry, thank you for your kindness. It meant the world.

To my second favorite distillery, whose family of employees opened my eyes, filled my ears, and warmed my heart . . . thank you, Bruichladdich.

To the barkeep at Balbirnie House in 1991—I may not know your name, but it should be crystal clear how much I am indebted to your labors on my behalf. And to Heathrow Airport's Rare Malt Shop—you folks have provided the most delicious (albeit expensive) tuition, so my thanks to you, as well.

To Dave Broom and Ian Wisniewski, I am so grateful you both took the time you did to give me the encouragement you bestowed. I hold your scholarly words in high esteem, and they have been wholly instrumental during these last many decades.

I owe a drink—or maybe several bottles' worth of thanks—to Robin Gott. I have admired, and laughed, and felt my soul benefit from all your brilliant sketches. I am so very fortunate to have a few of them grace these pages.

And finally, to my clan. Mom and Dad, may my words and my whisky always bring you warmth. To Charlie and Harper, you guys are well on your way to being labeled as "nearly as *interesting* as your dad," but, personally, I think you will far surpass him. Gabriel, it is worth it, you are worth it, persevere, my sweet lad. Chloe, one day I wish to grow up and become you with your fearless spirit and your big brave heart. Dave, I'm pretty sure you caught the monkey.